LOUISE RANDALL PIERSON

Roughly

Speaking

PEOPLE'S BOOK CLUB EDITION   Published by
Consolidated Book Publishers by special arrangement with
SIMON AND SCHUSTER · NEW YORK · 1943

THIS BOOK IS FOR

THE FAMILY

WHO LAUGHED WHEN I SAT DOWN TO THE TYPEWRITER

THEY DIDN'T KNOW I WAS GOING TO WRITE A BOOK

CONTENTS

OVER THE BODIES OF JOHN ADAMS
AND JOHN QUINCY ADAMS

M Y MOTHER was back from Boston, where she had gone for the reading of the will, and my sister and I tried not to appear too eager. We fortified her with a glass of hot milk, into which a pinch of salt had been dropped, and two saltines with butter carefully browned.

"The trouble is," my mother said finally, "your father endorsed notes."

We had never heard of trouble and we had never heard of notes. But we had an indefinable feeling that the glass through which we now saw darkly was in for a brisk polishing.

"Promise me," said my mother, "never to endorse notes."

We promised.

"Elinor may take my veil," she continued. "And Louise may unbutton my boots. Whistle down the tube for Christine. Mr. Myers says I must dismiss the servants."

I whistled.

"We will, of course, have to sell this house."

My mother rose rather unsteadily.

"Mr. Myers says I am really fortunate. I have my health and I have my two daughters and I shall have a yearly income of six hundred dollars, if I don't touch my principal."

So saying she burst into tears and went upstairs to bed.

"What'll we tell Christine?" said my sister.

"Tell her to get out!" I suggested, brightly. "She's fired!"

That was what my father told the bookkeeper he dismissed because nights he was being "The Veiled Lady Who Rides the White Horse Down the Cataract of the Ganges" at the Boston Theater. That was the stuff to give the troops, I thought proudly. That was what we hearty descendants of New England clipper-ship captains called "letting them have it in plain English."

"I'll tell Mama what you said," my sister said. "And you'll have

your mouth washed out with soap." My sister thought she knew it
all because she was eighteen and I was only twelve; and she went to
Miss Post's Friday Evenings.

"If you do, I'll tell Ma you said you didn't believe in God and you
tried on her red-satin corset!"

My sister paled. Atheism, though "bad taste," might pass muster.
But we weren't even supposed to know my mother owned a red-satin
corset. My sister had unearthed this entrancing if sinful proof that
my mother was human in a frantic search for some magic by which
she might achieve the languorous grace of her current idol—Princess
Flavia, heroine of *The Prisoner of Zenda*. We had gazed, awestruck.
"Quick, pull!" said my sister, clasping it around her and handing
me the strings. I pulled. My sister looked in the glass. "Of course,"
she said, "Princess Flavia wore a crown. And she didn't wear skating boots." I still felt something was lacking. "You're flying too
high," I said. "Remember 'He who has his head among the stars
falls in the ditch.'" I was more practical. My own idol of the moment was Trilby, a role for which I had been cast by nature. Trilby
had short hair, freckles, and big feet; her mouth was too large, her
chin too "massive." No special props were called for.

"You're—you're common," said my sister. "How can you be so horrible—now that we've lost everything!"

Lost everything! Were we going to be *poor*? If we were, I decided instantly, I was against it. The "poor" I had seen had not impressed me favorably. Tramps, mostly. "Tell the cook to set down a
plate of food for them on the kitchen steps," my mother said. "Then
direct them to the town woodpile." *Us* tramps? It was unthinkable.
My sister was crazy.

" 'Just tell them that you saw me but you didn't see me saw,'" I
hummed airily.

I crammed my stocking hat down over my ears and set out for the
barn to have a talk with Fred, our hired man, and a ride on my
tricycle.

"She's going to sell the house," I said to Fred as I circled the cement floor of the washroom where he was polishing harness. "Because Mr. Myers told her to. Twenty-three skiddoo for Mr. Myers."

"Yer ma don't like to be called 'she,'" said Fred. "And maybe she don't know what to do. The way yer pa flung money around, maybe she's busted."

"Oh go way back and sit down," I said rudely, giving the harness a good flick as I rode by.

"You'm a hard nut," said Fred. "You'll make out."

I shut my eyes tight to squeeze back the tears and whizzed out of the washroom on one wheel.

"Bury your dead at night," my father had said. "Where the enemy can't see them."

Once outside, I rode more slowly. "Busted." So it was true, then! Our house would have to be sold. But if the house was sold, I thought desolately, there would be nowhere to deliver the pony.

"Complete this picture," it said in the back of *St. Nicholas*, "and send it to us together with your name, address, and date of birth. You will receive a Shetland pony FREE. State color desired."

"Louise John Randall, 70 Adams Street, Quincy, Mass.," I had printed carefully. "Born May 18, 1890." Pure white was the color I had chosen.

No place for the pony! I wished I was dead. What a beautiful child in the snowy satin coffin with the heaps of roses! Oh, that is Louise John Randall. She was only twelve. They are heartbroken. Look, you can hardly see her freckles at all. What a clever undertaker! Yes, the best was none too good for Louise John. They are having *a solid gold pony* made to put on her grave.

A cold chill struck me. *Could* you get a decent solid gold pony for $600—without touching your principal?

I watched the fat pigeons bobbing and pecking their way across the stone ramp leading to the stable door. On the threshold, Litzer Hurgle, the cat, lay sunning himself, a small yellow lion. I could hear the horses move in their stalls, nuzzling at their water pails. "My gal's a highborn lady. She's dark but not too shady," Fred sang. I tried to grasp what had happened but I couldn't. All this was *ours*. Ever since I could remember we had lived like kings and been rich as Croesus.

Our house, my father said, was our castle. And a pretty damned good one at that, he always added. It had been designed by H. H.

Richardson and built in 1893 (panic or no panic) "above the bridge" on Adams Street, Quincy, at a cost of $48,000. The only thing our house needed to make it perfect, my father claimed, was a moat with a drawbridge that could be pulled up at a given signal.

"And I'll build one," he'd say chestily. "And if I'm bothered by any more fools like the one who came with that bosh about compulsory vaccination. No one can tell *me* what to do."

Our house was big. Make no little plans, my father said. So big, it took four Finnish maids to keep it clean. The Finnish maids always scuttled, leaning forward slightly, as if they could feel the whiplash across their shoulders.

"I like Finns," my mother said. "They are a subject race and therefore accustomed to taking direction."

I sometimes wished my mother hadn't felt it would give them "ideas" if their quarters were equipped with heat and electricity. At home they probably lived in a peat hut, she said. Not that I was upset because our maids had to break the ice in their pitchers to get water to wash with, or heat their curling irons over a lamp chimney. They were lucky to be working for people like us, people who had "plenty to do with" and things like clothes chutes and barn telephones. But their dining room was so cold, my teeth chattered when I went out after supper to play duets with Ole, Christine's beau. He made out all right with the banjo because he came from Finland, where it was always cold. But I couldn't do justice to *Three Blind Mice* on the comb with my teeth rattling. And the tissue paper slipped if I wore mittens.

The floors of our house were of soft wood. On top of the wood were layers and layers of newspapers. Then came carpet lining. Then thick Brussels carpet covered with ankle-deep Orientals. And, in front of the fireplaces, white or black bear rugs. Which just goes to show how near the feet of little New England girls in the last decade of the nineteenth century came to touching the ground.

I liked my bedroom. It was paneled in redwood and it had a fireplace. Next the bed was a tub in which I kept my alligators. On my bureau was a picture of Queen Wilhelmina. Queen Wilhelmina, my mother claimed, "always practiced, always brushed her teeth, always studied her lessons." If she did, I was disgusted with her. Why not "Off with their heads!" if you were Queen? No spunk, that was her trouble.

From my bedroom window, I could look down into the box-bordered garden of the old Vassall House and watch Charles Francis Adams III, and his sister Abigail, walking with their uncle Brooks, half a dozen squatty little black carriage dogs tagging at their heels. My sister and I were pretty jealous of young Abigail. She was allowed to drive her horses hitched tandem to a racing sulky. My father wouldn't let us do that. Our horse, Jim, had won two blue ribbons at the Brockton Fair and we figured we could have licked Abigail Adams to a fare-thee-well. Her name was also taken in vain at our house, spring and fall, when the dressmakers came.

"I *won't* have lace and I *won't* have ruffles. Why do I have to? Abigail Adams never wears anything but a blue-serge suit."

"How many times have I told you not to stamp your foot? If *you* were Abigail Adams it wouldn't be *necessary* for you to wear anything but a blue-serge suit."

Period!

But my cousin Harold Faxon's Herreschoff knockabout trimmed Charles Francis Adams' *Bat*, even if it did capsize later in Hull Gut. Let Charlie Adams try to wiggle out of *that* one, even if their house did have shutters with musket holes.

"I cannot allow you to refer in that tone," said my mother, "to persons whose ancestors were Presidents of the United States."

Forget it and remember the *Maine*, I muttered. Didn't our own ancestors come over in 1636? And wasn't my Grandfather Randall lost climbing Mont Blanc, even if he did have a wife and seven children and was cashier of the Granite National Bank? And wasn't my Grandfather Pickering's name Manthano, which showed he had Spanish blood in him? And wasn't he a graduate of Bowdoin, which was almost as good as Harvard? And wasn't he tutor for Thomas B. Reed? Let the Adamses stow *that* in their Chippendale spinet. They needn't think they owned Quincy just because they got there first.

Along about April, when she was sure they were out, my mother would leave cards at the Adamses'. Along about September, this barren gesture would be politely returned. I had achieved carte blanche to their domain, however, by reason of a feverish friendship I had struck up with their hired man. I was allowed to share in the sacred rite of washing the carriage dogs and I was permitted to exercise their fat, overfed horses in the field behind the house. This captivating pastime consisted of standing in the center of a circle around which the horse paced endlessly, moored to my middle by a half hitch of the rein. I was supposed to hold the rein in my hand, but it added an element of danger to act as a human post. More fun than teasing the Chinaman or retrieving clay pigeons for the Sturtevant boys.

I had the Adamses' greatness further thrust upon me every Sunday when my weekly bout with religion took place. Our pew in the First Unitarian Church was centrally located over the bodies of John Adams and John Quincy Adams. Not to mention Abigail and Louisa Catherine, their wives. It was also near the register, which was a help. The church was big and drafty, as it had been constructed simply by piling one great granite block on top of another until patience and money ran out. In Quincy, City of Quarries, they never ran out of granite. And, while the crimson curtains, which glowed like rubies at the long windows, pleased the eye and warmed the cockles of the heart, they did little or nothing for the feet. If it hadn't been for the closing hymn, I doubt that I would have survived. When it came to "Holy, holy, holy," I really bore down. "*Only thou* art holy, *there is none* beside thee." You could hear me all over the church. I shut my eyes so I couldn't see the two plaques testifying to the Adamses' glory.

But the Adamses were with me late and soon. It was to the John Quincy Adams farm my father and I drove, after church, to get the cream. There was some consolation in the fact that the entrance was right opposite the smallpox pesthouse. It was exciting to see if the red flag was out. The Adams farm might not be there much longer, my father said. The Charles Francis Adamses had already moved away from Quincy and the J. Q.'s were going soon. Taxes were too high. Because of the granite cutters. Who only paid toll tax. And spawned like rabbits. And then expected somebody else to pay for their kids' schooling. It was a shame, he said, to waste Shakespeare and Caesar on those squareheads, anyway. All they needed to know was how to cut granite. Besides, they were troublesome cusses. Why, those Knights of Labor packed the town meeting and voted for the town to pay men two dollars a day for nine hours' work, my father said. No wonder John Quincy Adams threw down his gavel and stamped out. It was downright robbery. No man living was worth more than one fifty from the neck down. Those fools didn't know when they were well off. First thing they knew, they'd drive all the white people out of Quincy.

"Will they drive *us* out?" I asked anxiously.

"Let 'em try it!" my father said. Nobody could drive him. In or out. He never did anything till he got good and ready.

I felt better. I didn't worry about the Adamses. If *all* the Adamses moved out, lock, stock, and barrel, it was all right with me. I had plenty to occupy my time.

Every morning, Father and I got up early and went out to the stable to give the horses sugar and watch them be brushed and curry-combed. I called on the cow but Father didn't. He hated her. Every Sunday night, he and my mother had a battle over her. As Fred had a few hours off Sunday to repent his sins, there was nobody to do the milking.

"But, John, she has to be milked!"

"Damn it, Louise," he'd sputter. "Let me do the worrying."

His worrying always resulted in a flat refusal to do the milking. As far as the cow was concerned, he said, it served her right for letting a habit get the upper hand of her. As far as he was concerned, he had long leaned toward the theory that Lincoln, in freeing the slaves, had acted too hastily. He would then pound out Audran's *Mascot Song* fortissimo on the piano to drown out my mother's groans and the cow's lowing.

When we had fed the horses, Father and I made the rounds. I had to hurry to keep up. He had a quick, light step.

"We'll see what there is in the garden."

"There isn't anything," I said stubbornly. I knew what he meant to do. What he always did. Find something new, like the first jonquil or the first strawberry, to put by my mother's plate. It was mortifying to see a grown man do a thing like that. Especially my father. I wondered what Christine, the waitress, thought. My mother was smug about it.

"John always finds *something* to put at my plate."

Once, I thought she would get left. It was fall. Everything was dead.

"Look," my father pointed. Above the swirl of shriveled leaves, one dark velvety Jacqueminot rose. "Your mother'll be surprised."

After breakfast, I drove with my father to the station. On the way back, Fred left me at Miss Wright's school. Everybody went to Miss Wright's; millionaires like the Rices and Kings; old families like the Adamses and Quincys. I didn't like it. Not because the schoolhouse had no "improvements." It was fun going to the outhouse, and putting coal on the stove. But "sums" bored me after two years of making out checks for my father and balancing his checkbook; and *The Village Blacksmith* was dull after *Jude the Obscure* and *Quo Vadis*. Longfellow and Whittier weren't poets anyway, my father said. Why read that slop? Read Shakespeare. Read Walter Pater.

After school, I went out to the barn again. I would ride my tricycle around the washroom till Fred finished polishing harness. Then we went upstairs to his room. Fred's room was small and dirty. It smelled sweaty. But there was an air of *laissez faire* about it. Fred never said, "Ladies are not supposed to relax in the presence of gentlemen" when I flopped down on my stomach on his straw mattress. Or, "Don't do that, your boots are muddy." Fred said, "Seen the new *Police Gazette*?" Or, "Got a new yellow-back by Ouida. Big print and nearly all conversation." Fred didn't think fiction was "demoralizing." Under the bed there were always a couple of Horatio Algers, *Max the Matchboy* and *Sam the Streetsweeper*, and the newest *What Si Perkins Saw*. All jokes and pictures. Fred would throw stick after stick into the airtight stove, till it turned red and then white, and steam would rise from the clothes hanging on a nail in the corner. Then he would tell about great fights he had seen or how Dan Patch and Croesus could step it.

"Faster than Jim?" I would ask anxiously. "Or the Whiteface?"

"Oh, them! They ain't nothin' but drayhorses along o' these babies."

"Then why doesn't Pa sell them and buy something decent?"

"Say! You otta be glad you ain't got to walk!"

"I'd rather walk till my feet dropped off than ride behind second-raters."

"Well, don't bawl about it. Come here and I'll let you feel my muscle."

After I felt his muscle, Fred let me examine the fascinating details of his gold tooth and his diamond ring, while he tossed off a couple of bottles of Bass' Ale he'd snitched from the wine closet. Then we practiced the songs he was teaching me:

> *Oh, give us a drink, bartender, bartender,*
> *For we love you as you know.*
> *And surely you will oblige us, oblige us*
> *With another drop or so.*
> *(Low growl) We want no wine of another vintage*
> *Or beer of another brew.*
> *But just one drop of your old red liquor*
> *Is all that we ask of you.*
> *(All together) So-o-o give us, etc. . . .*

The other:

> *Oho, the bead is on the pewter Mayme,*
> *And Nancy mind the shop.*
> *And 'Arriet I'm wyting*
> *For a little bit off the top.*

The jig was up at the first jingle of the barn telephone.

"Fred, tell Louise John if she doesn't come in and feed her alligators, and finish knitting the thumb of her mitten, she can't drive down to meet her father at the station."

If I couldn't drive down for my father, I was heartbroken.

"Have you been a good girl today?" Father would say as I took his bag and Fred held open the carryall door for him.

"No."

"What this time?"

I would recount my crimes.

"I kicked the cook," or "I swore, to tease my sister." "But," I would add hopefully, "I've been stood in the closet and had six raps with the ruler."

My father would laugh.

"Look in my bag. There *might* be something." In his bag I would find the box of Page & Shaw's with the little gold tongs in it. "For a thoroughly depraved character," he would say. "But you mustn't trouble your mother," he always added.

As soon as we got home, I had my supper served on a tray in the upstairs sitting room. When I had finished, I was entrusted with the keys to the wine closet. It was my proud privilege to guard Fred while he selected the wines ordered for dinner. Then I was hustled off to bed. After my mother heard me say my prayers, she sang to me. "I am a pilgrim; a-and a stranger. I can tarry, I can tarry but a night." It was a sad song. So sad, that after my mother left I had to get up and get my dolls for company. They weren't silly French dolls like my sister's Charlotte and Madeleine, who had trunks full of silk dresses and hats with ostrich feathers. One was a rag doll called Carint Caroose (a shortened form of Clarinda Clarissa); the other, a faceless colored doll named Dinah. I shoved them down to the foot under the covers. I didn't want my father to see them when he came up after dinner to tell me stories. "Sit on the chair," I'd say. That was so he wouldn't feel the dolls, and the gaslight in the hall would shine on the diamond eyes of his bulldog stickpin. I liked the story about when he visited his uncle Caleb Huse in Newburyport. Uncle Caleb was stingy. He had an orchard loaded with apples but he wouldn't let my father have one of them. One night, after Uncle Caleb was in bed, my father got up and took the pillowcase off his pillow. Then he sneaked down into the orchard and stuffed it full of apples and started up again. Just as he got to the top stair, Uncle Caleb heard him and came roaring out. My father was so surprised, he took the pillowcase by the wrong end. All the apples bumped down the stairs, and my Uncle Caleb whipped him.

"Tell about the cigars and cigarettes," I would beg.

My father had once brought from Cuba a trunkload of cigars and cigarettes for his friends. When the boat got to Boston Harbor, it was boarded by a mean and grasping customs inspector. When he told my father what the duty was, Father was furious.

"I'm a Mugwump!" my father roared, brandishing his sword cane. "I didn't vote for that damned Irishman who slapped on that tariff. No taxation without representation!"

He threw the whole trunkload of cigars and cigarettes into Boston Harbor. He didn't like the Irish, he said, because he had no respect for a nation that would let its religion interfere with breakfast. He didn't like Italians, either. They were Dagos. Swedes were square-heads.

"Why," my father said, "if it wasn't for the famines in India and the floods in China and a first-class European war every few years, this country would be overrun with foreigners. Good Americans like us would be worse off than Lo, the poor Indian."

I hoped the famines and floods and wars would keep up their good work because I liked the life we were living. Who wouldn't? The best was none too good for *us*, my father said. Quail and larded grouse and oysters by the barrel. Venison hanging in our own special booth in Faneuil Hall Market. Coffee at S. S. Pierce's of our own special blend.

"Nothing can be too rich or fancy to suit my taste," said my father. "If there's anything I hate, it's good plain cooking."

St. Julien claret every night and hock and dated Scotch and champagne.

"Don't forget you're a long time dead," said my father. "On with the dance. Let joy be unconfined."

Cape Cod in the summer, where I had my own deep-sea dory with tholepins instead of rowlocks, and I got drunk on the smell of fog, honeysuckle, and bayberry. The State Suite or the Imperial Suite at the Ponce de Leon or the Hotel Ormond, where we went in the winter, when the passes came.

"But, John, thirty dollars a day!"

"Hell, it's worth it."

"Just because you have a brown beard and have been told you look like King Edward," said my mother, "your every gesture doesn't have to be Edwardian."

"Gather ye rosebuds while ye may," said my father.

We gathered them.

Front seats at the Admiral Dewey Parade. Boxes to Denman Thompson in *The Old Homestead* and Joe Jefferson in *Rip van Winkle*. Visits behind the scenes to meet the cast. Landscapes to order by John J. Enneking. A miniature of my sister by Laura Hills. Diamonds for my mother from Bigelow and Kennard's. A bellboy suit made to order for me at Browning King's.

And then suddenly it was over and my mother was bending over me.

"You have no father but your Father in heaven," she said.

What fancy language, I thought. She had read that in a book.

"Get up, Louise. I want you to do some telephoning."

"Hello, George? This is Louise John Randall. Pa died last night. I said *Pa died last night*."

(He says he can't believe it. Why can't he? He knows it means he'll be Treasurer. He can believe it, all right.)

"Hello, Aunt Edith? Listen, Ma says to tell you Pa died last night. What? Pa! *Pa! Died!*"

(She's crying. What's she crying for? Dead's just a word. It doesn't mean anything.)

Tall, skinny undertakers with carnations in their buttonholes.

Nothing for granite cutters, daisies for people, carnations for Randalls, roses when an Adams dies. Gray gloves smelling of formaldehyde.

"I would suggest a smoke gray with ebony handles. A little darker gray than Ruth had."

"Get out, you black, cadaverous vultures with your casket memories! Get out of this house!"

"All who loved him are invited."

Dead is a word, but it's getting nearer.

"Kind hearts are more than coronets." That's from the firm. Roses and violets. Put it on the easel in front of the Enneking. Lilies. Put them in the library. Put them in the dining room. Put them in the upstairs sitting room. Put them in the hall. Don't tiptoe. Don't tiptoe. Don't you know you can't wake the dead? Those Mayflowers "in the coffin beside him." Who? Miss Small? She's got a hell of a—she's got a nerve! Speaker of the House of Representatives, the Honorable James J. Myers. Show him up front! No more passes for Florida. No more money for the party coffers. No more John Randall. No more John. Mr. Carter. Sober for once. "John, shake me a fiver." No more fivers. No more John. Mr. Haynes. What about that second volume of Burton's *Anatomy of Melancholy*? We know you've got it. You needn't think you can get away with it. Just because John's gone.

"All who loved him are invited."

Put them in the library. Put them in the dining room. Put them in the upstairs sitting room. Put them in the hall. Sorry, Pa isn't here. He never comes home until the 5:15. That there? That's just an effigy in Pa's blue suit. There's no brilliantine on the beard. That can't be Pa. Those people coming up the driveway? Line forms on the left. Standing room only.

"Lead, kindly light, amid th'encircling gloom."

Good heavens, we should have had the piano tuned. It must be another marshmallow on the strings.

"For some we loved, the loveliest and the best."

Stop rustling. It's the *Rubáiyát*. It's the *Rubáiyát*, all right.

> *That from his Vintage rolling Time has prest,*
> *Have drunk their Cup a Round or two before—*

Turn down a row of 'em. Every day and every night. On the shelf in the butler's pantry. No use to keep varnishing it. Whisky eats the varnish away. Salt takes out claret stains.

> *And one by one crept silently to rest.*
> *Ah, my beloved, fill the Cup that clears*
> *Today of past Regrets and future Fears.*
> *Tomorrow?—Why, Tomorrow I may be*
> *Myself with Yesterday's Seven thousand Years.*

"Let us pray."

Don't listen, Pa. Don't pay any attention to what they say. Remember the time you coasted down President's Hill right across the tracks under the freight train? Remember the time you drove the buggy into the little shed, with the top up? Remember the time you leaned against the railing at the duck stand and there wasn't any railing there? Remember the time after the Harvard-Pennsylvania football game, when you left me outside Young's Hotel in the herdic and you forgot me and I could see you drinking and playing billiards in there? Remember what I thought? I will be like you when I grow up, I thought. I'll be on the inside looking out. I'll never be on the outside looking in. Don't you worry about me, Pa. I'll make out. Don't you worry about me.

"The family first, please. Please, the family first."

Fred touched my shoulder "Hey! Yer cryin'!"

"You shut up. You mind your own business!"

I pedaled my tricycle savagely down the stone ramp over Litzer Hurgle's tail, scattering the pigeons. Fred laughed and shook his head. "You'm a tough nut," he said. "Anybody that tries to shove a curb bit between *your* teeth'll lose a finger."

I whizzed down the driveway, wiping the mist from my eyes with a muddy mitten. Let them sell their old house. Who cared? I'd make out. I was a tough nut. I'd always go lickety-split. Head up, and tail over the dashboard.

COHASSET was the place my mother selected in which to Do the Impossible. Not that she wanted to go there. It was the place picked out for her by a real-estate agent named Frank Crane.

"Got a little old farmhouse just your meat," he said to my mother. "Restore it and all that. Give you something to occupy your time."

My mother's life had been so completely shot out from under her, it didn't make much difference to her where we went. If Frank Crane said Cohasset, why not Cohasset? Besides, the little old farmhouse sounded interesting. It wasn't a "tenement" and it wasn't "in a row," two types of housing which strike terror to the heart of a New Englander. It might make a nice background for the Governor Winthrop desk and the secretary—"with a little fixing."

"But Cohasset!" my sister moaned. "It's so far away from our friends!" Ever since the decline of our fortunes my sister had lived in horror of being "marooned in some middle-class morass," as she put it. By friends, she meant the Sturtevant boys who lived next to us on Adams Street and had a Stanley Steamer.

"When you haven't any money," said my mother, "you haven't any friends. Besides, we have to live *somewhere*."

"Buy it!" I urged my mother. "Buy it!"

If it was really terrible, I could be a Little Heroine. In 1903, the entire Peter Thomson sailor-suit set was eating up stories about Little Heroines. The Little Heroine usually lived with two sourpuss old aunts and a pernickety old grandmother on a ramshackle farm, ten miles from a spool of thread. She eked out their meager substance by selling butter she had churned, the clever little rascal having thought up a new way of packaging it between cool, green plantain leaves. One day, as she is manning the well sweep or driving home the Guernsey, she is accosted by a handsome stranger. He asks the way. She knows it. A few weeks later, the handsome stranger comes by again. He sweeps the Little Heroine up onto the saddle beside him. They are married. It turns out he is in the wholesale notion business and almost intolerably rich. They have a fine house in the city with an iron deer on the lawn. But the Little Heroine never forgets. Every Christmas she sends Gramma and the aunts a money order so they can have the foolish boy at the corner do the milking and get a new washer for the pump. Of course, if the farmhouse in Cohasset proved *too* terrible, I wouldn't leave my mother and sister there. I would take them to the city with me.

Two weeks later my wildest dreams were realized. We were cozily ensconced in what my sister described as an unconverted pigpen. The unimaginative swineherd who built it along in 1790 had never heard of Adam mantels or pine paneling.

"Beggars cannot be choosers," said my mother, as, in her kitten's-ear broadcloth from Hollander's, she optimistically sounded for concealed fireplaces. "And it has very nice lines."

"Oh, don't start in about beggars," pleaded my sister. "It only leads to how we could have lived in Windsor Castle if you had taken all the change out of Papa's trousers every night and I hadn't bought this pink feather boa." My sister had bought the pink feather boa in an effort to capture the patrician elegance of Ida Conquest, John Drew's leading lady. Ida Conquest now held the high place in my sister's esteem formerly occupied by the Princess Flavia.

"I am only asking you to remember," said my mother, tearfully, "that it is very difficult to raise two daughters on six hundred dollars a year without touching your principal."

"If the barn was propped up a little," I said hopefully, "it would make a good chicken house."

There was a fortune, it said in the back of the *Youth's Companion,* to be made from raising bantams.

"I'm not worrying about money at this moment," said my mother firmly. "It will not take much to make this place livable."

But there was more wrong with our little heaven on earth than met the eye. The roof leaked. The plumbing didn't plumb. And the sills were rotten. It looked, my mother said despairingly, as if we would have to tear the whole place down and build it over again. This was where a pearl of almost prohibitive price, named Mr. Chandler, came in. Mr. Chandler, the agent said, would be "just the ticket" to take charge of our Restoration. For a good fat fee, of course. Mr. Chandler was a "builder of wide experience." He might *seem* like an extravagance, my mother argued, but he *wasn't*. He "just loved old things."

He certainly did. Show Mr. Chandler an old brick you'd found, and he'd go right down on his knees, in his good suit, and burrow like a dog until he'd unearthed another. Then he and my mother would gaze spellbound at these treasures and try to figure out what to do with them.

Since Mr. Chandler and his old bricks, my sister and I remarked frankly, were in our opinion a lot of bosh, we were demoted from prying up wide board flooring from the attic and placed on the pick-and-shovel gang. Our task was to remove rubble.

"Save any old bodies you find for Mr. Chandler," said my sister. "And keep the road to the stove and icebox open."

I hated Mr. Chandler because he wanted to tear down the old barn and build a pergola. We had no well sweep and no Guernsey. My sole hope of being a Little Heroine was pinned on bantams. My sister hated Mr. Chandler because he cost so much. While we had Mr. Chandler there was no chance of our having an Apperson. She thought it would go far toward restoring our shattered prestige, and attracting the attention of handsome strangers, if we could only buzz down South Main Street, swathed in veils and dusters, scaring chickens and scattering pedestrians, in our natty Apperson.

"Little Heroines went out when horseless carriages came in," my sister said. "Forget about bantams."

That was just like my sister. She always wanted to do things the easy way. Maybe *she* could get a rich husband just by buzzing down Main Street in an automobile. But she was nineteen, not thirteen. And she had red cheeks, and curly hair, just like a Gibson girl. She didn't have a snub nose and freckles.

"An automobile costs too much," I said. "We'll never get one."

"We'll get an Apperson when the Burlington and Hinesburg gets built," my sister said firmly. "Don't forget we own a majority of the stock in it."

We had the same fanatical faith in the Burlington & Hinesburg that "We Three Downandouters," 7959 East Stenchley Street, Queens, had in their sweepstakes ticket. And the same chance of cashing in on it. The B. & H. R.R. was a brain child of my father's. It was supposed, in some mysterious way, to lure away Northern Pacific's New York traffic direct to the Port of Boston. My father and an old General Somebody-or-Other with a rambling white mustache and a wooden leg had financed it. If it could be completed before the franchise and/or money ran out, it would make us rich and Boston the key point of transoceanic shipping. Since my father's death, we had had no word of its progress. But we felt sure that it would be Burlington & Hinesburg in a photo finish.

"If we only had our Apperson now," my sister said to my mother, "we could go up and inspect it."

"How could you learn to run an automobile when you can't even learn to run a sewing machine?" my mother said. "Besides, horseless carriages cost money."

"Millions for an old Dutch oven George Washington once slept in," muttered my sister, "and not one cent for an Apperson."

It was really all Mr. Chandler's fault, we agreed later. I wished I had my Daisy Air Rifle. It would be wrong to kill Mr. Chandler, of course. But a few close shots might serve to discourage him.

"If your hand slipped and you did shoot Mr. Chandler," my sister said, "you wouldn't be any better off. You'd never get time to raise bantams. Mama'd still make you beat rugs and make squash biscuit."

This, alas, was true. Just because our income was reduced, my mother said, and our house "temporarily upset," she saw no reason for relaxing her standards. Her standards had been assembled in New England, hotbed of perfect housekeeping, and geared to four Finnish maids, a hired man, a gardener two days a week, and an "accommodator" when there was company. Come hell, high or low water, she never relaxed them. All she had now, in place of this competent staff of coolies, was me and my sister, a couple of millstones who would probably have been a drag upon operations even in a mill.

I was strong and not very willing. My sole accomplishments consisted of skinning the cat, riding my bicycle no hands, and playing the comb. This left me three up on my sister, whose greatest activity to date had been sitting for the miniature by Laura Hills. My sister had taken lessons in practically everything—piano, singing, drawing, dancing—but she was so taken up with clothes and parties they had made no impression on her. Her usefulness was further impaired by an unshakable belief that if you charged anything it was paid for, and that hot water was piped in from the street. Besides, she had a habit of getting "nervous" when anybody asked her to shake a leg. This resulted in her having lessons—principal or no principal—from Annie Payson Call on "Repose" and having to spend most of her time in a "recumbent position." It is doubtful if, without hiring Mrs. O'Leary's cow to kick over a strategically placed bucket of kerosene, we could have achieved anything so elementary and necessary to survival as a kitchen fire.

But my mother, who had survived the ordeal of being born and raised in Portland, Maine, by the grace of God and the help of long flannels, was nothing if not determined. She might retire at night, defeated and discouraged, but she always rose next morning, recharged like a battery from a night's rest, ready to renew the attack with redoubled ferocity. Under her brisk tutelage (while my sister reposed) life for me became what I dourly regarded as a seething caldron of constructive activity.

I got breakfast, did the dishes, put coal on the furnace, and washed the kitchen floor before setting out on my bicycle for Cohasset High School. Public school, my mother said, would be good for me. It would teach me to hold my own. She did not insist, however, I travel by "barge," a horse-drawn vehicle resembling a stagecoach.

When I got home I emptied the pan under the icebox, weeded the strawberry bed, and washed the spinach in seven waters. I set bread, baked beans, made sea-moss blancmange, clam chowder *with* salt pork and without tomatoes. I mastered Miss Parloa's sponge cake and red-flannel hash, and was initiated into the mysteries of Indian pudding which curdles if you look at it. When dinner was ready, I served it. My mother, resplendent in her black foulard with the *soutache* braid, would sweep into the little dining room full of sawdust and cracked plaster as if she were entering the banquet hall at Buckingham Palace, and graciously permit me to pull out her chair. As I staggered in with the soup, trouble started. My mother would look at me coldly, as if she'd never seen me before.

"This soup is cold. Heat it up again. It should be piping. And brown the croutons as I told you."

While these orders were whirling dizzily around the kitchen, more faults would have been discovered.

"The butter isn't iced. And you didn't make pats. Why is the bread piled like this? It's so unappetizing. You didn't use the India-tree plates. Simply because we no longer live on Adams Street, Quincy, there is no excuse for our living like pigs."

"I haven't any napkin," my sister would add meanly. "Or aren't people using napkins any more?"

I would thank God when the meal was over and I was free to wash the dishes and scald the dish towels. When this was done, I would retire with my tail dragging, as my sister said, like a galley slave scourged to his dungeon.

Sleep was welcome. In my dreams I was myself again. One dream I used to dream over and over. It was about my last birthday party at home in Quincy. I had on my pink-silk dress my mother brought me from Liberty's, and my pink-kid slippers. Only I didn't have short, brown hair going every which way. I had long yellow curls. I stood at the door with my mother and shook hands with the guests as they came in, and my mother said, "Don't reach for the present before you shake hands and don't bite your nails." While everybody was playing pin-the-tail-on-the-donkey, I went in and looked at the dining-room table. It was set with the big damask cloth that came down to the rug and the gold ice-cream set from Tiffany's. At one end of the table was a big melon mold of chocolate ice cream with spun sugar all heaped up around it and, at the other, a mold of vanilla. In the middle, where the birthday cake should have been, was a little gold pony with diamond eyes. I was just taking a taste of the chocolate ice cream when Christine came in and began to light the candles on the Hepplewhite sideboard. She curtsied and said, "You look like a little princess," and I said, "I am. This is my castle." Then I went into the library to watch my father run the magic lantern. Everybody was sitting in chairs facing the screen. My father was back of them fussing with the lantern that set on a tall tripod. Swearing like an old salt, he said, "Somebody's been monkeying with this thing." Then he put his head under the black cloth that was over the lantern and began to throw pictures on the screen. I held my breath waiting for the picture of the little Russian girl with the fur coat and hat, driving two plunging horses hitched to a red sleigh. That was the best one. When it came on, I almost screamed. It was *me* driving. "If there isn't Louise John Randall!" everybody said. "Brave as a lion. Just like her father." Then, all of a sudden, the sleigh upset. The horses went tearing off. I was all alone in the snow, surrounded by wolves. I called, "Pa! Pa!" but he couldn't hear me because he had the black cloth over his head. That was when I always woke up. I wished some night I could finish it so I could see what happened.

While I toiled, my sister "reposed," my mother worried, and the ticklish work of remolding our little farmhouse nearer to the heart's desire gathered momentum. Accomplices were called in and placed on the payroll to ransack near-by towns for strap hinges and old wainscoting. No sooner did a paneled door swim into these wreckers' piercing kens than it was ripped from its moorings. The village green gave up its iron chains. They reappeared later, tastefully draped across the front of our property. They were more in keeping with the "period," Mr. Chandler said, than mere pickets. By the end of three months nobody who entered our farmhouse, and did not immediately have to go to the bathroom, would guess that anything at all had happened since it was built in 1790. By some rich burgher, no doubt. Adzed beams, wooden pegs, and a final three coats of white on everything inside and out finished off our little Revolutionary number and made a nice big dent in our principal.

"Painting is very expensive," my mother remarked dolefully. "I've had to sell one of my bonds. But Mr. Chandler said the wood is so old that three coats at least are needed to preserve it."

But even though, as she said, the worst was over, she could not seem to keep our expenses within our budget. Now that the house was finished, she branched out in other directions. She bought me a new Crawford bike with a safety brake. She bought my sister a black-fox muff. Every Saturday, she ordered a rig from the livery stable and we went riding.

The ride, to which we looked forward so eagerly, always degenerated into a bitter quarrel between my sister and me as to who should do the driving. The one who didn't drive had to sit in back with my mother and play roadside whist. A dog counted ten; a cow, twenty. An old lady in the window, knitting with a black cat beside her, counted one hundred. If my sister drove, we proceeded at such a fast clip that my mother complained she couldn't see anything. If I drove, my habit of slapping the horse on the rump with the slack of the reins would result in my sister's begging to be allowed to get out and walk. "I don't see," said my sister, "how you can be so *country*."

When we got home, I had to return the rig.

"Tell Mr. Penniman to add it to our bill," my mother would say, snapping down her carriage parasol. "And be sure and remind him that we were gone only two hours."

The first of the month, when the bills came in, she would say, "*Nobody* can live on six hundred dollars a year. I'm going to Boston and see Mr. Myers and see if something can't be done."

Mr. Myers was our lawyer.

"Ask about the Burlington and Hinesburg," we would cry eagerly, "and if we can have an Apperson."

We would watch hopefully to see her round the turn from the Beechwood Station. Invariably she would sail into the house and straight upstairs to bed. Obviously, Mr. Myers' reactions were not favorable.

She would reappear at breakfast pale but undaunted, full of new plans. If the old barn were torn down (good-by bantams), the rich soil underneath would be fine for a garden. We could set out currant and raspberry bushes. We wouldn't have to go to the expense of buying currants and raspberries when it came time for jelly-making. Mr. Chandler had his heart set on the pergola, but, with a few changes, it could be turned into a grape arbor. We could grow vegetables: parsley, radishes, and lettuce. That would be a saving. And she was planning to build a little ell on the shed. All old farmhouses had ells, Mr. Chandler said, and it would be just the place to make soap and freeze ice cream. She wasn't going to worry any more about money. Everything would come out all right if we were careful.

For *who* to make soap and freeze ice cream, I thought.

Before the long dark night closed in, I would take one last fling at being a Little Heroine. I would take care of the garden and market the surplus. My sister, in her brief moments of activity between reposes, could design labels for the grape and currant jelly. To make assurance doubly sure, I would kick in the profits on an Apperson.

As the tempo of my life increased, I feared I might give out. At thirteen, I no longer had the vigor which was mine in youth. In desperation I sent away for a Strength Course, the dictates of which I heeded religiously. These called for the eating of large quantities of cold boiled rice doused with sugar and cream and long hours of secret muscle flexing. The results were a surprise to me, though the prospectus was highly optimistic.

"Follow this course faithfully," it said, "and whatever your weight at the start, it will shoot right up to one hundred and forty."

It shot up all right. Unfortunately, the course did not tell how it could be persuaded to shoot back down again if the ensemble effect was not pleasing. The muscle flexing developed my back so spectacularly that it was difficult to tell from a distance whether I was coming or going.

"Now," my mother said, "I guess there won't be such a time made over it when you have to split a little kindling."

This was the last straw. The garden venture had flopped dismally. Currant and raspberry bushes don't bear the first year, it turned out, and the grape arbor couldn't be expected to amount to anything for a few seasons. Everybody in Cohasset had gardens of their own, so there was no market for radishes and lettuce. The only stranger who had accosted me was Dick Cushing, a local boy. He picked me and the wilted radishes out of the gutter when I rode my bicycle into Mr. Stoddard's ice wagon. Of course, he *did* name his boat for me. That is, after I went down to the hardware store and bought the letters L O U I S E and nailed them on the bow, he did. But financially he was a bust. When he finished working his way through college he would have to help his mother run her old hotel in North Scituate.

"I'm just a slave," I said to my sister. "Ma'll have me laying flag-stones days and chopping piccalilli nights, the way things are going. I'm going to run away."

"If you run away," my sister said, "we'll send the bloodhounds after you, the way they did after Eliza."

Of course, she explained afterwards, she was joking. But when Stanley Leary, the principal of our school, gave his talk on "Girls, What the Future Holds for Them," I was right in the mood for it.

"Women need no longer look forward to long years of household drudgery and financial dependence upon others," said Mr. Leary in his thrilling voice, "if they have had the wisdom and foresight to go to college. It is high time women threw off convention. There is nothing that boys can do that girls cannot do also."

It was not until years later that I realized Mr. Leary didn't say "better" and he didn't say "as well." "Also" was the word he had had for it.

To a college graduate, Mr. Leary went on, there were four main highroads open to Destiny: Fame, Fortune, Doing What You Wanted (otherwise known as the Pursuit of Happiness), and Service to Humanity. As none of these highroads appeared to be littered with parsley, radishes, raised bread, or scalding dish towels, I secretly determined to combine all four—I would buy back the Quincy house—we would have *six* Finnish maids to wash out the bathtub and turn down the beds—we would have a Winton. That was better than an Apperson.

"Do you think I could go to college?" I asked Mr. Leary anxiously.

"If you have the necessary stick-to-itiveness," he replied, "and the money."

I was thirteen. In three years, when I was ready to go, I thought, it could be managed.

I could hardly wait to get home and tell my sister.

"Bunkydoodle," she said, "you'll never get to college. You can't even read the end of *Swiss Family Robinson* ["And now came the worst parting of all. The mother from her two brave sons. But they were brave and hopeful"] without crying. Mama says that shows you're emotionally unstable."

"I'm going to ask Ma now," I said. "I bet she'll let me."

"I bet she won't," said my sister. "She's mad at you. When you took up the register in the hall to wash it, you forgot to put it back and she stepped down it."

By the time this had worn off, something worse happened. My mother received a letter from the bank saying her account was overdrawn.

"I shall go right to Mr. Myers," said my mother. "It is his business to see that such things do not occur. I don't understand it."

She returned heartbroken.

"I have bad news," she said tearfully. "We have spent too much money. Mr. Myers has had to sell another bond. That means our tiny income will be still further reduced. And the franchise on the Burlington and Hinesburg has expired."

"No Apperson," my sister moaned.

"Now I'll never get to college!" I wailed.

"College," my mother said. "To think that a child of mine who has the ambition and brains to go to college should be denied that privilege! What are things coming to?"

She burst into tears and went upstairs to bed. Next morning, she came down, radiant. She had been thinking, she said. Of course, I could go to college! When you came right down to it an *education* was an *investment*. Mr. Myers couldn't object to our making an investment, could he? I would have to have a good suit from Hollander's, of course. And some shoes from Thayer McNeil's. We *could* get them cheaper at Jordan Marsh's. But the best was always cheapest in the end. There was no use being penny-wise and pound-foolish.

"But—" I began.

But her no buts, my mother cried with sudden gaiety. Just let *her* manage, she said. Everything would come out all right if we were careful.

I PREPARE TO MAINTAIN MYSELF

*E*very morning, when I arrived at Simmons College, there was a note on the bulletin board telling me to report to the Dean's office. I reported.

"It has been brought to my attention," said the Dean, casting a jaundiced eye over the Daily Crime Sheet, "that you have been seen talking to the policeman on Ruggles Street. And you have been whistling in the corridors. Can it be," she asked, smoothing down her billowing black-taffeta skirt and blinking her eyes disapprovingly, "you are not aware that this is unladylike?"

I hadn't come to Simmons to brush up on the fine points of being a lady. I had come to be a Pioneer. I wanted to learn new and radical things, like business law and touch typewriting. I thought I was entering the front-line trench in the glorious battle for the emancipation of women.

There was nothing in the outward appearance of Simmons College to suggest it was the front-line trench in the battle for anything. It was a large, austere stone rectangle rising phoenix-like from the ashes of the burning dump on Boston's Fenway. The catch was that it "prepared girls for self-maintenance," an aim so epochal in its implications I almost fainted every time I thought of it. My enthusiasm, however, was not shared by the solid citizens of that day who regarded the whole dirty business as radical, if not downright disgusting. Why should ladies wish to spend long hours in dirty offices, risking possible insult from the sex whose sworn duty it was to support them? Would gentlemen be willing to tip their hats, or to give up their seats on "electrics," to abandoned creatures who preferred jotting down cabalistic signs in notebooks to exercising their God-given right to break their backs over washtubs and hot cookstoves?

I didn't care. I could do a jackknife dive and I owned a pair of blue-serge bloomers. They were pretty droopy but they were bloomers just the same. I had shuffled off the mortal coil of household drudgery. As far as gentlemen were concerned, their time might be better spent looking to their laurels. Besides, self-maintenance for me would be a necessity. By the time I had achieved a "knowledge of arithmetic sufficient for the application of fundamental principles," together with a high-school diploma, our finances had hit an all-time low. My mother had had to sell our little white farmhouse in Cohasset and we had come, via two rooms and meals at a boardinghouse, to the south end of a house going north in Wollaston. My sister, fed up with "repose" and weary of waiting for our overdue ship to come in, had enrolled at Bryant and Stratton's Secretarial School. To everyone's surprise, including her own, she turned out to be so smart that they were allowing her to work out part of her tuition by teaching. But the other part had to be paid. And the floors of the Wollaston house were so "disreputable" that my mother was "forced" to put down Chinese matting. Of course, she wasn't forced to plant Persian lilacs at the corners of the tiny lawn. But it looked "dreadfully bare" without them. Our bank balance was nothing. It was only thanks to my mother's diamond sunburst that I was able to take off one warm September day, in my green nun's veiling with the taffeta underskirt and the spiffy two-toned cloth-topped button boots, to crash the wide stone portals of higher learning.

Simmons was in its infancy when I got there. "Opened, October 9, 1902 with —— students," the catalogue said. Although this start was a little discouraging, things had picked up and there were about four hundred when I entered. The course was terrific. Simmons ambitiously aimed to combine the cultural with the vocational over a four-year period, with an eye to turning out a virtually foolproof product. Everybody had to take English, History, French, German, Biology, and Sociology. Outside that, you could name your own poison.

What did I want to be? Social worker? Their rats always showed, and they wore ground-gripper shoes. Laboratory technician? Laboratories smelled badly. Librarian? Stuffy. Dietitian? I had been taught to cook and cook correctly. "There is a right and wrong way to do everything, even to beating an egg," my mother and Mr. Ralph Waldo Emerson said. Besides, one of my main reasons for going to college was to escape the white woman's burden. There was no use jumping out of the frying pan into the double boiler. So I would be a Secretary; complete knowledge at my fingertips; trigger-quick judgment in a crisis. The power behind the boss.

I lived at home.

"Unfortunately," said my mother, "this pittance upon which we are supposed to exist cannot be stretched to cover your board at a dormitory. I shall shortly have to sell another bond, and if worst comes to worst we may even have to part with our autograph collection. However," she added, brightening, "I hardly think you would care to be one of a group."

I was sure of it. I had no desire to make fudge over a gas jet, or receive callers under the supervision of a "house mother." Besides, I liked commuting. Swinging out of the house to hop the 7:45 local to Boston was the 1906 version of standing on the steps of a sod hut on the prairie, shading your eyes with one hand to see if the grasshoppers were coming, while with the other you protected your little ones from the swift onrush of marauding Indians. It was Pioneering.

There was a thrill in trudging across the Fenway after dark, past the fitful fires of the burning dump. When I boarded the Boston-bound "electric," tired and book-laden, there was a spring in my step. I was a business girl! When we clattered past the Hotel Somerset, I would dart a contemptuous look at the striped awning erected to protect the patrons of the dance to be held that evening. I was glad I didn't have to fritter away my time like that! I didn't have to simper and giggle and stick out a dainty foot so the maid in the Somerset might draw off my fur-edged carriage boot. I didn't have to hope my dress was fluffy enough, my shoulders white enough, and my smile dazzling enough to lure some silly male into dancing with me and then, when he was off guard, swoop him up in my marriage net. I had work to do. I was going places.

Off the car, I shoved my way into Cobb Bates & Yerxa's for a free cup of sample coffee, like any commuter. I was as good as, or better than, they were. After four years at Simmons, I would be worth ten dollars a week of anybody's money.

Nights, when civilization crowded in on me, I would tackle Essex Street. In the daytime Essex Street was full of big dray horses, rearing and plunging as they struggled to back their huge drays, full of rich-smelling hides, up to the leather warehouses. It was narrow, crooked, and cobble-lined. At night it was dark as pitch, deserted, and considered dangerous. I would step out of the bright patch of light under the marquee of the Hotel Touraine, past the man selling violets, into inky blackness. Head up, I would march briskly along, hoping some thug with his hat jammed over his eyes would lunge out at me from a deserted doorway. I'd fold him up like a jackknife. There was a lift to a thing like that. It was part of trail blazing.

Even quiet nights devoted to "research" in the Public Library proved an inspiration. I would run up the little winding, musty stairs to the ivory tower where the "original sources" were kept, and pace up and down while the old custodian with the rumpled hair and thick glasses dug around in the safe for them. Here, right in my hand where I could look at them, were authentic records of the East India Company and the Pilgrims who blazed trails and sailed uncharted seas. I never thought to wonder if pioneering got them anything.

Friday nights were not inspiring. On Fridays we had Dean's meetings. There was a corroding air of lavender and old lace about them. At five o'clock, four hundred potential self-maintainers crowded into the assembly room on the top floor. Suddenly, the Dean held up her hand with the little white, lace-edged handkerchief dangling from it. When you could hear a pin drop, she addressed us. She was short and very round and wore a black-silk dress that completely enveloped her. Her hair was parted in the middle and combed down on each side in neat crimps. She looked like Queen Victoria, if Albert had never existed. She had an electric smile which she flashed on and instantly snapped off again. We were Pioneers, she said. Only she said it with a small letter. The world would judge women by how we comported ourselves. We must be efficient. We must be ladies. We must be careful. Above all, we must be inconspicuous.

She made me feel as if we weren't Pioneers at all. Who ever heard of Pioneers who were inconspicuous? Or careful? Or who lay awake nights dreaming up new and better ways to be "of service"? I wanted her to talk about how we were going to set the world on fire and the great things the future held in store for us. I pictured us, battle-ax in hand, storming the bastions of legitimate business. Simmons didn't.

Simmons wanted us to creep forward on all fours, whispering the battle cry of service. Well, I was going to be a Pioneer anyway. With a capital *P*. If she didn't like it, she could lump it.

But when I blazed up the Fenway next morning, hatless, and in my little Pioneer special of red-flannel shirtwaist, short skirt, and moccasins, the Dean didn't like it and she didn't lump it. There was the customary note on the bulletin board saying she "would see me" in her office.

"You might remember," she said, "that the world is censorious. Public opinion cannot be disregarded so cavalierly." This valuable pearl was allowed to kick around in the trough for a pregnant moment. "In later life," she went on crisply and with heightening color, "you may find it costly to maintain such an independent attitude. The law of compensation has not to my knowledge yet been repealed."

I gave her ten on phrasing but zero on content. Women were emancipated, true or false? Besides, the divine right of every inhabitant of one of the thirteen original states to do as she (or he) pleased, and the devil take the consequences, is not something to be lightly abrogated. And, after all, had not Dr. Dewing, the philosophy professor, said that true happiness was to be gained only through self-expression?

I felt pretty independent because though I was the youngest freshman ever registered at Simmons—I was barely sixteen—my marks were sensational. To one reared on such stout fare as Lanfrey's *Life of Napoleon* and Plato's *Republic*, most courses at Simmons were purely elementary. Shorthand and typewriting, however, I practiced day and night. Good students were sometimes given outside assignments, and I wanted to be one of them.

It seemed years—it was two years, actually—before I was asked to report the lecture by the Commissioner of Education to the Milton Parent-Teachers Association. A Milton newspaper applied to the college for a stenographer, and I was recommended. I was to receive the unbelievable sum of ten dollars.

The Commissioner of Education who addressed the meeting was a fast talker, but I kept two jumps ahead of him. When he came to

"(4) Children's Homework," he went into high. Homework he evidently regarded as bosh, and with a good deal of bitterness.

"The children just sit around and wave their pencils and draw pictures and talk hour after hour and get nothing done," he said. "Two or three hours' dawdling is positively disastrous."

At this point, one of Milton's doughtiest dowagers came out of her igloo.

"Just how much dawdling do you think *should* be allowed?" she asked in all seriousness.

The Commissioner blew up. He talked a mile a minute. But I got every word of it, question and answer. Next day, I transcribed it and sent it to the Milton paper. They printed it word for word. It looked pretty funny. The lady wrote in. The Commissioner wrote in. Everyone wrote in—and everyone was furious. The matter was referred to the college authorities. I was yanked to the Dean's office.

"Your typing and your shorthand may be perfect," said the Dean, with fire in her eyes, "but you have, nevertheless, made an error. An error in judgment, to be explicit. Has it ever occurred to you that there might be some things not worth reporting?"

"Not worth reporting?" I cried, amazed. "I thought it was priceless!"

The Dean didn't. By the time she got through, I doubted if the future held anything but trouble in store for me. There were things, she hinted blackly, that Simmons didn't like about me.

Well, there were things I didn't like about Simmons.

One was that there was nowhere for me to eat the little three-thousand-calorie snack I brought along every day to keep my strength up. We were forbidden to eat lunch upstairs in a classroom. "Crumbs," it said on the bulletin board, "breed rodents." Of course, bloated capitalists with twenty or thirty cents to squander could trek over to the dormitory on Brookline Avenue and eat a lunch prepared by the Household Ec. Students on a trial-and-error basis. The only haven for the underprivileged was down cellar with the janitor. As Simmons was built on not-very-well-made land, when it rained the tide rose, and the down-cellar-eaters had to sit on crates and put their feet on duckboards.

I complained loudly to the Authorities. They passed the buck to the Trustees. I bearded Robert Treat Paine 2nd and Guy Lowell in their lairs. Redress was promised, but our wrongs continued. So I headed Boston's first walkout. Over at the Boston Art Museum there was a lunchroom where, it was bruited about, the chicken-salad sandwiches and marshmallow cupcakes were exceptionally yummy. These tasty tidbits, sold at cost, were designed to bolster the waning morale of foot-weary art lovers. We landed, however, in the wake of a stampede. I had reckoned without *Bacchante*.

Bacchante was a statue. Her unveiling in the courtyard of the Boston Public Library had disrupted Boston. *Bacchante* was nude. She held in her arms a fat cherub before which she lusciously dangled a bunch of grapes. Nudity and joy in one dose were too bitter a pill for Boston to swallow. *Bacchante* was "dirty"! Families divided. Breasts were beaten. *The Boston Transcript* was deluged with letters. Why not a pair of Plymouth Rock pants for *Bacchante*? While the controversy raged, she was snaked out, chastely swathed in burlap, and bundled off to the Art Museum.

That was the day I appeared with my hungry little band of insurrectos. *Bacchante* had just blown in, and all Boston had come to disapprove of her. Every last chicken-salad sandwich and marshmallow cupcake had been wolfed down by the disapprovers. Hungry and crestfallen, we returned, but our absence had been noted.

"One classroom," it said on the bulletin board, "will be designated for eating purposes."

Although this was my round, I stayed in my corner. I did not want a showdown on my newspaper career. The Dean regarded all newspaper publicity as "conspicuous." If she found out about it, she might put a stop to my "publicizing" the college in the Boston papers. That would have been a blow. I gloried in my unsigned column, at five dollars per, in *The Boston Transcript*, and my free-lance reporting for *The Boston Herald*.

I am sure the Dean would not have approved of the fight I had with the *Herald* about money. I was mad because they not only cut to one inch my full-page story of a fire which caused damage estimated at twenty-four dollars, but they ignored my spirited requests for cash on the barrelhead. I descended upon the *Herald* office in high dudgeon. How could they pay me, the editor asked fretfully, unless I brought the items in and let them measure them? As I'd thrown them into the wastebasket, I told him, this was impossible.

"Dad blast it," said the editor, removing the toothpick from his mouth and taking his feet off the window sill, "if that isn't just like a fool woman."

"Dad blast it yourself," I said heatedly.

No man in a derby hat could cast aspersions on *my* sex even if he *was* editor of *The Boston Herald*. The matter was ultimately settled by negotiation. Quite amicably.

My happy discovery that discretion was the better part of valor encouraged me to further suppression of the truth. I decided to keep strictly under my hat the fact that I was doing a little offside pioneering at Harvard College. Simmons discouraged any association with members of the male sex as "distracting." However, I felt I was doing a real service to the cause of the emancipation of women by disposing of the base canard that unchaperoned girls were not safe at Harvard. I felt I was just the girl for the job. I was so wholesome.

I must admit, after critical examination of old snapshots, that I did not *look* wholesome. In spite of my tailored Gibson shirtwaist, neat bow tie, serge skirt, and pigskin-leather belt, my twenty-two-inch waist taken in conjunction with my thirty-eight bust produced an effect which I can best describe as startling. This effect was further accentuated by the fact that, eschewing corsets as unhealthy, I had adopted a contraption entirely innocent of bones, known as the Flynt waist. And even though my serge skirt was the customary eight inches from the floor, it was apparent to the observant that I possessed what were known in those days as "Frankie Baileys" or, currently, "Petty legs." My luxuriant black hair I wore twisted loosely into a "French roll" to save time and hairpins.

My passionate appearance concealed, however, as my admirers soon found out, only an intemperate zeal for sports and an almost fanatical interest in business. I have been told that my first words to a new partner at a dance were always, "What business is your father in? What's the overhead and what were last year's gross sales?"

I hope that is an exaggeration. But I wouldn't guarantee it. My entire knowledge of sex had been gleaned at an act put on by John Daniel, the baboon, at Keith's, which I am sure wasn't in his contract. I was interested but hardly enlightened. I adhered to my mother's admonition not to let boys "take any liberties" with me. I assumed this referred to kissing. Kissing led, I gathered from reading *Tess of the D'Urbervilles*, to illegitimate babies. I had no desire to have one.

If all this sounds forbidding, let me add that I not only could paddle my own canoe but if necessary carry one end of it. This was rare in 1910, when girls had to be waited on. I was, moreover, possessed of a limitless fund of physical energy, known then as "vivacity." It is possible that my swains hung on in the hope that they could direct it into what may have seemed to them more productive channels. Anyhow, they hung on. Maybe they were attracted by my uncanny ability to figure out intercollegiate track-meet possibilities to fourth places. The fact remains they were attracted. Gardner Boyd, a Harvard student who lived near us, even tried to hang himself in the attic when I refused to abandon my career to marry him. There were skeptics who ascribed his act to a quarrel with his mother over taking violin lessons. But he told me himself, while I was helping him put back the clothesline, that he had been "driven to the point of madness" by my "cruel attitude." This attention I received from the male sex was, of course, in spite of the fact that I went to Simmons. Simmons girls, as a group, were regarded by Harvard students, and even Tufts students, as "pills." Radcliffe girls were "horse marines in shell-rimmed spectacles."

Naturally, the nucleus of my admirers was at Harvard. All the boys I had known in school, as well as the sons of old Quincy friends, went there. I would have done well to stick to this group. If I had, my first little job of pioneering wouldn't have proved so disappointing. I led off my campaign by going to three baseball games, unchaperoned, with the man who held the Strength Test Record at Harvard. He was not a local product. I was invited to meet him when he came to near-by Quincy to address the boys of the Sunday school. He was not only strong. He was a DKE, a member of Phi Beta Kappa, and relief pitcher on the baseball team. He was also tall, dark, and handsome and had a pompadour haircut. One of those all-around personalities who fascinate women and registrars. I knew he was respectable because his parents, who came to visit from up in the Catskills, wore little white ribbons to signify they were members of both the WCTU and the Epworth League. My first shock came when he refused to match me for the fare when we were on the way out to our house for dinner. (Pioneer or no pioneer, I was not allowed to stay out with a man after dark unchaperoned.) I was further bewildered by the fact that when he went up to the bathroom to wash his hands he turned the nude print, which hung over the bathtub, face to the wall. My sister suggested that he was crazy. But my mother said it was because he had no background; he didn't know a good etching when he saw one. He kept pestering me to admit we had an understanding, and I didn't know what an understanding was. But when he said if we had one he would give me his Harvard banner and his DKE pin and his sweater with the H on it, I said yes, we did. Then an awful thing happened. He wrote me a letter saying that as Taft, who was running for President, was a Unitarian, he and his family were *praying* for him! A Unitarian to be prayed for by a lot of Methodists! I sent back the DKE pin, the Harvard banner, and the sweater with the H on it.

"You did just right," my mother said. "After all, we didn't know *who* he was. And I always said he had flat feet."

After that, I was more careful. I spent many bracing afternoons with two members of the gun team who lived in a converted apartment house called the Brentford, shooting pigeons off near-by Trinity roof. Pigeon pie, properly prepared, can be very good and it isn't bad when made on a chafing dish. The social position of the gunners was unimpeachable. My mother had exchanged calls with their mothers.

"But even if I hadn't," said my mother, "there would be no chance of your going wrong there. Both Hauthaway and Higginson are *good* names."

She approved of my going over to Harvard. But of course she didn't know I was cutting classes. She thought I waited till my last class was dismissed.

With the gun team lived an unhappy soul named Bert Rogers. He sang in the quartet. Bert had a habit of shaving openly at the end of the hall. This was the signal for his sharpshooting roommates to pick off the toothbrushes and other paraphernalia which surrounded his mirror.

Another member of this vicious circle was a large bird dog named King. It was King's duty to retrieve the pigeons. If he brought them in mangled, we stuck pins in them and threw them out again. When King went out to retrieve them we shouted from the window, "Don't mouth, King, don't mouth." King was so large and furry, his owner, "Coots" Hauthaway, used to take him to class and use him for a pen-wiper.

The gun team had in their room a copy of the suppressed number of the Harvard *Lampoon* which I considered excruciatingly funny. The cover showed a pretty lady wrapped in the arms of a huge Russian. Title "GetoffmylipskiIwantospitovitch." Another joke: Student in Shop, "How much are Wigglesworth?" Clerk, "He's your quarterback."

My association with the gun team had a sad ending. A play called *Brown of Harvard* had come to the Castle Square Theater in Boston. In it an actor named Woodruff wore a sweater emblazoned with a big H, an honor to which he was obviously not entitled. My friends greeted his appearance on the stage with a barrage of lemons. There was a fine. There was incarceration. I wrote a post card to Mr. Bert Rogers, Mr. "Coots" Hauthaway, and Mr. Maynard Higginson, begging them to address the Bridgewater Normal School on "My Glimpse of Prison Life, or Forty Dollars' Worth of Fun." I forgot to mail it, and my mother found it, at a very inopportune moment. She was low in her mind anyway because she'd just had word from Thayer McNeil's that due to changing styles they would be unable to dispose of the last shipment of bedshoes she had sat up nights for weeks knitting for them. Bedshoe revenue plus the money my sister and I earned summers "substituting" was all that kept us from being whisked over the hill to the poorhouse. In the same mail as the bad news from Thayer McNeil's had come a letter from the Dean demanding an explanation of my "unaccountable absences." The Dean said that when I had been asked to explain, my answers had been "equivocal." She also added that my mother might like to know that in getting out the college yearbook, I had been guilty of "blackmail, sacrilege, and libel." Junior Lewis, who fixed our furnace, said he could hear my mother right down the register. If there were any more rows like that, he said, he could make five dollars by renting the rocking chair he sat in while he waited for the coal gas to burn off.

The college yearbook was my special pride and my most ambitious bit of pioneering. I had got it out over everybody's dead body. Simmons had never had a college yearbook, so why should they have one? "Do you *forbid* me to get one out?" I asked the President. He said he washed his hands of it. I solicited the advertising, wrote most of the articles, and authorized the printing. I named it *The Microcosm*. Things were coming along fine, when the President called me into his office. He had thought I would appreciate being given a free hand, he said. But no! I had construed liberty as license. The Trustees were up in arms. They had learned that I had told the firms doing business with Simmons that unless they advertised in *The Microcosm* the college would withdraw its patronage. *Blackmail*. I had referred to the statue of Phillips Brooks in Copley Square as "hailing an electric," when—all unbeknown to me—he was really gainfully employed in blessing the multitude. *Sacrilege*. I had insinuated that the Burroughs Adding Machine was wearisome to operate. Quote! "The pressure on the lever of this machine is something like ten pounds to the square inch. As we take our somewhat stubby lead pencil in hand to pen this article, a telegram comes in from the camp of that greatest American of modern times, Mr. James Jeffries, future defender of the supremacy of the white race. 'Can Jeff come back? Well, we guess yes. The Burroughs Adding Machine has done it.'" End of quote. *Libel*.

Guilty as charged. But I didn't think the authorities would be so mean as to tell my mother. They not only told her, but they added baldly that unless I made a very high average in the "Jones Manufacturing Company" the college would be regretfully forced to withhold my diploma.

The Jones Manufacturing Company was a trial by fire which climaxed the four-year secretarial course at Simmons. The Irish curse of the three black crows on him who thought it up. It was a mythical company in whose employ the secretarial seniors, for a frenzied fortnight, found themselves. But brief though its existence was, it was definitely spectacular.

On the desk of each secretary, when she arrived in the morning, was a large wire basket full to the scuppers with telegrams, letters, bills, notes, contracts—every conceivable disaster known to man. These knotty problems, which would have set a battery of International Business Machines back on its heels, were supposed to be solved speedily and *in toto* by one lone secretary. Where was that shipment of thread? Where was the receipt from the express company? Why didn't the checkbook balance? Clue. "There is, you may notice, a check missing for which the stub has not been filled out. What course is indicated?" What course, indeed! And as a sorrow's crown of sorrows, coyly snuggling at the very bottom of the basket, yes, a note at the bank three days overdue. "Attend to this." (Business of kneeling, arms outstretched in supplication.) Every night, having brought order out of chaos, the secretary would stagger out, if possible in her right mind, because the next morning the whole thing would begin all over again.

I don't know what ever became of the officials of the Jones Manufacturing Company. But I will make a little wager of ten to one that they're on relief. Nothing else, in a country where justice allegedly holds its head high, could possibly have happened to them.

I skimmed along nicely until the fourth day of the second week, when I suffered a slight attack of claustrophobia. This turned rapidly into a severe attack of the twitches. My ability to co-ordinate cracked up completely. I began writing Bones instead of Jones. No erasures allowed. No place to throw the spoiled sheet. In the office of the Jones Manufacturing Company no such defeatist suggestion as a wastebasket was allowed to intrude. Every page had to be letter perfect when handed in at the desk.

"Yours sincerely," double space, and my hands would begin to sweat. Slower and slower. Dear God, let it be J. I know I'm a Unitarian, but let it be J. *Please* let it be J. Bones. I took the letter up to the monitor, a mean-looking woman who wore bifocals.

"What is the matter with you?" she asked severely. "Are you doing this on purpose?"

I walked out and slammed the door.

"I can't help it if you don't give me my diploma," I said stubbornly to President Lefavour, who was now pinch-hitting for the Dean. "I've got my education. You can't take that away from me."

He tipped himself back in his chair and looked at me quizzically.

"Do you always have to swim upstream?" he asked.

I didn't answer. I couldn't think of the words to express my conviction that that was the only way *to* swim.

Well, I'd come to Simmons for an education and I'd got one, I thought, as I walked slowly down the corridor. But I couldn't help thinking of a theme a classmate had written way back in freshman year. "Simmons is a new enterprise, a daring scheme which plans to give training in those arts and sciences which will help women to earn a living wage. We who answer her call are Pioneers. Thousands will flock to our standards. We shall sweep onward strong, brave, and indomitable. Our names will be shouted from the housetops. We shall be heralded as those who come to regenerate a man-made world!" It had brought tears to my eyes. "Tripe!" Mr. Hastings, the English instructor, had scrawled across it.

I hurled my books into my locker. The way of the Pioneer, like the way of the transgressor, was hard. But if they thought they had us licked, they had another think coming. Wait till we got out into the world! Just watch our smoke!

I got my B.S. But not in person. White dimity was not my idea of what the well-dressed Pioneer should wear. Nor did dancing on the grass in white cheesecloth to Mendelssohn's "Spring Song" appeal to one whose soul was clad in buckskin. I went over to Brookline the morning of graduation and spent the day in a Turkish bath.

SIXTY DOLLARS A MONTH

I AM putting a postal card addressed to me in your purse," said my mother. "Be sure and write a few words on it and drop it in the first mailbox you see when you get off the train."

I hardly heard her. With heart beating like a trip hammer, I buttoned my spats, put on my black sailor hat, and drew on my dogskin gloves. My great moment had arrived. I was about to plunge headlong into the maelstrom of life. I was leaving home to become a career woman.

The job was in New Haven, and everybody came down to the station to see me off. Flowers, candy, fruit, even a pair of silver sugar tongs. You would have thought I was going on an expedition with Peary rather than to another New England city three hours away. Even my baggage, which included two iron suitcases, two tennis rackets, and a baseball bat, was impressive. I can't imagine why I took the baseball bat. Possibly I remembered that "Harvard was old Harvard when Yale was but a pup" and fancied myself strolling over to the village green after supper to knock up a few flies.

My mother, who had been brave up to the very last, broke down completely when she heard the train whistle.

"My little baby," she cried, "my little baby," and burst into tears.

The other seer-offers regarded this outburst callously. How anyone, even a mother, could refer in these tender terms to someone who, from the rear anyway, resembled a fullback on a college football team was beyond their comprehension. It was not beyond mine. I felt pretty teary myself. It was the first time I'd ever been away from home. The fact that I was twenty years old and large for my age didn't alter the fact at all. It was still the first time. Besides, I had a sneaking feeling that I was being selfish. My mother was having her usual struggle to get along. True, my sister had a promising secretarial job with a well-known brokerage house. But I'd never made any return for the money my mother had spent on me. Maybe I ought to have got a job near home and paid board.

My gone feeling gradually gave way to elation as I settled myself carefully in a seat on the shore side. This was the moment to which I had looked forward during four years of grueling preparation at Simmons College. I was standard-bearer in the vanguard of the irresistible army of women who, in 1910, had the courage to thumb their noses at public opinion and fight for financial independence.

Taking a hard-boiled egg and two hermits out of my lunch—an army travels on its stomach—I reread the letter from the Dean summoning me for an interview with a "prospective employer."

I don't know what I expected in the way of an employer. But I certainly didn't expect an old Yale Professor Emeritus with a white mustache and derby hat. Nor could I possibly have foreseen the epic nature of the work which would engage us.

The Professor, it seems, was about to embark upon the preparation of a series of readers for pupils in the elementary schools, readers which would revolutionize human nature. They would contain no silly stories about how Cock Robin got killed or Epaminondas, he careful how he step on dose pies, he step—right—in—de-middle-obevery one. No wonder, he said, that children turned out badly when they tooled up for manhood and womanhood on such ungrammatical and subversive pap. Each story in *his* readers would point a moral. But obliquely. The innocent victim would be unaware that it was creeping up on him till, bingo, it pierced him right in the conscience. From then on he would quit throwing spitballs and swiping cookies, and his life would become one long sweet song of helpful and constructive activity.

If this seems vague to you, let me say right now that to Professor Cronk it wasn't. This was no hit-or-miss proposition, so he informed us. He had diagrams and he had charts; he was fuller of unasked-for and detailed information than a college catalogue. Take cats. There was cats, kindness to rewarded; cats, unkindness to punished. My task would be to thumb through fairy tales, folklore, juvenile thrillers, and what not till I found a story with vocabulary suitable for use in the lower grades where justice met cat. The child who read that story would never again pick pussy up by the tail and give her a good larrup. Not if he had any sense he wouldn't.

It wasn't only cats. Professor Cronk was thorough. It went on from cats through cheetahs and leopards and tigers till it started at the bottom again with dogs. Every conceivable animal was included, even those that nobody knew existed till they turned up years later in a crossword puzzle. He had not, however, included fathers and mothers. Evidently on the theory that if you had learned to be kind to a lion or a ferret, your resistance would have been sufficiently broken down so you could take parents in your stride. The only real trouble he had run into was with flies. What might constitute kindness from a fly's point of view might constitute unkindness from a human's. But it would clear itself up. The thing was to get started; to get along.

He had, so he informed us, because of the colossal nature of the undertaking, enlisted the services of two confederates. One was an English dean whose name would look well on the title page. The other was the Superintendent of the New York City schools, whose name—if everything worked out according to Hoyle—wouldn't. But who could doubt that with such an eminent collaborator the books would be specified as they came hot off the press for use in the New York City schools? Not me. Even if we never solved the one about flies, I thought the whole thing was a pushover.

The salary? I could hardly consider such an insignificant matter, so anxious was I to be included. He knew, he said, that fifty dollars a month was regarded as ample for a beginner, but because of the encouraging account of my ability he had received, he was willing to go a little higher—say sixty dollars? I looked at the Dean. She nodded her head almost imperceptibly.

"Yes," I breathed. The Professor beamed. Not knowing, of course, he could have had me for nothing.

"Mrs. Norton's, where you will board, is about two miles due north of the New Haven station," Professor Cronk said.

When we arrived at the New Haven station, I airily waved away beckoning cab drivers, picked up my baggage, and set off at a rapid pace in the wrong direction. Having walked what I estimated to be two miles, and gathering from the smell of the clam flats that I was approaching the coast, I sat down on my suitcases to rest. It did not seem as if Mrs. Norton could keep house in a bolt-and-nut factory, so I inquired. My error, it seemed, had resulted from the fact that the ocean had moved on me while I was traveling. While it was due east of Boston, it was south of New Haven. Picking up my impedimenta, I set out again. When I arrived at the boardinghouse, they had given me up for lost. But they thought I'd done the right thing in not taking a cab. Why should any New Englander squander money on a conveyance when he can still put one foot before the other? I was glad, though, when Professor Cronk's car showed up for me next morning. My blisters were pretty bad.

"Ever see *her?*" said the chauffeur as we bowled along Whitney Avenue. No, I said, I hadn't. "Well, you will," said the chauffeur brightly, "and don't say I didn't warn you. She wears the pants."

Before I had time to inquire further, we had arrived at the Professor's house, a huge Elizabethan structure reeking with turrets, towers, and batten doors. When I lifted the carved bronze knocker, a peal to wake the dead resulted. I fully expected Robin Hood and a couple of other medieval soldiers to pop out at me. Nothing happened but a frightened maid who pointed wordlessly to a button neatly concealed in a wooden panel. Everything in the Cronks' house was like that. Mrs. Cronk, it seems, had made a fortune from her inventions.

Mrs. Cronk was lying in wait for me, ambushed in the dark hall. I wasn't to expect to be called for every morning, she told me. This was only to show me the way.

"The Professor's former secretary, Mrs. Carter," she added, "always used the back door."

"Did she?" I said. I figured the Professor's wife would bear watching.

I found the Professor on the porch in woolen gloves, overcoat, and rubbers. It was evident that he was a fiend on fresh air as well as a bear on morals. We would work on the porch, he said, and pointed to a neolithic Woodstock typewriter. I could start right off on Grimm's *Fairy Tales.*

By the time I went home to lunch I was a little discouraged. I had acquired cold feet and a hearty dislike of the neolithic typewriter. I had found nobody who had been unkind or kind to anyone but a dragon and a stepmother and they, according to the chart, were un-called for. But I felt sure everything would come out all right. I had been taught, and I believed, that there was nothing (except pos-sibly the fickle fancy of the populace) to keep me from being Presi-dent of the United States if I didn't speak to strangers, worked hard, and kept my bowels open.

After the first day—for a while, anyway—things went better. I even found snakes and lizards someone was kind to. But the Pro-fessor got to worrying more and more about flies. If you didn't kill them, you might get sick. If you did, it was: "Flies, unkindness to."

Mrs. Cronk made it her business to see that my duties were not restricted to the preparation of readers. I tutored Henry in Math, Margaret in French, I read aloud to William when he had the measles; not to mention balancing her checkbook and writing invitations when she gave parties. If I was allowed the proud privilege of helping her pick out a new hat or suit, I had to make up the time afterward. I spent so much time being a Companion and Mother's Helper, I hardly had any time left to revolutionize human nature.

Evenings I devoted to catching up on being a career woman. Alice, my roommate at the boardinghouse, was a kindred spirit. She had a cataloguing job at the Yale Library that paid ten dollars a week. She was a tall, willowy blonde whose demure expression was far from being an index to her character. She had refused to pay five dollars for a sheepskin at Simmons, on the ground of both economy and principle. Unable to afford silk, she attended both junior and senior dances at college in cotton. As her family had come to this country in 1635 and were among the incorporators of the town of Andover, my mother considered her an "eminently suitable companion." Like me, she had always gone to bed at 7:30 unless she had callers. Like me, she had unbounded confidence in her ability to handle any situa-tion. Alice and I both felt the boardinghouse was a tough place for career women. We stayed because it cost us only eight dollars apiece for room, board, and the "privileges of the laundry." Our room was on the north and didn't have any heat. The mattress was so thin we had to put newspapers under it. But the gas jet was fine. It didn't give much light but it was splendid to heat your curling tongs over. You had to be careful, though, if you were curling your hair with your cotton flannel nightgown on. Mine got afire once and all the nap burned off. "I hope it will not be necessary for you to experience real disaster," my mother wrote, "in order to learn that no flannel is worth buying but Viyella."

Next to us lived an old engineer with a mustache who was all of twenty-six; next to him was a graduate student named Lawton Mackall who didn't do anything but play Brahms with one finger and then put his hat on and go out. He was nice in spite of the fact that he had red hair and stammered. He said we could use his room if we had callers, because Mrs. Norton didn't like anyone to have callers in the parlor. The couch had no back to it and their hair got the wallpaper greasy. In return for his largess we were supposed to dust his bisque dogs. He had a large collection, garnered during extensive foreign travels. He claimed one bisque dog was interesting; two were stimulating; three were fascinating. We did not share his enthusiasm. However, we dutifully dusted them till his mother, who was a Lawton from Baltimore, came to visit.

"No lady dusts!" said Mrs. Mackall, snatching the dusters out of our hands. "Dusting is for servants."

Lawton originally took his meals at the boardinghouse. But when Mrs. Norton dropped the brown Betty on the floor and burst into tears, he said it was too sad, he couldn't stand it.

The only other boarders were four old ladies over eighty. One was the oldest living graduate of Mt. Holyoke. She was small and thin and stone-deaf. She had a habit of appearing suddenly in doorways out of nowhere like an eccentric ectoplasm. It was hard to realize that in her time she too must have been a career woman.

The old ladies were pretty outspoken old parties. They said decent girls didn't go traipsing off to work every day. They stayed at home where they belonged and got married. We got around them by introducing Oscar Wilde to them. We started them in easy on *Lady Windermere's Fan* and then increased the doses gradually. Before long, we had them clamoring for all kinds of forbidden literature.

Mrs. Norton, our landlady, thought woman's place was in the home and didn't hesitate to say so. She was the wife of a former missionary to China. She was very proud of it and we couldn't see how she could be. In Massachusetts, where we came from, nobody liked missionaries. They were people who wanted to travel and didn't have the price, so they got the church to pay for it. Worse still, they were proselyters. Alice said there was no need to worry, because after Mrs. Norton got through cooking for all those boarders she was too tierd to do any proselyting. But I said I wouldn't trust a missionary around the corner. I gave Mrs. Norton to understand she needn't try any of her old hocus-pocus on me. I was a Unitarian.

Although Mrs. Norton frowned, the old ladies said loyally they thought it was "perfectly proper" for Alice and me to put on our hats and coats and go out after supper. We liked prowling around New Haven. Sometimes we just walked up and down Chapel Street, looking in store windows. We haughtily ignored the rude stares of passers-by, which we attributed to their hidebound notion that women should not go out after dark unattended. It never occurred to us that our appearance might be striking. Alice, with her two enormous braids of golden hair wound round her head, looked like a tall, slim Madonna. I was dark and chunky, and attired in a mannish blue-cheviot suit with stiff white Eton collar. Occasionally, when we were flush, we stopped in at Huyler's and blew fifteen cents on an ice-cream soda. Just like that! It was our *own money!*

Some nights, when we were too tired to walk, we would go out on the little balcony off Lawton Mackall's room and look out over the city. Its lights were bright and made a glow in the sky. The engines in its factories throbbed and hummed far into the night. Things were being made and created. It was as if we could hear the city's heart beating.

When the night was still, we could hear the long low rumble of freight trains pulling into the train yard to change engines. Sometimes from far out in the harbor came the beckoning, lonesome call of a boat whistle. It was breath-catching. Home was a million miles away. This was the maelstrom of life. And we were the New Woman.

We were unpleasantly surprised, however, to find that our social position, which at home was unquestioned, was nil in New Haven. We were just "working girls." We had stepped out of the Boston orbit, where family and background were the supreme requirements, into the New York orbit, where money and clothes were the criterion. If it had not been for Lawton Mackall, we might have blushed unseen. Lawton had been plying me with silver belt buckles and hatpins with Yale seals on them, object matrimony, ever since I arrived in New Haven. (Hell-bent on a career, I spurned his attentions.) He became our press agent. Assiduously, he spread the rumor that despite our lowly occupations we were "ladies."

Bob Haas, Yale 1910, was the first to bite. He had a fur-lined overcoat and a Simplex racer complete with chauffeur, which he was grooming for the Hill Climb in New Haven. Our stock rose by leaps and bounds when we were driven home from work by Vittorio in the Simplex. In no time at all, Lawton's room became a Mecca for Yale students who came to scoff, but remained to toast marshmallows over the gas jet, and make the welkin ring with gems from *The Pink Lady*. The "old" engineer begged to be allowed to join us but we wouldn't let him. We were afraid the sounds of revelry might disturb the old ladies on the third floor. Far from it. They left their doors ajar, we found, so they wouldn't miss a note of it.

But our life wasn't all beer and skittles. Just to be sure we weren't stagnating mentally, we went to lectures. One lecturer told such a harrowing tale about how hard Woolworth girls worked, and how little they got paid for it, that we got up a club for them. We found an empty loft and organized a basketball team. Every two weeks everybody would bring sandwiches and lemonade and we would have a "social." The Woolworth girls didn't like it much, but we enjoyed it.

It was Mrs. Cronk's nephew, who was going around with one of the Woolworth girls, who told Mrs. Cronk about it. She said it was silly to do anything for the poor; it made them discontented. She didn't approve of my going out nights, anyway. I was getting myself talked about. She said I made myself conspicuous by wearing a white-rubber raincoat and sneakers. Ladies did not do things like that in New Haven. She even said that when Alice and I had gone down to the station to see the Dartmouth train go through, people had criticized.

The Special stopped at New Haven to change engines on its way to Princeton. A couple of Dartmouth boys we knew had said that if Alice and I were at the station when the train pulled in, they'd wave to us. We were there. They couldn't get out. The train was sealed just as if they were exiles being sent to Siberia. Only half a dozen cases of rye had been sealed in with them. They waved. We waved back. The train door couldn't take it. Yielding to the terrible pressure within, it burst open. Hordes of exuberant exiles poured out. They lifted us to their shoulders and carried us through the train triumphantly.

"My nephew was at the station," said Mrs. Cronk. "He saw it."

I forgot that an employer's wife is always right. I said I could take care of myself without any help from her. Or her nephew. I said why didn't people mind their own business. This was 1910. Not 1890. The old ladies at the boardinghouse were very indignant when they heard about it. They said Mrs. Cronk was nosy. They advised me to write my mother. My mother wrote back reminding me to guard my tongue, an unruly member. There was no necessity of offending Mrs. Cronk. Though she herself was amazed at her attitude. It was *who you were*, not *what you did* that counted. If you were *somebody*, it didn't matter what you did. If you were *nobody*, it didn't make any difference. Personally, she had no doubt about my ability to take care of myself. She wasn't worried. (My sister would have added a word, my mother concluded. But she had gone in town to look for a suitable hat. She had been invited to a football game by the Mayor of Salem!)

These votes of confidence were comforting. But after my experience with Waldo Frank, I wasn't so sure of myself. Lawton Mackall introduced me to Waldo Frank, and he invited me to go and see Mordkin and Pavlova. From the first, I was a little afraid of Waldo. He was sophisticated. His behavior had been suspicious at the very start. Why chocolates from Sherry's in hand-painted boxes lined with quilted satin? Chocolates were chocolates. Lowney's were cheaper.

Then there was the engraving on his letter paper. It was so thick. In the middle of the performance at the theater, my worst fears were realized.

"Do you know," he whispered, "that Pavlova has never had a liaison?"

"No!" I whispered back.

I was a little hazy about what a liaison was. I decided uneasily that it was an illegitimate child. I found when I got home and looked it up that I had put the cart before the horse. But I was glad and proud that I had coldly refused his invitation after the performance to have a snack at Heublein's.

When X, several weeks later, invited me to take a buggy ride up East Rock with him I didn't know what to do about it. (I refer to him as X because he now has a position of almost overpowering importance.) X was good-looking, a member of Skull and Bones, and had a line. I caved in like an old-law tenement every time I saw him. He couldn't decide whether to be a minister or an actor, so he spent his time milling around the YMCA, reading poetry. I was an anomaly to him. A working girl with a broad *A*. He asked questions. Was I an Episcopalian? Could I ride horseback? ("Can you write shorthand?" "No," replied the boy in homespun, "but I can try.") I tried. I sent home for a divided skirt and spent hours with an old army sergeant plugging around the ring in the armory. But X never invited me to go riding. I even learned the Episcopal service and tried it out privately once or twice, though it is hard for a Unitarian to kneel, especially after horseback riding. But that subject was never brought up again, either, and I should have been warned.

I wasn't. With the invitation to the buggy ride, I thought I had him. Of course, it was dangerous. But should a soldier of the Irresistible Army show the white feather?

It was moonlight. He quoted Browning: "Ride, forever, ride." My cheek was like velvet, he said. A kiss. The stars above. Below, the city lights. More Browning:

> "*Were you happy?*"—"*Yes*"—"*And are you*
> *Still as happy?*"—"*Yes. And you?*"
> —"*Then more kisses!*"—"*Did I stop them*

When a million seemed so few?"
Hark, the dominant's persistence till it must
Be answered to!

The next morning I got a letter. I had *failed* him! Those kisses! "When I think of my sister," he wrote, "when I think of Jesus."

I read the letter on my way to work. I was pretty depressed. But I was more depressed an hour later when Mrs. Cronk got through with me.

There were a number of things, she said as I entered the front door, she had been meaning to tell me for a long time. She said she didn't like my persuading Professor Cronk to ride a bicycle (so he wouldn't stand behind me eight hours a day breathing down my neck). She said I was too forward. She didn't like the openwork yoke I wore on my shirtwaist. She didn't approve of my taking a course in English at Yale with Henry Seidel Canby. Even if I did make up the time. Ladies didn't do things like that in New Haven. Besides, she'd heard me talking about Theodore Roosevelt as if he was somebody. Everybody knew Theodore Roosevelt was a drunkard! Mrs. Cronk hated Theodore Roosevelt; she owned stock in the New York, New Haven & Hartford Railroad. She said there was a trail of crumbs from the cookie jar in the pantry out to the porch every day. She said mice couldn't have done it. She said she could see I didn't like typewriting. That when I typewrote, waves of protest just *radiated* from me.

But one thing she wanted me to understand. Clearly. I mustn't think that when Mr. Cronk rode over on his bicycle to bring me a box of Huyler's on my birthday, she was *angry*. She was *worried*. He wasn't responsible, poor thing. It might interest me to know that Mr. Cronk was suffering from neurasthenia and that was why she encouraged him to embark on the readers. She was defraying the expenses. But she didn't really give a hoot about cats, kindness or unkindness to. It was all silly!

Silly! My job silly! I felt my face getting red. I mustn't do anything foolish, I told myself. Jobs didn't grow on trees. Maybe all employers were mean. My sister had just had a terrible experience with hers. She'd arrived at work one morning early. She was just about to take off her hat when she heard footsteps. She assumed it was Foster Hitchcock, the office boy. We'd known Foster years before in Quincy. Thinking to surprise him, my sister crouched down behind the wicket. As he put out his hand to open it, she sprang out at him with a piercing scream. Unfortunately, it was not Foster. It was Mr. Reece, the senior partner.

"I cannot conceive of a daughter of mine doing anything so undignified," my mother wrote. "It is so unlike her. I can only conclude that it must have been the Randall in her. The Randalls would resort to any extreme to be amusing. I recall once walking past the gingham counter at Hovey's with your Aunt Maud. Mr. Denham, with whom we had dealt for years, was bending over, his back toward us. Your Aunt Maud seized a measuring stick from the counter and struck him. She then dodged quickly out of sight, leaving me to bear the onus. I have never considered such antics humorous."

After the jumping incident, relations between my sister and Mr. Reece were strained. When my sister asked for the afternoon off to go to the Pi Eta baseball game at Harvard, Mr. Reece *refused*.

"*Naturally,*" my mother wrote, "your sister resigned."

Although it was evident that my mother approved (if, indeed, she had not instigated) my sister's resignation, she might get discouraged, I thought, if we *both* resigned. I'd have to swallow my pride and stay on. I'd have to grin and bear it.

If Billy, Betty, and Ben hadn't taken a hand, the whole thing would have blown over. Billy, Betty, and Ben were brain children Professor Cronk dreamed up for the purpose of being kind or unkind to animals nobody else would have any truck with. Guided by his nimble pen and my faltering Woodstock, these little perverts succeeded where others failed.

That afternoon, while the Cronks were out, Billy, Betty, and Ben got restless. They felt like being unkind to someone and they picked on Mrs. Cronk. I forgot to tear up their little story, and Mrs. Cronk found it. Next day I received a note to the effect that after the first of the month my services would no longer be needed.

"It's outrageous," said Mrs. Norton, our landlady. "You worked your heart out, even if you did have queer notions."

The old ladies were all for marching over to the Cronks in a body and giving Mrs. Cronk a piece of their mind.

"I'll have to get a job somewhere else," said Alice. "I can't stay on in New Haven alone after we've had such good times."

Lawton Mackall said he hated to see me go but he had to admit he'd be glad to have the use of his room again. He'd spent so many evenings wandering around New Haven it was a wonder he wasn't picked up for vagrancy.

Grimly, I packed up my baseball bat and skates and tennis racket. My first dive into the maelstrom of life had been a belly-whopper. The Irresistible Army was in full retreat. But never fear. It would re-form on new lines and attack again with renewed savagery. I'd get a new job. A better job. A job that would knock everybody's eye out. The field of the cloth of gold wasn't even tarnished.

I would miss the old ladies at the boardinghouse, and hearing the city's heart beat. I would miss Alice, and Lawton Mackall. But there were compensations. It would be wonderful to sit down once more with my own family, to a table set with damask and candles and Canton blue china, treasured vestiges of our Imperial Past, unworried by the unsolvable problem of flies, kindness and unkindness to.

$\mathcal{N}$ow THAT you are engaged," said my mother, "you will, of course, give up your position at the Fore River."

"But we'll never be able to be married," I said, "if I give up my job at the Fore River."

"The place for a wife is in the home," said my mother.

"Don't forget this is 1911," I said. "Things have changed since 1876, when you got married."

"Maybe things have," my mother said. "Men haven't. They like to be the center of attention. Why, if your father came home and I wasn't back from the Friday Club, he went right out again."

"Well, other women can sit around being parasites, embroidering and running up bills you can chin yourself on while their husbands slave," I said. "I don't want to. Marriage is a fifty-fifty proposition."

The men she'd known, my mother said mildly, never objected to paying for things. They liked it. It made them feel smart. Men enjoyed feeling smarter than women. Most women she knew weren't parasites, anyway. They kept pretty busy. By the time a woman had cooked three meals, cleaned house, spanked the children and put them to bed, she didn't owe her husband anything.

"But who wants to cook three meals and clean house?" I demanded. "Why should a woman drag around in a Mother Hubbard with her hair in curlpapers, breaking her back over the sink when she can get a job and pay someone to do it for her? Housework is very stultifying. The only thing those poor drones have to tell their husbands when they get home is how the laundry man didn't come, or how Al the butcher cheated them. How much better to keep young and fresh and alert working in an office, and come home bursting with interesting topics of conversation. A man doesn't want a bedraggled slavey. What a man wants is a companion!"

The men she'd known, my mother said, didn't want companions. All they wanted when they came home tired at night was to smell supper cooking. And they didn't want to be told anything. They

53

wanted to do the telling. I might not like to hear it, she went on, but the best way to keep a husband was to make things pleasant for him. Men went where it was pleasantest. Maybe it ought not to be so, but it was. I might as well accept it.

Accept nothing, I thought. The truth was, I'd never intended to get married. "You'll never catch me spending *my* life with my nose pressed to the windowpane," I told my friends. But love, like death, is no respecter of persons. I'd weakened. But that didn't mean I was going to let my marriage be stymied by a lot of outworn old customs. My marriage was going to be different.

"What the institution of marriage needs is a good overhauling," I told my mother.

Maybe it did, said my mother, but she still doubted if Rod would allow me to support him.

"Rod," said my mother, "impresses me as a gentleman."

This from a Bay Stater corresponds to being kissed on both cheeks and decorated with the Croix de Guerre.

Rod and I had met in New Haven. He was one of the Yale students who had been lured to the boardinghouse by Lawton Mackall. A mutual liking for Goldberg cartoons, F.P.A.'s column in the *Evening Mail,* and Joe Jackson's bicycle act at Poli's had ripened into what was euphemistically referred to in New England as "warm affection." Rod was an only child who had been raised behind screens by two doting aunts and a doting mother. He was six feet two, tailored by Brooks Brothers, and had won six Latin prizes at Yale. Not that I was ever one to sit up nights playing games with gerunds and gerundives. But I felt that an erudite touch like that would put my Harvard friends in their places. Of course, he *was* a little thin, but I felt that at twenty he might not have got his full growth yet, and would fill out later: it is always a matter of grave concern to New Englanders that the stock doesn't run down mentally or physically. His sartorial splendor fascinated me. He was a veritable glass of fashion. He not only carried a cane, had different gloves to go with different suits, but he wore an outsize white carnation with pink spots in his buttonhole every day. He also kept several extra pins on the underside of his lapel in case of emergency. I thought this was wise.

I didn't realize till years later that it was an Indication. I was much impressed by the terrific bunch of violets he sent me every Saturday, not knowing at the time that he had arranged with a florist to take off his hands all flowers which might not weather Sunday for the lump sum of fifty cents. When he threatened to jump in the river if I didn't marry him, that clinched it. I didn't want to be a murderer. I remembered the near-suicide of Gardner. It was just luck, I felt, that he had reconsidered.

At first my mother had been doubtful. But when she heard that Rod's mother was a Van Benschoten, she felt better.

"Still, I had hoped you might marry someone with money," she said wistfully. "Wisdom is a defense; and money is a defense."

I knew she was thinking about the Sturtevants and Kings and Rices who were all multimillionaires and who had lived near us on Adams Street, Quincy. I thought she was being very sordid.

True, at the moment Rod had only the $2.50 weekly allowance his mother gave him on which to support me. But he had been promised a job in a New York bank as soon as he learned shorthand and typing. As I had the job at the Fore River, I didn't see why we couldn't whiz right down to the town clerk's office and get married. I could support us while he was learning.

My sister said the whole plan struck her as distinctly bizarre. She felt competent to advise on financial matters because she'd landed a secretarial job that paid twenty-five dollars a week, an unbelievably high salary for a young girl in 1910, especially in Boston. "Can't you see it would be bad form for you to support Rod?" she said. "But why talk about it? He has sense. He'll never let you."

She was right.

"We couldn't do that," he said, when I broached the idea. "People would think I couldn't support you."

"Well, you can't," I said. "People aren't going to think you can just because we don't get married."

He couldn't see it. He agreed with our families that there were certain preliminary rounds to marriage before we qualified for the finals. These included an amethyst hatpin from his aunt, a moonstone brooch from his mother, notices of our engagement in the Boston and

New York papers, and a diamond engagement ring which I regarded as a barbaric symbol of superstition and a shameful waste of money.

These sops to Cerberus were followed by a lot of palaver about "suitable income" and "household furniture." What did love, I asked hotly, have to do with prosperity?

"For the last time," I said, "I'm getting fifteen dollars! Why can't we get married?"

"It just isn't done," he said flatly. "I'm sorry."

When his family heard of my indecent proposals they promptly dragged him off to feed the pigeons in St. Mark's Square, Venice. I lodged a spirited protest. I was told that a trip to Europe was indispensable to a well-rounded education. Besides, his aunt had helped put him through college. He owed it to her to act as courier.

The day they sailed, Jim Claflin and Charlie Nichols, two old beaus, came over. They said I shouldn't take a thing like that lying down. So we took Charlie Nichols' father's knockabout and ripped the spritsail off it trying to jibe off Nantasket. I felt better.

"Let them gallivant around Europe," I said. "I've still got my job at the Fore River."

"I was hoping you would give it up whether you got married or not," said my mother. "I don't see how you can do anything so *common* as to work at the Fore River."

My mother hated the Fore River Shipyard. So did everybody else in Quincy. It might seem a little captious to anyone who didn't know New England that Quincy, left economically high and dry by the dwindling demand for granite, could afford to hate a solid, industrial enterprise like the Fore River. But Quincy would rather have drowned peacefully in the stagnant pools forming in its abandoned quarries than be rescued by a "foreign" agent like the Fore River. Everything about it, including its owners—their names didn't "mean" anything—was alien to Quincy. It was big, it was inefficient, it was impersonal. A man who worked there lost his identity. He had no name, just a number. He had to punch a time clock when he entered; as if a man didn't know enough to get to work on time, and if he was late, he probably had a good reason. They thought they were smart, funnying things up with a lot of red tape and fancy book-keeping. The place was so big, anyway, they couldn't keep track of anything. What was the use of a man doing an honest day's work in a place like that? His boss didn't know him from Adam. He was working for a "soulless corporation."

When sprucely uniformed naval officers and shipyard officials had the temerity to crash the Tennis Club dances at Faxon Hall, they got the brush-off from Quincy society. They weren't ushered up to the patronesses. They weren't even spoken to. They were left to huddle shivering in the corner of the unheated hall, listening to the discordant five-piece orchestra and wishing wanly there was something more bracing than lemonade in the punch glasses.

It was with fear and trembling, once, that I had to admit to my mother that I had been so bedazzled by the brass buttons on a lieutenant's uniform that I had given him permission to call on me. She was quite well impressed when he turned up at the fashionable hour of eight in full evening dress. But it soon came out that he not only *read* but *liked* the New York *Journal*. This yellow sheet had never been allowed to cross our threshold. "Just one more proof," said my mother, "that you *cannot* judge by appearances."

My mother did let down the bars to a Mr. Frick who had made millions, people said, in coal or coke in some dirty place like Pittsburgh. But that was because she had been told that he was, like herself, a Dickens addict. And she was influenced, in spite of herself, by the fact that he wore glasses.

The funny thing was that the Fore-Riverites seemed so unconscious of their inferiority. You would have thought they were the salt of the earth to hear them tell it. A teacher in one of the schools reported that she had caught the children of these immigrants concluding the Lord's Prayer with the words *"Fore-River forever."* The crust of some people!

However, after the panic of 1907, a number of Quincyites—while cussing it up and down and sideways—had taken jobs at the Fore River. Among these were my cousin Ethel Randall, who had not only picked up a cinch in the boss' office but a husband in the welder's division. She was drawn to him by the wonderful stories he told about the English public school he had attended. The one that ended

"And they jolly well pumped on me, d'ye know," always got the best hand from the assembled workers. My cousin Alan Arnold, Harvard School of Forestry, '08, was also an employee, paroled as "Architect" on his own recognizance. Days it was too hot for strolling, he said, he just peered out the window about four o'clock in the afternoon and fixed up the plans on the drafting board to conform to whatever they had been building. "Altering," as he put it, "the cases to fit the circumstances."

If they weren't too proud to work at the Fore River, I wasn't. Besides, it was only a nickel fare from Wollaston, where we were living.

My job was in the battleship department. The government was raising a row over the cost of a battleship built by the Fore River. It demanded an accounting. The Fore River had apparently forgotten what they put into it. My task was to type out endless lists of nuts, bolts, and rivets which would, in the words of the foreman, "impress them buggers down in Washington." I made a good many mistakes because the foreman sat all day with his derby on and his feet on the desk, singing "Ain't it funny how all the cunning little oil stoves grow up to homely men?" But it was a wonderful job. I got fifteen a week for it. Of course, rivets and bolts grow tiresome when you get up in the hundred thousands. But I figured if I hung on, when the pigeon feeder came home from Venice he might be so glad to see me I could slip marriage over on him when he wasn't looking.

When he did come home, he had a constructive suggestion.

"Why not come over to New York and get a job?" he wrote. "You can be near me. And New York salaries, everybody says, are simply fabulous."

We were twenty-one now, and if we waited much longer, I thought, time and old age would overtake us. Maybe, if I were near him, and the salary fabulous enough, I could wear down his resistance.

I wrote that I'd come and that I hoped he was getting on fast with the shorthand and typing. I had read in the papers that some doctor said long engagements were dangerous. I didn't know exactly what that meant but I thought it would throw a scare into him.

My mother was so glad to get me away from the Fore River that she gave the plan her blessing. She was a little disappointed, she said, that I couldn't have had a little time at home to put up jelly and pickles. Crab apples were just coming in. There was nothing nicer to have on the pantry shelf than a few jars of crab-apple jelly. She never hinted that without my twelve dollars a week her financial affairs would once more be reduced to chaos. That might have "held me back." No mother had a right to hold back her children.

No one would have guessed her little world was coming to an end the morning I left. Just "Be a good girl" and a cheery wave of the handkerchief as I set out for the Great Metropolis in my black velveteen with the hobble skirt, and five dollars.

The hobble skirt split when I leaped off the curbstone at Forty-second Street. I hadn't seen the curb, I was so busy looking at people. I was not well impressed to see so many foreigners.

"Where," I shouted to the policeman directing traffic, "is the Hotel Manhattan?"

"You're standing under the marquee now," said the cop. "But you can't do business there, baby. They won't stand for it."

I wished I was back in Boston. I would have written a good stiff letter to the *Transcript* about him.

In the lobby I found Marion Cole, a former classmate at Simmons, waiting for me. I hardly recognized her. She was wearing rouge and silk stockings. Her good looks and my split skirt attracted a good deal of what is known at home as "undesirable attention."

Marion said New York was wonderful. She was a Cambridge girl who "had everything" but found New England unexciting. So she'd left Simmons and come over to Barnard, to "broaden her horizon." I'd written her I was coming to New York and she had located a job for me. She said Frank Alvah Parsons, Director of the School of Fine and Applied Art, wanted a secretary. He hoped to get one for twelve dollars but he would go as high as fifteen if he had to. She had a room for me, too, on One Hundred and Sixteenth Street. It was small. It had a cot, chiffonier, and clothes stand. But there wasn't room for a chair. It was really a converted broom closet. The heating pipe went up through it and the window opened onto the air shaft where they put out the ash and garbage cans. It was pretty noisy at four in the morning. But it was the best she could get for five dollars.

Mr. Parsons turned out to be a choleric, red-faced man with the soul of Bismarck. The minute I stepped into the office he snatched off the little pink-satin rose with the green-satin leaves which my mother had made me to pin at my collar.

"Terrible," he hissed, "terrible," and threw it into the wastebasket. "But you look fairly intelligent," he added, after his blood pressure had let up a little. He tapped his forehead. A secretary with brains, he said, was what he wanted. He was about to embark upon a new and colossal undertaking. He was going to sell art by correspondence.

All I knew about art he could put in his eye, I told him, honestly.

"Very refreshing," said Mr. Parsons, "very refreshing."

But I wasn't to worry. He would teach me. Poof. Just like that.

"Come," said Mr. Parsons mysteriously, and took me by the hand. We tiptoed into the art classroom and stopped behind a cherubic-looking boy with rubbers on, who was painting.

"He comes from Brooklyn and looks like an angel," said Mr. Parsons. "But ah! What dirty thoughts he must have. Look at his nudes. I've never seen the like of them."

Neither had I. I turned red as a beet and gritted my teeth. I felt like Little Billee in *Trilby*. Never before or since have I seen the female form painted in such glowing colors.

"Every human being has hidden depths," said Mr. Parsons, back in his office.

"Do I have to teach people to draw nudes by correspondence?" I asked anxiously.

"My poor innocent, no," said Mr. Parsons. "Our first lesson will be a design for sofa pillows."

He explained. After landing a student, we'd write him a letter asking him to submit a design for a sofa pillow. A bunch of violets in the middle rated zero. It was a bust on two counts. First, it would hurt your head if the design were embroidered. Second, it would make your artistic soul suffer. A design for sofa pillows should leave the center pure and unsullied as driven snow. The design—which I visualized as a series of skriggles—should go round the edges.

Simple, what? I had only to remember one rule which covered

everything—"Fitness to use." That was the criterion. I wasn't to come to him with questions every minute.

"But what about color?" I asked. "And material? Suppose a student wanted to work out a design on pink chiffon?"

"Yummy, yummy, yummy," said Mr. Parsons, and careened out of the office.

While I was working on the first letter, Mr. Odom, Mr. Parsons' assistant, came in. He said Mr. Parsons talked as if it was all a joke, but I'd better follow his directions carefully.

I was very proud to have such an important job. It was much more exciting than listing rivets. But I wasn't allowed to mention it to Rod's mother. The idea of her son's future wife's working was too disgraceful.

Fortunately, I saw his family only on occasional week ends. His mother and aunts were always saying how wonderful he was. They showed me pictures—at the age of eight, in a Lord Fauntleroy suit with ruffles and his feet turned out; at the age of sixteen in knicker-bockers and checked cap. He'd always been "perfect." They said it right in front of him. I was shocked. "Praise to the face is open dis-grace," in New England. I could see they thought he was throwing himself away on a "stenographer." They were always telling about the rich girls he could have married. It made me pretty mad. I felt like telling them I nearly broke the engagement when I found out he lived in a row of seven houses just alike and the living room had a golden-oak table and a fireplace with a gas log. They said how wonderfully Rod was getting on with his shorthand and typing, but they talked about our marriage as if it were years away. If only I could work up a larger clientele for art by correspondence—and keep the present members from dropping out—Mr. Parsons might raise my salary, I thought. I could see Rod's mother would never consent to his living on fifteen dollars.

I went at the art work hammer and tongs, advising right and left, and writing the students long, encouraging letters. Our enrollment increased by leaps and bounds. As Mr. Parsons left me strictly alone, I got to handing out praise in bigger and bigger gobs. I found praise was a much better enrollment builder-upper than criticism. One day,

I glanced up to find Mr. Parsons looking over my shoulder. He gazed with glazed eyes at a bright-red rose design with glossy green leaves intertwined with blue bachelor's-buttons. "This," I had written enthusiastically across the drawing, "is the best thing you have done yet. Let us have more of this rich imagery and riotous color."

The next thing I knew, I had my hat and coat on and Mr. Parsons was pressing the down button at the elevator.

Now we could *never* get married! This finished it!

Back in my broom closet I found a letter from Simmons College. Dr. Simon Flexner, at the Rockefeller Institute, it said, needed a "mature" secretary.

I flew over there. Mr. Jerome D. Greene greeted me. I was a little younger, he said, than they expected. They wished someone to obtain case histories of the diseases they were studying. At the moment, they were concentrating on syphilis. Had I heard of it? No, I said, I hadn't. It was quite an old disease, he said, and a very serious one. They were having quite a time eradicating it. The plan was for me to go into the patient's room and sit behind a screen while the doctor asked questions. I was to take down the patient's answers. Later I was to transcribe them and devise some sort of filing system. The job would start at twenty-five dollars.

"But the prospects are limitless," said Mr. Greene, smiling.

I went out in a daze.

Twenty-five dollars!

I called up Rod and told him about it. There was a horrified gasp at the other end of the wire.

"But Avenue A and Sixty-sixth Street!" Rod exclaimed. "They aren't halfway lighted. There's no way to get to them. They're full of goats and thugs. And syphilis! It's impossible!" he shouted. He'd do anything rather than have me do that. Even get married. After all, he said, in a few weeks he'd be getting $66.66 a month at the bank. And there were little apartments up near Two Hundredth Street you could get for eighteen dollars.

"But if we do get married," he added, "I hope you'll never throw that job you could have had in my face." (I wish I could truthfully say that I hadn't.)

At last, I thought, as I hung up, at last, we can whiz down to the city clerk's office.

But could we? We couldn't. Everybody but us, it seemed, had to be considered. One after another, my cherished plans for a modern-istic marriage were torpedoed. I "must" wear white. I "must" be married in church. If I didn't change my name and include the word "obey" in the ceremony, people would think I was crazy. Step by step I was worn down. But when it came to filing health certificates, I got stubborn. "And I *will* be married on time," I maintained defi-antly. I'd never seen a wedding that wasn't late starting.

The health certificates were particularly important to me. Eugenics was getting a big play in the papers. I felt that health certificates would *guarantee* us superior offspring. John Haynes Holmes, who was going to marry us, was quite pepped up when he heard about the health certificates.

"It's so rare," he said, "to see people do the progressive thing on their own initiative."

Well, I had got *something* the way I wanted it!

The doctor who examined Rod wasn't so optimistic. "No good will ever come of your marrying the kind of girl who wants such bosh as this," he said dourly.

We were to be married in the Church of the Messiah, three days before Christmas—a thrifty New England notion of my own. We could take advantage of the Christmas decorations. The audience was to consist of Rod's family, mine, Mr. Theodore Hetzler and Mr. Algernon Frizzell representing the Fifth Avenue Bank; and Mr. Robert K. Haas, Mr. James Shaw, and Mr. George Endicott, repre-senting Yale, Columbia, and Princeton. Five was the hour appointed. Rod was to meet me at four-thirty. No hocus-pocus about not seeing the bride till the bridegroom met her at the altar. I'd slipped that over on them.

At four I met my mother and sister in the Hotel Manhattan. My sister looked lovely. She had on a gray broadcloth suit with a chin-chilla collar, and a big chinchilla muff with a bunch of violets pinned to it. My mother looked positively regal. She had a new surah silk trimmed with passamenterie, and she'd had her sealskin coat made over. She was "wearing her face on top" as Fred, our hired man, used to call it. She and my sister never breathed a word about the fact that they'd had to give up the Wollaston house, and I never guessed it. It turned out they'd put the furniture in storage just the day before they came over.

My mother walked up to me and took my face between her hands. "Now let me take a long look at my daughter before I lose her," she said. She smoothed up the hair at the back of my neck just the way she used to do when I was little. "My baby," she said. "My little baby." I started to cry. I couldn't help it. "Now, Mama," said my sister. "You've got her all upset. This is a wedding, not a funeral." My mother wiped my eyes with her handkerchief. I'd forgotten to bring any. They said I looked very nice in my *peau de soie* with the layers and layers of white fringe and my gold lace hat that cost forty dollars. They refrained from commenting, however, on the seventy-five-dollar Burberry overcoat suitable for a Russian droshky driver I had insisted on buying in place of the customary fur dolman. It was a gesture. To prove my spirit wasn't broken.

As soon as they left for the church, I ordered two club sandwiches and a pot of hot chocolate. My knees were weak. I didn't know getting married would be so taxing.

Suddenly, I looked at my watch. It was half-past four. Where could Rod be? The Manhattan was only a step from the Fifth Avenue Bank where he was working.

Quarter of five came, but not the bridegroom.

I gnashed my teeth and peered from the window.

At five-fifteen he burst in with the news that his mother and aunt had *insisted* that he drive over from New Jersey with them, that the bridge was up, and where were the flowers?

What was he doing at home! I'd been right to be worried.

"Didn't you go to work today?" I asked horrified.

"No," he said. "Where are the flowers?"

"How do you ever expect to get anywhere if you take a day off whenever you feel like it?" I demanded. I'd forgotten all about the wedding.

"Can't a man take his own wedding day off?" he shouted. "*Where are the flowers?*"

"*No! Not if he wants to get anywhere in this world, and I haven't seen the flowers!*"

We leaped into a cab and tore over to the church. The flowers had been there and gone back to the Manhattan. We went back to the Manhattan. The flowers had been there and gone back to the church. For half an hour, the flowers chased us and we chased the flowers. We caught up to them in a traffic jam on Madison Avenue.

It was six when we tramped up the aisle. The organist had to give Wagner all he had to drown out the mutual recriminations.

"Aren't you going to kiss the bride?" Dr. Holmes asked after it was all over. Rod was so slow, Bob Haas beat him to it.

Mr. Holmes took me aside. He had had a little trouble about the health certificates, he said. The city of New York had never heard of such nonsense. They were not disposed to file them without a special dispensation.

"Then get it," I said. I was in no mood for trifling.

An hour's ride in a taxi up to One Hundred and Eighty-first Street, and we were at our apartment in the Anita.

"My God!" my husband exclaimed, as he went to make change for the driver. "I gave Dr. Holmes only ten dollars. The organist got the twenty." Then he rushed up ahead to unlock the apartment and turn on the lights.

I started slowly up the three flights of stairs, tripping over the hated white fringe and dragging the wilting flowers. I'd been balked at every turn. Tomorrow I would be a parasite with nothing to tell my husband but how the laundryman didn't come, or how Al the butcher gypped me. Rod met me at the door.

"Why, darling," he said. "You're crying." He put his arms around me and drew me inside. "You poor kid. Nothing went the way you wanted it. It was awful." Gently, he took my hat off and brushed my hair back from my forehead. "Don't fight things so," he said. "Just take them as they come. We'll be happy. We've got each other. That's all that matters."

He took my face in his hands and kissed me. I stopped sobbing. Sure. We had each other. Let the rest of the world go hang. We'd be happy.

Only, there was one thing I drew the line at. I was darned if I'd embroider.

THE ANITA

I KNOW you think an apartment house is a tenement," I wrote my sister, "but our apartment in the Anita is wonderful. It has a tiled bath and continuous hot water, and a dumbwaiter that brings the ice up and takes the garbage down."

I didn't tell her that if you forgot to leap like a gazelle when the bell rang, it took the ice down, or that if Shand, the janitor, was drunk, it brought the garbage up again. Nor did I mention that the cockroaches, as well as the hot water, were continuous.

Oddly enough, my sister was living in an apartment herself. She'd joined forces with a cousin who had a big comfortable "flat" on Falmouth Street, Boston, when my mother decided to return to the fastnesses of her native Maine. But my sister had predicted that I wouldn't like an eighteen-dollar-a-month apartment in New York City. I didn't want her to know she'd hit the nail on the head.

"I will like the Anita," I said to myself, "I will like it if it kills me. If other people can be happy in this hellish combination of cell block and rabbit warren, I can."

"Home-loving hearts are happiest," I wrote firmly on a pad and referred to it several times a day when I felt myself slipping.

Nobody else, least of all my husband, shared my low opinion of the Anita. It was regarded by experienced cliff dwellers of 1912 as very high-class housing. Its location at the corner of Northern Avenue and West One Hundred and Eighty-first Street, which seemed to me an all-time high in utter desolation, was referred to by the other tenants as "very healthy." Of course, it didn't have elevators like the Nathan Hale—Nathan "Hagel," as it was known on Washington Heights. Nor was it a seven-story skyscraper like the Rockhurst. But it had imitation mahogany doors on all the closets, and the bathrooms were "throughout modrunn."

The Anita was really twins. If you turned left as you entered, it was the Kathryn. If you turned right, it was the Anita. It two-faced the Hudson. Our apartment was on the back, as the front ones cost twenty-five dollars.

"You don't got river, yes," the agent said, shrugging his shoulders. "But you got country, no?"

No.

Unless he meant the field with three goats munching grass outside our living-room window, on which the orange girders for a new apartment house were already rising. At one side of the field was a large cave where several dirty little boys and one dirty little girl played cops and robbers. They looked dirty and they talked dirty. They would have had their little mouths washed out with soap and their little bottoms spanked till they were red as cherries if they'd talked like that in New England, where I came from. As it was, they kept up their noisy and repulsive little activities every afternoon without let or hindrance till the dot of five. Then a window slammed open and a voice screamed shrilly, "Stanley! Git a *Joinal!*"

"You go chase yourself," Stanley shouted back without conviction.

"Ya, ya, ya," the children chorused. Stanley was the keynoter.

"You want me to come out there?"

At this, Stanley yanked his cap down over his eyes and trudged sullenly across the field. The band straggled off one by one with parting kicks at the goats.

This little drama was one of the few bright spots in my life at the Anita. But when I had callers I felt it pulled me down socially. Nor was it possible to seat them so they couldn't look out of the window.

The whole place baffled me. I didn't think the way the architect must have thought. In fact, the apartment seemed to be the answer to what the builder did with some space the architect had left over. You got into it through a long dark hall. A caller instinctively reached for stalactites and demanded a ball of string for the purpose of orientation. When the hall reached the dining room, it came out into the open like the subway at One Hundred and Twenty-fifth Street. Then it pulled itself together again and went smashing past the bedroom into the bathroom, ignoring the living room entirely.

Where the hall crossed the dining room it was really just an imaginary line like the equator. On the offside of this equator was the "kitchen." This was a row of fixtures against the wall, icebox, stove, sink, and garbage can.

It was a frank arrangement. The person manning the kitchen was completely at the mercy of kibitzing diners. A piece of butter dropped on the floor was pronounced dead by onlookers before it could be retrieved, washed off, and put into circulation again.

The frazzled cook was on the receiving end of a lot of constructive suggestions.

"You better mash those potatoes a little more, or they'll be lumpy."

"Look out! Look out! The toast's burning!"

To discourage audience participation I bought two fourfold screens. When these were stretched across in front of the kitchen it was officially open for business. All communication between the outside world and the cook was strictly taboo. I operated behind the screens like a disembodied spirit. Only dense clouds of smoke, a slight billowing of the screens, and muttered curses gave proof through the meal that our flag was still there. When I came bursting out with a dish of string beans in one hand, and a platter of roast lamb in the other, diners must presume I was Dr. Livingstone.

This gave the place more atmosphere, I tried to think. I'd have blacked up if that would have helped any.

At least the novelty of the arrangement distracted attention from the fact that the dining-room window opened on the air shaft. Directly across was Mrs. Babcock's kitchen in the Kathryn. Mrs. Babcock never pulled the shade down. Mr. Babcock was an engineer on the Valhalla dam, and he ate in the kitchen. He had a Gargantuan appetite. Great heaps of crisp-looking French-fried potatoes and a huge sirloin steak set before him made my little budget menu look skinny.

When we had company, I used to pray that the couple next to the Babcocks wouldn't get quarreling. About suppertime we'd usually hear them scuffling and screaming.

"Take back your ring! I'm going home to Newark to Mother!"

The bedroom presented a more serious problem. It was heated at all times, usually to a temperature of one hundred and four, by pipes which led to the floors above it. The window opened onto the fire escape where, in 1912, it was considered *au fait* to park dogs and garbage cans. After I waked up one night to find two large white chows standing on my chest, I decided in favor of suffocation.

But there was no use moaning. It was conquer or die. I tried doing what the Anitans did.

Every morning I gave the apartment a ferocious cleaning. Then I braced myself for the battle with the dumbwaiter. This wasn't easy, as we had got off to a bad start the first morning I was alone with it. As I was doing the dishes, I had heard a rumbling noise that suggested a California earthquake. Then a bell rang. I rushed to the dumbwaiter, opened the door, and peered into it. Sitting in the middle of it was a piece of ice. Standing on the other side was a man, stark naked. He didn't know our apartment had been rented. We both slammed the doors quickly. After a few more furtive rings it rumbled down. As it came to a crashing standstill at the bottom some hearty Italian curses drifted up the shaft.

If you didn't watch it like a hawk, it played tricks on you. Sometimes you'd hear the bell, open the door, and it wasn't there. As you leaned in to see where it was hiding, it dropped playfully on your head and knocked you senseless.

Getting the ice was a job in itself. After staggering to the refrigerator with it you were supposed to return and put fifteen cents on the dumbwaiter. The only chance of the money arriving at the bottom without being taken off on the way was to get in and ride down with it.

But the meanest thing was what it did with my old clothes. I had a merino skirt, a hat with a frayed cock's feather, and a covert-cloth coat I'd worn faithfully for five years. But there was no wear-out to them. I got to where I thought I'd die if I ever saw them again. In a fine frenzy, I put them on the dumbwaiter and slammed the door. As it rumbled down, I laughed the high-pitched, crazed laugh of a happy murderer who has successfully hidden the body. Next day the woman that lived below me blossomed out in them.

After the dumbwaiter came errands. The other tenants loved errands. They would haggle for hours over a bunch of carrots, leap at the butcher's throat about a shoulder lamb chop, and come home beaming over the top of a thousand bundles.

A New England errand-doer on Washington Heights was a sorry figure. I couldn't find an iron muffin pan heavy enough for popovers. I couldn't find a frying pan because I asked for a spider; nor a saucepan, because I demanded a porringer. When I tried to locate a cobbler to have my boots tapped, the boy at the newsstand looked at me as if I were something out of *The Red Fairy Book;* I had to do a Charlie Chaplin to indicate I was looking for a shoemaker to have my shoes half-soled.

They cut the meat wrong in New York. There was no rump or tip of the sirloin. And when I asked, as I used to ask at S. S. Pierce's, for my own mixture of mocha and java, Gristede's offered me something in a package already ground. As if I didn't have a coffee grinder! Corned beef wasn't corned, it was saltpetered. And they'd never heard of swordfish.

"Maybe you'd like some nice shark meat, or a slice of dragon," the butcher asked facetiously.

When I finally tracked down unsalted butter, the clerk said, "It don't appeal to the gentiles, but we like it, don't we?" He passed me up, however, when it turned out I preferred brown eggs to white ones.

I found no one anywhere who'd ever heard of cracked wheat. And I had never heard of Charles'.

After the errands, I took my camp chair down to the sidewalk. Fat ladies jiggled perambulators and went into grisly details about their adhesions, gas on baby's stomach, and the very, very gorgeous little crepe de Chines you get at Macy's for only sixteen dollars.

When I'd absorbed all the punishment I could stand, I moved my chair out onto the untidy, overgrown plot where an old mansion overhung the Hudson. I'd read the *Tribune* from stem to stern, even stooping to such items as "Rates on Foreign Exchange" and "Fire Department Trial Decisions." Then, head in hands, I watched the tugs breaking up ice with their snub noses.

Finally, driven back into the Anita by the cold, I would look in the glass to see if my hair had turned white. I was always surprised that it hadn't.

"What kind of day have you had?" my husband asked brightly each evening.

"Fine."

"That's good," he replied, and played the "Whistler and His Dog" on the phonograph. Then he read *The Saturday Evening Post,* while I looked at the furniture. It was considered pretty snappy in 1912. I thought it was awful. But I didn't trust my judgment. I could tell Sheraton from Chippendale at a hundred paces, but was lost in any period later than the eighteenth century. Ours was mission style of the bilious-green variety. It was the contents of my husband's college room mated with wedding presents. I had diffidently added candle shades with bead whiskers, and my husband suggested we didn't need anything else.

"Pretty nice," my husband would say glancing up from the *Post.* "I bet after all the kicking around in offices and boardinghouses you've done, a home looks good to you."

I remembered my father saying he'd rather die any way than be bored to death. I doubted that I would escape that fate.

"Didn't anything at all happen at the bank today?" I'd ask desperately. "Didn't *anybody* say *anything?* They can't have *all* sat there all day like a lot of fishfaces."

I asked it so many times that my husband got a little notebook. During the day, he would jot down (1) bright sayings of coworkers and superiors, and (2) interesting happenings. Every night at dinner he would set down the notebook, open, beside his place at the table. From time to time, as conversation lagged, he would read from it. He was a very literal person.

Once in a blue moon, we went downtown to dinner. Old college chums of my husband would join us at Still's Oyster House for chicken hash with green peppers. Then we would go to see Eva Tanguay or Alice Lloyd ("The Lloyd") at the Palace.

Every Sunday we went out to New Jersey to visit my husband's aunts and mother. I used to try to beg off, but my husband said if we didn't go they'd be heartbroken. They tried to be kind. They always had pumpkin pie because I liked it. They paid our fares both ways and sent us back to New York loaded with cake and cookies. But I didn't understand them. Once when I was out there I found a little stray kitten. I set down a saucer of milk for it on the back steps. Rod's aunt saw me from the window. She rushed down and shooed the kitten away. Then she broke the saucer. It was a little thing. But I never forgot it.

It was the deadly, unbroken monotony of our life that got me. Nothing to look forward to. After an interminable evening of old phonograph records, I used to get up and go into the bedroom and twist my face all funny ways in front of the glass. If I was really going crazy, I thought, it would show.

I tried counterirritants. One evening, when my husband was at a bankers' meeting, I burst from my cell with a terrible yell. I went downtown on the subway. I smoked a cigarette in the lobby of one hotel after another. I was thrown out of all of them. On the way home I got the policeman at One Hundred and Eighty-first Street to let me ride his horse. I was thrown off twice. It hurt but it was better than an insane asylum. I had heard they beat the patients with rubber hoses.

It was the day I set the apartment afire that I realized that I wasn't gaining. I was frying doughnuts and the fat blazed up. I rang every bell in sight and Shand, the janitor, came up.

"We ain't got no sand. Will we throw water on the fat?" asked Shand desperately.

"Yes," I said.

With fascinated eyes, I watched the flames spread and consume the gold-lace hat I was married in.

It was a two-alarm fire. Damage was small but the smoke was terrific.

I brooded and brooded. I knew better than to tell him to throw water. Subconsciously, I must have *wanted to burn up the Anita.*

I decided to take steps. "I have run across a girl in New York," I wrote my friends hastily, "who is practically a shut-in. Her family is very strict. What she needs is a job of some kind. One which would take her out of this unhappy environment for a few hours daily. If you know of anyone who needs the services of a stenographer—the girl is very ambitious, she picked it up herself—I wish you would write me. If the work was in the nature of public service of some kind, it would be perfect. I am positive, under these circumstances, she could obtain the consent of her family."

It was deceit. But better than arson.

For two weeks, I waited anxiously. Then came a letter from Josephine Dodge Daskam Bacon. There was an association just being formed in New York to get vacations for working girls. This association needed a secretary. The person to get in touch with was Gertrude Robinson Smith.

"Have you ever thought how awful it is that working girls don't have vacations?" I asked my husband, at supper.

"Hell no," he said. "Why should I?"

"Well, I've been worrying over this matter of vacations for working girls for some time," I said, toying with my lettuce. "Have some more steak. And some of this good gravy right on your potato."

Funny we should be talking about vacations for working girls, I went on, because I'd had a letter about it that very day. An association was being formed to help them get vacations. It needed somebody to write a few letters. I thought I'd help them.

"Why don't you just sit around and enjoy yourself?" said my husband. "Just live!"

"But you have to have some excuse for living," I said.

He laughed. "You come from New England. You mean justification."

"All right," I said, "justification."

"If you really loved me," he said, "you'd be contented."

I didn't answer. He was always saying I didn't love him. Of course I loved him. But to me loving him didn't mean I had to rush to the door every time I heard his footsteps and throw my arms around him. It would make me pretty mad if I came home tired at night, and someone came racing out and flung themselves on me before I'd had time to get the key out of the lock and my coat unbuttoned. To me, loving Rod meant "doing for him"—picking up his dirty socks, heating the egg cup so his eggs would be just right, remembering to buy tooth paste, not complaining when I couldn't "have things." Besides, I wasn't brought up to be demonstrative. Naturally, I didn't love him blindly. I saw his faults and didn't hesitate to mention them. This was what we in New England called "speaking your mind." But Rod regarded it as criticism. It hurt his feelings. He resented my wanting to do anything that wasn't connected with him. I didn't blame him for expecting the earth to revolve around him. I'd never seen a man who didn't. But I couldn't see moping around all day just to foster the illusion. Love, for me, could never be a full-time occupation.

"Go ahead and take the job, if it makes you any happier," he said grudgingly, when I came into the living room after doing the dishes. "But I hate like hell to see you at somebody else's beck and call. I wouldn't give them too much time if I were you. I'm not much for eating out of tin cans. And I'd be hanged if I'd do it for nothing."

"Oh, I expect they'll be willing to pay my expenses," I said. "Maybe a little bit over."

Next morning, I put on my good old blue-serge suit and thumbed my nose at the Anita.

I found Miss Robinson Smith at 4 West Fortieth Street. This was the office of Josephine Wright Chapman, a redheaded architect weighing about two hundred. Miss Smith, besides being interested in working girls, was engaged with Miss Chapman in a side scheme of interior decorating.

My interview with Miss Smith was short and sweet. In the middle of our talk, she decided to change her clothes. She stepped out of her skirt and said, "Somebody pick that up." I didn't pick it. She said I wasn't co-operative.

"Why don't you take her?" she said to Miss Chapman. "I don't want her."

"I will," said Miss Chapman. "I like her."

Miss Chapman said that because of a peculiar situation which had arisen she needed a secretary. It was very peculiar. Number 4 West Fortieth Street was not only an office but an apartment. Miss Chapman lived there with a friend named Miss Foster. Miss Foster had come to New York to be an actress and had landed a part in George Ade's *College Widow*. When the show closed, Miss Foster was out of a job, but had thought up a way to keep in practice. Every morning she got up, put on her hat and coat in the back bedroom, picked up her bag, and strode into the front office.

"Good morning, Miss Chapman," she'd say distantly.

"Good morning, Miss Stevens," Miss Chapman would reply.

Miss Foster-Stevens then removed her hat and coat and spent the day acting the part of Miss Chapman's secretary. The trouble was that it got so real to her that she carried it to the extent of conducting negotiations with customers.

One of these customers, feeling that he had got gypped in a house Miss Chapman built for him, sued her. It went to court. The judge inquired into the identity of Miss Stevens, secretary. The fact that Miss Foster and Miss Stevens were the same confused him. It took trouble and time to prove to the judge that they weren't all crazy. Due to their long absences in court, Miss Chapman needed a secretary. Ten A. M. to four P. M. daily would be good for a weekly honorarium of eight dollars. What could be fairer?

Of course, it wasn't *quite* working for the association to get vacations for working girls. But Miss Robinson Smith *was* connected with it.

"How'd you make out?" asked my husband.

"Fine!" I said. "It's ten to four and I'm going to get eight dollars."

"Don't work too hard," he said. "And that's not saying the eight dollars won't come in handy. How was this Robinson Smith?"

"She was all right," I said. "But I won't be working for her so much as I will for Miss Chapman. Miss Chapman's in with her."

I didn't say in *what* with her. He didn't ask me.

Every morning I tore through my housework and flew down to 4 West Fortieth Street. Housework wasn't boring at all if, when you finished, you were going somewhere.

My office was a little outer hall where I presided over a table with a typewriter and took on all comers. Reaching from floor to ceiling back of me were shelves loaded with every known brand of liquor laid in against the inevitable Saturday-night parties. This lent an air of informality characteristic of everything connected with Miss Foster and Miss Chapman. A steady stream of callers poured through the portals of their office-apartment, ranging from customers to process servers; from plasterers and carpenters to Mrs. August Belmont, Laurette Taylor, and Carl Van Vechten.

My favorite caller was an old Irish contractor from Brooklyn. He had gone bust on a contract his firm had got with the city. Counting on cut to make fill after careful measuring, they had struck bedrock at eleven inches. We exchanged opinions on many subjects. Take immigration: I ranted against agents of steamship companies who roamed southeastern Europe, seducing suckers with the promise of gold in the streets and free transportation. He came back with the retort that bringing in cheap labor was a good thing because Americans thought they were too good to dig ditches and lay sewers at a dollar and a half a day. They'd rather go to the poorhouse.

Take war:

"I found out in college, when I studied the Peace Conferences in Geneva, all the nations are arming. What do you think of that?"

He thought war would come but for a different reason. "Keep educatin' people up and beatin' 'em down, an' sooner or later you're bound to have trouble."

We both mourned the fact that we were ahead of our time and that nobody would listen to us.

It was a whole lot more exciting than gas on babies' stomachs and bargain crepe de Chines at Macy's. My husband was quite resigned to it. He said I didn't "pick on him" so much now that I was busy. He meant I didn't keep at him about getting ahead. I was always urging him to work harder and take courses in things. He said the only way to get ahead in a bank was to wait till death removed your superiors.

I didn't write my mother I was working. I thought it might worry her. My sister approved of it. "*Now*, you can get a maid," she wrote. "As long as you have a head, why work with your hands?" I didn't want a maid. I reveled in my ceaseless activity.

Everything might have gone all right, if I hadn't got an "outside assignment." It was to collect a bill from a man hat designer on Fifth

Avenue. Miss Chapman and Miss Smith had undertaken to decorate his bedroom. He got the idea he was being cheated at the price asked for the gold edging on the bedspread.

"Show him this bill," said Miss Chapman, "here, where it tells what *we* had to pay for it. God knows, we have to make some profit. If he acts up, tell him to go to Hades."

I found the man striding up and down the aisles of a loft where rows of girls were working on hats. He suggested that we go to the bedroom and take a look at the bedspread. As I was married, I made no objection.

The bedroom was as big as our whole apartment. The *raison d'être*, not to mention *pièce de résistance,* was an enormous four-poster which looked as if it had been salvaged from a medieval castle. Over it was a crucifix. In it was a large, beefy, red-faced man. He was a friend, the designer said.

I showed him the bill. He showed me the edging. Then came a free-for-all over bedspreads, women decorators, the price of eggs generally and gold lamé in particular. The friend, from under the covers, joined in freely.

Suddenly, the telephone rang. It was Miss Chapman.

"I got nervous you were gone so long," she said. "I should never have let you go there. I called your husband. He's coming over for you."

Neither my husband nor I said anything going down in the elevator.

"Some association to get vacations for working girls!" said my husband, as we stepped out on the avenue. "Was that a working girl on vacation under the bedspread?"

"This is a side line of Miss Smith's," I said.

"Listen," he said, "the best place for you is right home in the Anita." He got ready for me to hit him but I didn't. I knew why I had laid all before me a week before when I got home. And it wasn't because I had tripped and fallen on the roof of 4 West Fortieth, where I had gone to watch General Grant's son's funeral. It was because I was going to have a baby.

While there's new life there's hope.

I would beg, borrow, or steal, and commission Miss Chapman to build us a house in the country. No child of mine was going to howl its first howl in a tenement called the Anita.

BRANCHES IN MOSCOW AND
ST. PETERSBURG

I ALWAYS go right downhill when I read somebody quit peddling shoelaces, or a good job in the canned-rattlesnake business, to become an author. I didn't become an author because I had "a book in me" or a message to deliver direct from the Almighty to an already suffering humanity. My motives were purely ulterior.

I became an author to scare up thirty-five dollars we needed for awnings. And I kept it up till cut off at the height of my career by the doubting Thomas who edited the *Bankers' Magazine*.

We needed awnings to conceal the fact that the house we built in Larchmont turned out so terrible. As a matter of fact, Larchmont turned out terrible.

"The trouble with Larchmont is that it isn't anywhere," said my mother, when she came down from Maine for a brief visit. It was, and it wasn't. She meant it wasn't a tight little town like the kind we had in New England, where everybody knew everybody else, went to the same church, had the same doctor, and assembled once a year in the Town Hall to vote down all improvements, including the new school, for fear it would raise taxes.

Larchmont was just a piece of the tail of Mamaroneck, expanding in 1913 along lines apparently bastard Spanish and far-from-pure colonial; and around whose Sound end a group of porte-cochered Queen Anne monstrosities perched like buzzards. I had been drawn to it because the circling sea gulls that came screaming in from the Sound, and the lighthouse that winked its eye nightly, spelled home to me as much as anything within commuting distance of New York could spell it.

Our little dovecot, which appeared on the blueprints as an adorable Anne Hathaway cottage, eaves deep in hollyhocks, turned out to be dirty gray, gaunt, high-shouldered Norman, set on a rock that moss couldn't cling to.

"Awnings," I said to my husband hopefully, "might take the cuss off it."

But awnings, the man who came to measure said, "wouldn't run to no less than thirty-five dollars."

We didn't have thirty-five dollars because my husband was still getting only $66.66 a month, and the Grand Panjandrum who came to investigate for the Building and Loan had been so narrow-minded.

"I will come out and inspect your residence," he said grandilo-quently, "and if things are as you represent, I think we shall have no difficulty in arranging a loan of three thousand dollars."

Unfortunately, the two thousand dollars (my share in my father's estate) which my mother turned over to me when she found we wanted to "build a home" had barely covered the price of the lot and construction of the first story. In order to finish the house we'd had to borrow from my husband's aunt, who had doubtfully taken a mort-gage. Three thousand dollars would have paid her off and left a nice margin for extras. But I never thought the investigator would come on a Sunday.

"I will bring sherry and lobster," my sister had telephoned Sunday morning, "if you will toss off a lobster Newburgh."

My sister was now living in New York City. A few months before, she had married a brilliant young Yale graduate who was well on his way toward an editorship on the *New York Tribune*. They were ab-solutely congenial and very much in love. It was fun to see my sister so happy. As her husband was busy Sundays she often came out bearing Major Grey's Chutney and a can of curry, or the makings of a lobster Newburgh.

If I'd made the Newburgh strong enough that Sunday, the sherry bottle wouldn't have been on the table. And if she hadn't generously kicked in a dollar and a half for a quick ride in a rig from the livery stable before she went back to the city, that sherry bottle and the unwashed dishes would never have been in sight. It was the first time in my life I'd ever left the dishes. Everybody in New England knows that God punishes you if you leave the dishes. He did. While we were out, the investigator came, found the door unlocked, and investigated. Two days later the letter came.

"We cannot make loans," it said, "to irresponsible housekeepers, or to potential inebriates."

This left us high and dry. Every nickel over and above the contractor's bill I had shot on the interior. In an effort to escape my early love of authentic colonial I had rushed headlong into the arms of early English. The iron-hinged batten door opened directly onto a rush-bottomed hickory chair (nineteen dollars), set by a sea chest (forty dollars) whose crude reds and blues were echoed in the twelve dollars-a-yard Delft-blue English chintz with the stylized red fruit on it, recommended so highly by the man with the cleft chin at Altman's. These crude reds and blues were re-echoed by the red Welsh tile floor that cost God knows what—the Welsh turned out to be a very grasping little people—and some Canton-blue china requisitioned from my mother. This striking *décor* was eked out with trestle table, benches—everything but stout knaves quaffing from flagons—to lend atmosphere.

All this damn junk, my husband remarked fretfully, had run into money.

So had the two little bundles from heaven we had on hand, and a third we had on order.

Of course I wanted the children. I planned to have nine. Though when Barbara, the oldest, arrived January 16, 1913, I was bitterly disappointed. After months of having my stomach pumped out with a stomach pump I thought I would at least bring forth something that didn't have argyrol in its eyes and had teeth as standard equipment. I also resented the three days she had taken to be born in. My muscles were so strong, the doctor said, they had no give to them. There was no such dilly-dallying when John was born eleven months later. In my eagerness to answer the doorbell I fell downstairs. John was born before I could answer it. As he wasn't due for two weeks, this resulted in his "looking a little underdone," according to the doctor. I hoped the third would be a boy, too. I wanted four boys so I could send one to West Point, one to Yale, one to Annapolis, and one to Harvard. I felt that in education, as in farming, diversification was the answer. At the moment, however, my little jewels were playing havoc with the budget.

In a desperate effort to make frayed ends meet I corralled a boarder. The boarder's name was Robert Miller. He had been a classmate of my husband's at Yale, and thought twelve dollars weekly was exorbitant. For someone who stirred a capsule of castor oil around nauseatingly in a glass of water every morning at breakfast, it was niggardly. I was nauseated enough without any peccadilloes on the part of the boarder.

But even the boarder's twelve dollars, plus the money I saved by serving meat left over from the children's broth in nine ingenious disguises, didn't run to thirty-five dollars. And I was restricted in my campaign to raise that sum, by my regular eighteen-hour day as wife, mother, and landlady.

Inspiration came when I was mulling over a pan of boiling diapers one night about eleven. I thought of slaves. My mind drifted to *Uncle Tom's Cabin*. Harriet Beecher Stowe wrote *Uncle Tom's Cabin* with seven children and a husband milling around her. She made plenty of money. I would take a leaf out of her book, so to speak, and rewrite it.

I ran across a little article in *Collier's* called "Writing as a Profession."

"Never write until you have something to say," said the article. "Then picture in your mind the person to whom you wish to say it. Say it with clarity and force and success will crown your efforts."

I had something to say all right, and I had no difficulty in visualizing the person to whom I wished to say it. This person was my husband's employer. He attributed his success in life, he said, to encouragement and help given him by my husband's father. He wished to repay that debt. "I want to do for you what your father did for me," he told my husband. Maybe he thought he was doing the Big Thing by giving my husband a job rolling pennies in a bank at $66.66 a month. I didn't.

Next morning, bracing a pad firmly against the handle of the baby carriage, and writing as I pushed, I whipped up a little article called "Banking with a Pull." I got in quite a few good licks at my husband's employer.

"Just wait till I'm cashier and the present cashier's son, Princeton, 1933, comes to me for a job," my article concluded. "I'll say to him, 'I want to do for you what your father did for me.' And believe me, I'll do it too!"

This little gem, duly published by the *Bankers' Magazine*, proved a sensation. It lost my husband his job and paid for the awnings.

Although I didn't sign my name, my husband's employer found that the shoe fitted and put it on. Rumor had it that he threw the issue of the magazine on the floor and stamped on it.

I told my husband not to worry. The *Bankers' Magazine* had contracted at a cent and a half a word for my future output. This I had glowingly described to them as a couple of articles entitled "The Woman and the Bank" and "Selling Bank Services," guaranteed to take the bunk out of banking.

"If worse comes to worst," I told him, "I can support everybody on my earnings."

To show how much confidence I had I took our last cent, hired a slavey to sit on the children's chests, and treated my husband and the boarder to a movie on "How to Cut Ham." An added feature was a lantern-slide lecture on the cell-block system at Sing Sing, by Thomas Mott Osborne. As we walked home, my husband was still uncheered.

"You'll drop dead," he said. "And I'll never be able to get another job. I'll be blackballed in every bank in New York City."

I felt pretty low myself, though I wouldn't have admitted it. Here I'd had such high hopes and tried so hard and everything had gone sour. But nobody thought of trying to cheer me up. They just acted as though I'd tried to make trouble.

At this point the boarder decided to guide Fate's guiding finger. Throwing his castor-oil capsule into the ring, he announced that in the interest of keeping a good breadmaker from becoming a bum breadwinner he'd use some secret weapon he claimed he had to get my husband a job at the National City. But I had to agree not to write any more articles after the two I had promised to the *Bankers'* *Magazine*. I agreed.

"But only," I said stubbornly, "if the job pays enough so we can go over to the Red Lion Inn and have a Welsh rarebit occasionally."

It paid eighteen dollars a week. My husband became secretary to a new vice-president, Samuel McRoberts. Mr. McRoberts, the boarder told us, was very important. He was being paid some ungodly sum to find new worlds to conquer. The United States was feeling its financial oats and wanted to sow them internationally. When he invited my husband and me to dinner to consider new plans, I was elated. I felt I was on the Big-Time Financial Circuit.

"Please," said my husband as we set out, leaving our little ones to the tender mercies of the boarder, "keep your trap shut and let McRoberts do the talking."

"And for heaven's sake," shouted the boarder from the batten doorway, "don't try to be helpful."

When dinner was over, we repaired to the living room, and Mr. McRoberts took out the world atlas. "South American nitrates," he said, "I've sewed up tight." His finger strayed to the Eastern Hemisphere. "Russia," he said impressively, "is the next place to exploit."

He planned to lead off by establishing branches of the National City Bank in Moscow and St. Petersburg. This task was confided to Number One Exploiter, Mr. Harry Meserve. My husband was to go along as secretary and Exploiter Number Two. At $1800.

I joined in a hearty toast to the successful exploitation of Russia.

"Why did you chime in with everything McRoberts said like that?" demanded my husband when we got outside. "Do you want me to get killed? Don't you know there's a war on?"

"Russia," I said dreamily. "Crown jewels. Volga boatmen. Wolves. The Kremlin."

"It's too bad you can't go in my place," said my husband.

I thought, "It sure is." I'd have given one thousand bowls of Farina and six dozen huck diapers for one glimpse of the stout little donkeys climbing the steppes of the Caucasus, dragging ammunition trains.

My mother-in-law thought I was a murderer to insist on her son's going. So did he. But I was adamant. New worlds were being conquered. Even though I was left at my old routine at the washtubs and cookstove, my husband would be among those present. He'd tell me how it was. I knew letters would take some time to get to me. But I could follow his peregrinations in the papers.

I invited my mother to come and spend her birthday tending the children while I went down to see him off. When I got home, it seemed kind of lonesome. I went down to the drugstore for some ice cream. My mother and I sat out on the hot little porch, eating it. "When I think of the eleven-course dinners your father used to give me on my birthday," said my mother, dipping into the ice cream, which tasted faintly of pasteboard, "and the diamonds from Bigelow and Kennard's or Shreve Crump and Low's—I don't know what he'd think——" Her voice broke. I looked out over the dusty little hill. I didn't know what he'd think, either. The best was none too good *for us,* he always said. It all seemed fantastic, somehow. My mother in her worn challis. My husband; Russia. Me; the children; the stucco Norman villa; the drugstore ice cream. My mother leaned over and flicked off a loose piece of stucco. "This house," she said, "is of very cheap construction. You ought to do something about it." I ought to do something about a lot of things, I thought. But I couldn't seem to. My mother wouldn't understand that. In a way I was glad she was going back to Maine.

Ten days later I read in the papers that the camouflaged liner my husband was on had been blacked out in Liverpool during a dirigible raid. I was excited. Then I learned that the port of Archangel was icebound. They would have to cross into Russia by dog sled. When my husband's first letter arrived, I opened it with trembling hands. Now for adventure. Life in the raw. Far horizons. I started to read. ". . . food is good . . . buying a fur hat . . ." What! No blacked-out stars over Liverpool? No mushing over Arctic wastes? I read on angrily. "You ought"—I turned the page—"to hear Baby MacCulsky sing 'Little Gray Home in the West' to Ambassador Francis." I threw the letter on the floor. Then I picked it up again. And "was that Babe built!" She was a "pippin!" Although he admitted that Raymond T. Baker (who afterwards married Delphine Dodge Cromwell after he'd married Margaret Emerson, the Bromo Seltzer Queen, after her first husband, Alfred Gwynne Vanderbilt, was lost on the *Lusitania*), well, this Mr. Baker said Baby MacCulsky looked as if she combed her hair with a sponge.

A sponge was nothing to what I'd have combed it with, if I could have got at her. I read on. He'd sent to Brooks Brothers for a new tuxedo. Baby MacCulsky didn't like tuxedo trousers with braid! Then I realized I had in my hand another letter still unopened. It was a forty-dollar bill from Brooks Brothers for a new tux shipped to my husband at the Hotel Europe in St. Petersburg.

I had had no idea that Mr. Meserve had a stepdaughter named Baby MacCulsky. Or that she didn't like tuxedos with braid. If I had I might not have been so insistent on my husband's going.

I considered the situation as I hung out the diapers. Forty dollars. Here was I dragging around, as big as a house, with no help and two kids tagging at my heels. There was he dancing with Baby MacCulsky at the Hotel Europe. Of course he hadn't wanted to go. I had to admit that. But the least he could have done was not enjoy himself. It was downright mean. Well, if I could raise thirty-five dollars, I could raise forty. The bill had to be paid.

Why not tear off a little red-hot piece on "Inside Information on International Finance"? Why not? Sandwiched in between the items about Baby MacCulsky was a lot of dope. The boarder had gone. He'd left to marry a girl named Gertrude, so my agreement with him was nullo. Maybe I could make more than forty dollars. Maybe I could make enough to buy a Model T Ford. It wouldn't be as good as a dog sled. I couldn't drive the children to the Kremlin. But I could drive them to see the elephants in the Central Park zoo.

I thought I'd never get the piece written. It seemed that every night I wasn't too tired to work on it, the minister came. He'd got in the habit of dropping around to urge me to initiate my little band of infidels into the mysteries of religion. He was quite good-looking. He would walk up and down with his hands behind him, discoursing on the merits of the Almighty, with Whom he seemed to be on intimate terms, while I devoutly wished him elsewhere.

"But I *can't* have the children baptized," I told him finally. "I'm not even baptized myself. Naked I came. Unhallowed I've remained."

He was furious.

"You don't understand the fear of God," he said, his eyes blazing. I told him that in New England, where I came from, nobody understood the fear of anything. He stopped coming after that, and I got my article finished.

The response from the *Bankers' Magazine* was instantaneous, not to say encouraging. Did I have any more like that? Sure. But they might have to wait a little.

The next letter was a gold mine. Russia, it seems, was more in need of a good stiff loan to carry on the war than of branches of the National City Bank. Wall Street figured there were more than enough widows and orphans who didn't know a ruble from a ruby to float one. My article was a humdinger.

"Through the pleasant haze of orchids and vodka which encircles these financial negotiators at the Hotel Europe," I wrote, drawing heavily on my imagination, "they catch no glimpse of the ominous clouds of oncoming revolution. Not only has the loan been arranged, but—surprise! The money will be spent in America!"

The letter of acceptance from the editors was not worded very cordially, and although I received full price for all words submitted, on publication the article was cut.

I'd never get the price of a Ford at this rate. I was depressed.

"Six months shut up alone writing articles and taking care of children," said my neighbor, Mrs. Merritt, "would kill anyone. You need a little social relaxation. Come on with us to dinner at the Hubbards' in Pelham."

I envied Mrs. Merritt because she had a car. And her husband was graciously permitting her to help him build model houses in spite of five children, a cow in the garage, and two hundred chickens.

So I got somebody to stay with the children, let out the seams of my wedding dress, and set out for Pelham with the Merritts' in their Chandler. Turning our tired backs bravely on reality, we rang a bell and were ushered by a butler into a Pelham dream world of maids, candelabra, marcelled wives, and Chinese Chippendale.

But as the evening progressed I didn't get pepped up at all. I got lower and lower.

"But my dear! Chaliapin!" somebody caroled. "Voice, yes! Interpretation, no!"

"George wouldn't dream of allowing me to drive the car," said a gorgeous creature. "Silly old thing. He won't let me lift a finger!"

I looked at Mrs. Merritt. She slowly closed one eyelid. Taking a hearty swig of Lafite, I opened fire.

"*Our* husbands are only afraid," I said, "that we'll fall into one of those tubs of diapers we're washing at twelve o'clock at night, and they'll have to *hire* somebody to take our places."

There was a moment of silence.

"Have you noticed what U. S. Rubber is doing?" someone asked.

After that I felt fine. I felt peppier and peppier.

When the next letter came from Russia I went to town on it. There were two dandy items. Apparently, when the first boxes marked "Ammunition U. S. A." arrived at the Russian front, where the Russians were holding the enemy at bay with their gun butts, they were found to contain stones instead of cartridges.

The second was more personal. When the loan was finally negotiated, the Russian baron, who was taking the money out of the bag the Americans were holding, threw a party. He invited them to hear the gypsy singers. Nobody noticed that Charley Rich, an executive vice-president who had come over from America to back up the line, was bearing down on the vodka. He kept it up, too, when the party was continued at the baron's castle. When it came time to leave, the baron helped Charley on with his coat. Charley *tipped him!* For a moment it looked as though the baron would flick a glove across his face. It was hastily explained that Charley was a financial wizard who had once been a newsboy on the streets of Chicago. Remembering those nights he'd spent shivering on sleety corners, dreaming of miracles, he always kept a pocketful of gold pieces with which to make them. All was forgiven. It was then "O, là, là, these odd, but undeniably well-heeled Americans!"

I was so proud of this article that for good measure I threw in one on Foreign Exchange, a subject which has always been as mysterious to me as the Sphinx. But I wanted to get on with the Ford.

No sooner were they dropped in the mailbox than a cable arrived from the exploiters.

"We are on our way home. Meet us at the pier tomorrow."

"Did Baby like the new forty-dollar pants?" I asked my husband nonchalantly as we walked toward the car.

"Baby MacCulsky?" he said as if surprised that I'd heard of her. "Oh, three weeks ago she married a French baron."

I felt fine. I didn't tell him we were going to have a Ford. I kept that for a surprise. As we bowled up Fifth Avenue in Mr. McRoberts' Crane-Simplex I waited spellbound for the first words of financial wisdom. More grist for my literary mill. He turned to my husband. I leaned forward.

"I see they're wearing 'em higher than when we left," said Mr. McRoberts. My Source was gone!

And at home, a letter from the *Bankers' Magazine*, another body blow.

"We are holding your last articles," wrote the editors, "pending an interview. We find the one on Foreign Exchange a little confusing."

An interview!

What would the editors of the *Bankers' Magazine* think when they found the author of "The National City Bank Throws Widows and Orphans to the Siberian Wolves" was not a retired financial wizard writing under an alias? I could guess. Good-by Ford!

"What are you so blue about?" asked my husband at supper. "Don't you realize? *I'm home!*"

"I do realize it," I said. And burst into tears.

"There, there," he said, putting his arm around me. "I'll tell you now. I was saving it for a surprise. Mr. McRoberts says it's a shame the way you had to stay at home all alone working your heart out. So he's buying us a car. He uses a Marmon mostly himself but he says there's nothing for young people like a Model T Ford. Why, where are you going?"

"To write a letter," I said.

"We regret to inform you," I wrote the editors of the *Bankers'*

Magazine, "that the author of the Russian articles has passed away suddenly. It will be impossible, therefore, to grant you an interview."

Signed, Haig & Haig, Solicitors.

They were sorry. But I wasn't. I'd got what I wanted. If I harbored a few secret regrets over the sudden demise of my literary career, they vanished into thin air in the presence of the Ford phaeton. It was gorgeous. We all swarmed out and stood open-mouthed beside it. Then we leaned against it jauntily and had our pictures taken. We were not fearful of it all but piled brightly in and drove off lickety-cut. The children in the back. My husband at the wheel. And me, sitting beside him, reading aloud from the book of directions.

ARMONK, FIRST DISTRICT TO REPORT

I ALWAYS feel conscience-stricken when I think how mad I was when the armistice came. It cut me off at the height of my most colossal and public-spirited undertaking. If they'd let me alone, in another month I'd have marched to Berlin and hanged the Kaiser.

In 1916 I started worrying over the state of the nation. We were living in Armonk, twelve miles from the White Plains railroad station. The instant my husband had been raised to $2500 a year, we'd embarked on a back-to-the-land movement. I say "we," but I was the prime mover. I had long nursed the idea (in secret) of tutors instead of schools for the children. We would have a garden. Everybody would hoe it. We would have a pony. I saw hope of carrying through this ambitious plan when Mr. McRoberts, my husband's employer, said we could get a farmhouse near his country estate for thirty-five dollars a month. When my mother wrote that if we would pay the freight we could have her furniture, nothing could have held me back. It would be heaven to junk the mission furniture and be reunited with the Governor Winthrop desk and the secretary. We immediately sold the Larchmont house at a terrific loss and moved to Armonk.

My happy hopes for a new life were quickly dashed. The children proved too young for tutors and they fell off the pony. Of course, Rodney at fourteen months and Louise at two weeks could hardly have been expected to ride it. But I felt that Barbara, about four, and John, going on three, could have ridden it if they'd wanted to. They insisted it looked like a lion to them, and it was too slippery. Mr. Stirling, who owned the farmhouse we were living in, said he didn't want the yard dug up for a garden. He even refused to let me have the pond-lily paper I picked out for the bathroom. "Who wants to be a damn bullfrog?" he said. It was very dispiriting.

Days I was pretty well occupied battling for survival against four children under four, a gasoline water pump that had to be drained in eleven places, and the Model T phaeton. But nights I worried about the state of the nation.

Here was the United States with a war coming up and no weapons to fight it with. Yet apparently nobody was giving a tinker's damn but me and a little girl named Margery. Margery had taken the bit in her teeth by sending to the *New York Tribune* ten cents toward the purchase of a battleship.

For a moment it looked as if Margery had hit the bull's-eye.

Hearst, it was rumored, said he'd have given $50,000 if Margery had sent her dime to the *Journal*. Stung to the quick by this base implication that they didn't know a God-given combination of human interest, national interest, and free publicity when they saw it, the *Tribune* snaked my brother-in-law off the night city desk with orders to slap "Margery's Battleship Fund" onto the front pages. A huge benefit was staged at the Hippodrome. Bands played; flags waved; the crowd went crazy cheering a skater who did the split on ice and after a little prodding from the manager gave a rather feeble hip-hip-hooray for Margery. Everybody slapped everybody else on the back and agreed that what this country needed was a good ten-cent battleship, more people who could do the split on ice, and more little girls like Margery. Then they forgot the whole thing in their eagerness to get back to their manicurist and see if she had any more hot tips like Electric Boat and Anaconda.

This left me as Sole Worrier over the state of the nation, but I felt I could work something out if the children would quit wetting their sheets and blankets and mattresses, and hurling them out of their cribs, long enough for me to get started.

I had never knowingly shirked my civic responsibilities. At the age of ten I wrote a letter to the Quincy *Patriot*, protesting against the removal from the Square of a granite horse trough, which I characterized lovingly as "a boon to man and beast." On Founder's Day at school, scorning such sissy subjects as "The Influence of Rosa Bonheur," I decided in favor of a polemic denouncing practically everything. My speech, which began burningly "As that eminent jurist, the late Charles O'Connor, so aptly said," was acclaimed by the

Ledger as the most amazing political commentary ever delivered by a twelve-year-old girl. It certainly was. Nobody, including myself, could make head or tail of it.

In 1912 I kicked in the fifty dollars I won for an essay on "Why Women Shouldn't Vote" on a blue-serge suit at Hollander's to wear in the Suffrage Parade.

Later, I put my family on a diet of hamburg and dried lima beans in order to squeeze out twenty-five dollars for the Anti-Saloon League. Not that I was afraid for myself. A childhood habit of sneaking downstairs after parties in my woolen nightgown and drinking up all the leftover claret, champagne, hock, and sherry had left me the happy possessor of an asbestos stomach. It was to demonstrate my passionate desire for civic betterment.

When I received my pallid orders from suffrage headquarters to take voters to the polls, I rounded the corners on one wheel, haranguing them every instant of the trip. I trailed them to the very jaws of the voting booth, breathing hot on their necks a final threat that a good kick in the slats was the least they could expect from me if they didn't vote "Yes" to woman's suffrage. Then I was led away by a state patrolman.

I felt the end justified the means, as John Hay said about the little revolution they whipped up in Panama. Armonk went for suffrage by a nice margin.

Since then, neither snow nor sleet, nor the receipt of Four Little Bundles from Heaven, had stayed me in my determination to give mankind a good swift boot in the right direction whenever the occasion warranted.

The job of arousing a sluggish electorate, lying doggo under the delusion it could lick its weight in wildcats, would be duck soup to anyone accustomed as I was to public service.

Before I could swing into action, the Germans beat me to it by announcing unrestricted submarine warfare. On April 6, 1917, America declared war. This saved me a lot of rabble-rousing, but left me with a world war on my shoulders.

My first efforts led into hearty opposition right in my own family. My husband stoutly resisted my suggestion that he enlist, pleading five dependents and no means of support but a salary of $2500. This meant I couldn't have a flag with a star on it on the Ford. I thought if he'd had the spirit of a mouse, he would have deserted us and left us starving.

Balked in my efforts to organize the family, I got busy on Armonk. I summoned six leading citizens to a meeting at our house to discuss a War Garden. "You can be Moderator," I told my husband. He said he didn't want to be Moderator. "What do you want to mix into a lot of stuff that's none of your business for?" he asked. He wasn't strong on public service. And he thought it was suicidal to proceed in any undertaking without due authority. "I'm going to bed," he said. "You can run your own meeting."

Only two leading citizens came. One smoked his pipe, kept mum, and glowered. The other said maybe I'd like to know that this war come at a damn inconvenient time for him. He'd just about made up his mind to shingle his barn. What happened? This war come! He couldn't git no lumber. After they'd gone I lay awake fuming.

Next morning I descended upon my husband's employer, now *General* McRoberts. I drew him a heart-rending picture of loyal Armonkers, with hoes in their hands rarin' to do and die for dear old cucumbers and radishes. Would he care to contribute? Visibly touched, General McRoberts forked over generously for a giant flag and flagpole to make it legal. His contribution was so lavish, in fact, that I was able to skin enough out of it for a mammoth sign: WE ARE DOING OUR BIT: THIS IS ARMONK'S WAR GARDEN. Armed with these two Gargantuan bits of propaganda, I now had to find a place to erect them.

The spot I selected turned out to be owned by a loyal citizen who said go ahead, he didn't give a damn, but the soil was so sandy it wouldn't grow a cabbage. I explained to him that in our War Garden, as in all great public enterprises, it wasn't so much the results as the spirit (and publicity) that counted.

The results were astonishing. Our grubby field was on the main highway. Our flag and flagpole were worthy of Gettysburg. Our sign would have done ample justice to the coming millennium. The first thing Armonk knew, it was lifted from obscurity onto the front pages of the New York newspapers. Headlines announced that a metropolitan populace, inspired by the patriotic get-up-and-get of tiny Armonk, would follow the progress of our project with breathless interest.

It was now root, hog, or die. Armonk rooted. Every man, woman, and child faithfully fertilized, watered, and tilled his carefully measured portion of that communal desert. It actually disgorged peas, beans, squash, and corn that Burbank would have envied. What's more, my neighbors loyally tilled my particular section as a tribute to my having coaxed fame and fortune to their little hamlet.

This was lucky. For not only does one look from me blight all growing things; I was up to the ears in selling Liberty Bonds. Armonk's quota was set at $63,000. This meant I'd have to crash the butlers of summer places. It wasn't that I was afraid of butlers. But the way they always look me up and down makes me want to commit mayhem. And since winter had set in I was having worry enough getting the Ford and pump started.

Starting motors in zero weather is a man's job. But my husband took the train at White Plains every morning at 7:23 after a wild ride around the lakes, and his position with the Bond Department of the National City Bank didn't call for a costume suited to starting motors. He hated the Ford anyway. He regarded it as a hateful thing he was too tall to drive and he had to climb out over the side of. He didn't know what went on under the hood and he didn't want to. He felt it tore him down socially when the children and I drew up alongside the Marmons and Pierce Arrows at night at the White Plains station. If we were early, I'd throw the children a loaf of bread to keep them quiet and they'd crouch down in the back, tear the middle out, and eat it. When the train pulled in they'd stand up on the back seat and cheer. I thought it was funny. He didn't. It was all I could do to get him to drive the Ford, let alone start it. I was of the more athletic type, anyway. So I took over.

To start a Model T in winter it was necessary to jack up the rear wheels, then rush around front and crank till your arms dropped out of their sockets while some accomplice put boiling rags on the carburetor. You had to be quick, like a fox, if the car started. The terrific vibrations of its powerful four-cylinder motor invariably caused it to leap off the jack and lunge forward. You had to jump for your life to avoid being pinned to the garage wall by an angry phaeton.

The instant I got the thing going, I sprang in for the quick twenty-four-mile trip around the frozen lakes, with curtains flapping.

Then I was ready for my daily bout with the bulldog engine that pumped the water supply into the house. This better be good. No startee, no water.

First, remove nails from drains. Then kerosene priming. Then insert two fingers in the hole of the flywheel, and ease it back and forth till it was loose enough to spin. Take a long breath and *spin it*. If there was a clattering explosion followed by a cheery rat-tat-tat which shook the pump house to its foundations, it was all right to go in and do the dishes. If it died with a gasping whoosh, it was half a mile down the road on foot to the spring with buckets and pails for water.

By nine o'clock I could usually count on being ready to stick a bottle in the baby's face, put her on the floor in the back of the Ford in a washbasket firmly held in place by the feet of the other three children.

Then off, tra-la, on our merry round of bond selling.

The children, in their little fur coats, objected to side curtains. They obstructed the view. So we rode with the top down, I, pressed for time, still in my starter's costume of stocking hat, sheepskin coat, knickerbockers, and riding boots. As the radiator cap was always blowing off, I put it into my pocket. Our general ensemble, as we approached the palaces of the mighty, suggested a battered and eccentric engineer driving a steaming teakettle full of rabbits.

Instead of drawing sneers, as I feared, our appearance proved an open-sesame with butlers. They were so baffled they could hardly wait to see what the master could make of it. And once my eyes were set on the Rajah of that particular Put, no whines that his Wall Street office already had hicks on his Liberty Bond purchases could save him. I had to work fast to get in and out again, before the Ford froze, or somebody was murdered. I got a personal letter from William G. McAdoo, Secretary of the Treasury, about the three weeks flat it took me to sell $63,000 worth of bonds. It was some kind of record.

As our fame spread, I was bothered by Democratic politicians from Valhalla who claimed I was an unauthorized upstart and they'd been "instructed by headquarters" to take over our war effort. I brushed them off with the news that women had the vote now and if I had another yip out of them I would set the women on them.

"They're really right, you know," said my husband. "If they wanted to get tough, you wouldn't have a leg to stand on. You may think you're Mrs. Bernie Baruch. But that's just *your* opinion."

"You ought to be proud of me," I said. "You ought to be glad *somebody* in this family's public-spirited."

I didn't pay any attention to his beefing. Drunk with success, I broadened my scope. I arranged a talk on food conservation for the ladies of Armonk, but the ladies of Armonk took an instant dislike to the speaker, a lady from Mount Kisco.

"There's a most marvelous sort of white cornmeal you can get," she suggested from the depths of her sables to the sulky audience. "Stone ground and all that sort of thing. Most interesting."

There was a dead silence.

"Where can you get it?" I asked encouragingly.

"Where can you get *anything?*" the speaker asked, aghast at our ignorance. "Naturally, at Charles'!"

"I'm sure we all want to do everything we can to win the war," I said vapidly.

"If you ask me, there wouldn't have been any war," said the lady in the back row, "if it wasn't for the rich like her being friends with the British."

"Well, well," I said hastily, standing up and smiling kindly. "Shall we all thank the lady from Mount Kisco for her very, very helpful talk?"

"Thank her yourself," said the lady in the back row. "I don't want to."

I felt perhaps I'd better let my community war efforts lie for a little and devote myself to the personal sacrifice the papers stressed

as so necessary. So I hired a girl to take care of the children two afternoons a week, and went down to the White Plains Armory to learn
ambulance driving.

When Colonel Weeks cast his eye over the little group of future
chauffeurs assembled for his instruction, he didn't hesitate to express
himself as pretty damn disgusted. Their waists were too tightly laced.
Their French heels were too high and wobbly. The whole thing was
too silly. But we'd see how they stood up under drilling.

They didn't stand up at all after the first few minutes. But week
after week, despite pained cries and thinning ranks, Colonel Weeks
drilled them. I was teacher's pet in my neat black dress, large white
piqué collar and cuffs, and low-heeled shoes.

One afternoon, while skimming merrily over a newly tarred road
toward the Armory, I blew a tire. By the time I had jacked up the
car, taken off the tire, removed the tube, mended it, replaced it, and
pumped the whole thing up with a bicycle pump, I looked like the
original Tar Baby. Half an hour late, able to see out of only one eye,
black from head to foot, I presented myself for inspection.

"What the devil!" shouted Colonel Weeks. "Go home and stay
there!"

"All right," I shouted back, "but I'm the only one in the whole
blamed outfit who knows a gasket from a gusset!"

The hell with the ambulance driving! I dove into the campaign
to sell War Saving Stamps. It didn't go so well until I put up a list in
the post office of all Armonk citizens who had *not* purchased them.
This smoked them out. One victim came to me with tears in his eyes.

"I'm busted," he said, "but rather than have some damn suffragee
put me to shame, I'll pay out the money."

But it was the man who didn't have a cent in the world who came
through with an idea that was worth its weight in gold; a plan that
made everything we'd done to date look like child's play.

"Why couldn't Armonk," he demanded, "stage a rally?"

I was ashamed. To think here it was the fall of 1918 and I hadn't
thought of having a rally.

"Tell you what I'll do," he said. "I haven't a nickel to bless myself
with, but if you'll take my name off that list, I'll let you have my place

for a rally. I've got a lot of cider in the cellar I'll throw in, and you can make some of your raised biscuits. We'll ransack the town for jellies and give the Red Cross the money we make from selling the whole kit and caboodle."

We rode around Armonk like Paul Revere rousing the citizenry. We ended up hoarse but agreed that if the war were never won it wouldn't be because Armonk hadn't put on a rip-roaring rally.

We strung banners across the highways from tree to tree. We brought chairs from every house in town, and ransacked the churches for benches. Boards were laid across sawhorses and loaded with edibles from stove and cupboard. The roads were lined with cars for miles and miles.

My husband claimed he couldn't get off from the bank to be there. But my sister loyally showed up with her Dodge patriotically plastered with red, white, and blue, and her two baby girls on the front seat, clutching flags. My mother wrote that she "lauded" my efforts and she only regretted the fact that she was prevented from coming down from Maine by lack of carfare.

I kindly consented to open the rally with a few well-chosen words. Once started, nobody could stop me. I was finally dragged from the platform in favor of a speaker supplied by Democratic headquarters —to show there were no hard feelings. He instantly won the hearts of the crowd by sawing the air with his arms and bellowing glittering generalities.

While he was at it, someone rushed up to tell me the cider was hard. Nobody minded. And my Parker House rolls were bringing a dollar and a quarter a pan. My real worry was our *pièces de résistance* —Three Blue Devils—without whom no patriotic rally could be authentic. The New York agency that specialized in these much-sought-after French chasseurs assured me they'd arrive in A-1 condition. But they were belligerently resisting all efforts to be helped to the platform. They had taken advantage of my long, impassioned address to slip up to Byram Lake Inn for a few last snifters. I sped their faltering footsteps to the dais with a little pantomime and some pidgin French, "*La mouche socko.*" As soon as they appeared on the platform, the applause was deafening. The crowd, not speaking French, interpreted their loud cries to mean not "More American whisky," but—"Long live America!"

It was a big moment. Reporters from far and wide gathered around me, clamoring for facts and figures. ARMONK DOES IT AGAIN, I saw as a heading. Then one of them whispered something: did I know an armistice was coming?

The glad news that the last pan of rolls had brought three dollars, and that the woman had given back the pan, fell on deaf ears. I slunk home utterly routed. The next day the rumor of an armistice was confirmed, denied, confirmed officially.

My heart, which should have soared, fell dismally. That armistice came at a very inconvenient time for me and Armonk. We were just getting set to go over the top.

YOU HAVE TO BACK OUT OF THE
PRESENCE OF KINGS

I HAD very dynamic and far-reaching plans for my children's education. But after the armistice was signed, I felt it was my duty to send them to public school. Hadn't four million men died to make the world safe for democracy? I'd give it a whirl. Although the level of intelligence was rather low at the particular school they attended, my children would be the leaven.

After a year, the only result was that they got lice in their hair so their heads had to be shaved, and they'd learned a dirty poem called "Fire, Fire, False Alarm!"

I sent for prospectuses of the best schools in the country. After all, my husband had been made an officer of the National City Bank at a salary of $7500. We could afford to splurge. But the catalogues all sounded old-fashioned and stuffy.

Then I read about Mr. Frank Vanderlip's School at Scarborough-on-Hudson.

"This school," I said to my husband, "is the answer!"

Children at Mr. Vanderlip's school were to be given advanced, progressive education, under the most aesthetic conditions. He wished to attract bright children of intelligent parents, irrespective of economic status, and the tuition was only one hundred dollars. Under these ideal conditions all his pupils would learn to be leaders.

Louise, at the age of three, was a little young for leadership. But she could go to kindergarten. Rodney, at four, could carry a hod of coal in each hand and swear like a trouper. He ought to make a leader of something, if only the Hod Carriers' Union. John and Barbara, at five and six, had already shown definite indications of leadership. They could boss me around.

"It seems like carrying coals to Newcastle," said my husband, "to send those children to the Vanderlip School."

My husband felt that the children had turned out to be little savages because of their free and easy upbringing. He was not receptive to new ideas. If he missed the tie of the year at Brooks Brothers, he didn't buy next year's tie. He bought the one he'd missed. Experiments of any kind were anathema to him. He attributed his success in life to the fact that he'd taken a cold tub bath every morning, gargled with Glycothymoline, and never missed an editorial in the *New York Tribune.* It was due to some overt act of God, he felt, that his hair had receded.

I was so enthusiastic about the Vanderlip School, however, that he finally said he'd rather send the children there than have to hear any more about it. So when our lease was up, we moved to Ossining, a short bus ride from Scarborough.

Even before I'd had children my ideas were very definite about bringing them up. They were not going to be brought up as I was brought up and have their little spirits broken. Of course, when I was young, it was still the Dark Ages when people had the horrid notion that parents came before children.

"Drink your milk," my mother would say. "Put on your rubbers."

"Why?"

"Because I tell you to."

I resented this dictatorial regimentation. Why wasn't I told that milk contained valuable properties necessary to proper growth? Why wasn't I informed that sudden chilling of the extremities might lead to illness? I would have been only too glad to comply. As it was, I simply maintained stubbornly that milk was too white and rubbers too sissy. And incredible as it may seem, brute force was at this point often brought into play. If I'd been of a less hardy nature I might have got the impression that the race was to the swift and the battle to the strong. Many children did. They are now presidents of corporations.

I had had private methods of holding my own, however. They were the precursor of the sit-down strike. It was croup that taught me. I didn't have ordinary croup. Mine was so complete that all I could do was make a low rumble in my stomach. I had to get up and patter into my parents' bedroom and stand by the bed till I could work up a short bark. Usually they supposed it was Bruce, our St.

Bernard. I hesitated to touch them because my father was quick on the trigger since we'd had burglars. When they finally gathered that it was me and the croup, they'd hustle me back to bed, rig up a croup kettle, and get the Arabian Balsam.

"You can have three Maillard caramels," my mother would say, "if you take the Arabian Balsam."

"Give me the caramels first," I'd croak hoarsely. Gripping them in my hand, I'd shut my teeth against the Balsam, with the inner assurance that my parents, monsters though they were, would hesitate to beat a sick child. It led to a lot of disagreeable remarks, however, and a distinct lack of camaraderie. Their mistake, of course, was bribing instead of the Appeal to Reason.

They had never even heard of Listening to the Child's Side of the Story. Once my mother went to Boston and left word that if I didn't play in the brook while she was gone I could have some clams when Selma steamed them for the chowder. When I demanded the clams, Selma seized the broom and chased me from the kitchen. I cornered her in the back hall and let her have it in the teeth with my #6 orthopedics. But was Selma made to apologize for her refusal to carry out orders? She was not. I was dragged to Dr. Ordway's and forced to have a wiggly tooth yanked out without gas and was rapped on the back of the hand so hard with a ruler my garnet ring got broken. They wouldn't let me tell them what had happened. It was the unfairness of it all that got me.

Take the little matter of the dimity dress. At my mother's suggestion the seamstress let it down by inserting a large piece of white lace just above the waist.

"I won't wear it," I said reasonably. "It makes me look like a cup and saucer."

"You will wear it," my mother said. "That's just a notion." I was thereby cornered into the act of throwing the shears through the bedroom window.

"You were so abused when you were little," my mother said long afterward, "it's miraculous you turned out so well."

That was the point. I *didn't* turn out well. But I might have, if I'd been handled intelligently.

When I was having my first child I read books on child guidance. "If you say no to a child," these books in 1913 asserted, "you may forever blight its little ego. Never say 'don't.' Make constructive suggestions. If a child breaks a dish or upsets its milk, it is not deliberately being naughty. It doesn't *know* any better. Explain; don't punish. You will establish such a bond of love and understanding between you and your child, he will be heartbroken if he feels you are out of sympathy with him."

It all sounded so sensible. I pictured my little offspring bursting into tears if I so much as raised an eyebrow.

"Come, darling, it's time for bed," I would say.

"Yes, Mummy, yes, yes, yes," the child would cry eagerly.

By the time my four children were one, two, three, and four respectively, I was but the shadow of my former self. Nobody ever cried, "Yes" to anything. Their egos had budded and bloomed, but mine was practically nonexistent.

I did everything the book said. When I received in the face a mug of beef juice that had taken me half an hour to press from a pound of tough round, I just smiled woodenly and retired to the kitchen to count a thousand.

When they climbed on three chairs, got the old razor blades, slashed their wrists, and painted the bathroom red, I said, "Wouldn't you like me to read Uncle Wiggly to you?"

"No, no, no," they cried eagerly.

The book said, "If you must punish, make the punishment fit the crime."

I tried it and was almost mobbed. Down at the beach one day the children were making sand castles. I was reading. Every little while one of them would come over with a shovelful of sand and throw it at me.

"If you do that," I explained sweetly, "the sand might hurt Mother's eyes and she would be blind."

"Then we could have a big police dog to lead you around!" Barbara said eagerly.

"If she's blind we can have a police dog!" I heard her explaining to the others. The next thing I knew I got four shovelfuls of sand right in the beezer. I walked over to the sand castles.

"You've made it so disagreeable and impossible for me to read," I explained firmly. "Now *I* am going to make it disagreeable for *you*."

I kicked down the sand castles and flattened them. The children began screaming. People got up and milled around us threateningly.

"Would you think a grown woman would do a thing like that to those poor little children!"

The people built up the sand castles again, while the children watched, now and then glancing up at me menacingly.

One thing the book admitted frankly. If the children's lives were endangered, steps must be taken. When we went out in the Ford we kept the top down. The children sat in the back and when we went under low trees, they'd grab at the branches. Sometimes they'd hang on until the last second, and I had visions of driving out from under them, leaving them hanging. I explained how dangerous this was. But they didn't stop it. So I got a long switch and when we came to a tree, I warned them. It was, I felt, a blatant example of brute force, but warranted.

"If you grab a branch," I said, "I'll switch you. And this is not all. The next child who grabs a branch will have to get out. We'll drive off and leave him."

We came to a low-hanging tree. Barbara grabbed it. I reached over and switched her, but she didn't let go. I stopped the Ford.

"Get out," I said. She climbed out. The tears began to run down her face. The other children's faces puckered and grew red. I started the car and left the pitiful little figure.

The children grabbed the switch and beat me over the head with it.

"You bad, bad, horrid mother!" they yelled. "We hate you!"

This was very discouraging. But the Vanderlip School would clear everything up.

When they started off for Scarborough that first morning in the bus, I sank back feeling at last like the mother who had done the right thing. I thought of the beautiful buildings and gorgeous grounds where they were to learn to be leaders. It was Mr. Vanderlip's own estate, and the landscaping had been done by Olmsted Brothers. Wide green lawns swept down to the Hudson. Deep-green pines hung low over a swimming pool of sky-blue water. A theater lay in the hollow, with three sets of scenery, and official dressing rooms. There was shop for boys, where they could tear down and build up automobiles. There was a little house which the children themselves were to build. Throughout all was an air of utter freedom. And my children's I. Q.'s had come through with flying colors.

The telephone interrupted my reverie. It was the bus company. Would I please come to headquarters?

I found Rodney, a lady, and the president of the company.

"This boy," said the president, "kicked this lady in the face. What are you going to do about it?"

The book said, "Never condemn a child without hearing his side of the story."

"Why," I asked gently, "did you kick the lady in the face, Rodney?"

"Because," said Rodney, "her face is so homely."

"We cannot transport this boy on our bus line any more," said the president of the company. I took Rodney home. The book didn't say what to do after you'd heard the child's side of the story. Moreover, I'd had a good look at the lady. Her face *was* homely.

Because the bus line outlawed Rodney, we got the Marmon. It was eighty feet long and all made of aluminum. It had everything but antiaircraft guns mounted on it. Every time it roared into the yard, my husband said he expected a general and five aides to hop out. It had belonged to Joseph P. Day, the real-estate man, who had used it to run up to Canada. Lots of people used to run up to Canada in 1920. It had trick tires that had only one lock nut on them. Sometimes a tire would shoot right off and up somebody's front steps while you were driving. On the level, you could get three miles to a gallon. The children loved it.

"Beat that old Lizzie! Beat that Essex!" they'd yell from the back seat, and we'd beat them. Mr. Rapp, the garageman, sold me a trick jack because I had so much trouble with the tires. It cost sixteen dollars. If you stepped on it hard, it raised the car right up as far as you wanted it to go. That's what Mr. Rapp said. But it took an elephant to step hard enough. I could jump on it and not raise it an inch.

"Jump, Mom! Jump!" the children yelled encouragingly. I thought of how my mother would glare at Fred, the coachman, if he failed to put the wicker guard on the wheel of the victoria when she stepped out of it. Could there possibly be something wrong with progressive education?

Besides the Marmon, we still had the pony. There was no barn, so we kept him in the chicken house. Nobody wanted to brush or currycomb the pony. When we drove down the street in the pony cart, onlookers jeered. There were wisps of straw and grain all over him. Nobody wanted to ride him. The book said there was no more salutary thing for children than to care for an animal. But they didn't care for it.

I waited eagerly for the children to learn to read. I was pretty tired of droning through Peter Rabbit and Uncle Wiggly. But months went by, and they didn't. I went to see the teacher. She said nobody was forced to read. That wasn't progressive. Nobody was forced to do anything. When the children came to school each morning, they found the room full of interesting activities. They were free to join whatever appealed to them.

"What activities have my children joined?" I asked.

They hadn't joined any. They preferred kibitzing.

I was so mad I called my sister. "I just don't think," I said wearily, "that my children have any ambition."

"Why should they have?" she replied. "They've watched you for years, all full of ambition, knocking your head against stone walls. They're too smart to stick their necks out. Why do anything if you don't have to?"

"But the book says children are naturally active and love to *do* things. I'm afraid my children have something the matter with them."

"Oh, throw that book away!" said my sister.

My sister was bringing up her two little girls by the most outworn methods. She had moved to Yonkers so they could go to a conservative private school. Yet they were turning out beautifully. It was very puzzling. It was true that they displayed a lamentable lack of enthusiasm when she took them to an exhibition of Chinese armor at the Art Museum. But she said that was because nobody they knew in

Grade B at Halstead School wore Chinese armor. I had to admit my own children's trip to the Museum of Natural History was scarcely more successful. On the way in they'd seen a dead horse lying in Fifty-sixth Street which proved infinitely more diverting than anything in the museum. When their father asked them at dinner what they'd seen, they described the horse with such accuracy and detail that he couldn't eat anything.

I didn't actually throw away my book of directions, as my sister advised, but I was worried to find myself slipping back to some of the old methods and theories that had blighted my own early years. I found myself not wanting to play Helpful Brownies when we got through supper and the table had to be cleared. I longed to say, "Take those dishes off the table and be quick about it." I realized that this was very wrong of me.

It was all very confusing. Especially when the first report cards said my offspring were "antisocial." Again, I hot-footed it down to the school. It seems that John didn't want to be in a play about a far-from-reluctant dragon which had a long waggly red tongue and electric-light eyes. He'd been found cowering in a ditch in his pink-cheesecloth costume. He wouldn't be in it, he said, because it was "too awful." Barbara was antisocial about Rhythms. She had teased and teased to take Rhythms. At a cost of forty-five dollars. I made a white-muslin costume, and provided the required scarf to be held floating over the head. But when she got there she wouldn't join the class. "They look too silly," she said, "hopping around barefooted."

Some children turned out wonderful plays, and poetry, and paintings. Mine did not. Some learned ancient history by building little forts and triremes. Mine didn't care to. They did not choose to learn. When the school wrote me, "What are you doing about Rodney's arithmetic?" I wrote back, "Nothing." Barbara failed entirely in arithmetic. Three times two, it said. She wrote, "Five *or* six," just to be sure to be right. The pretty covers on the arithmetic books didn't fool my children. They knew there were tables inside. Nor could I yet read Barbara's writing. She maintained that skriggles were writing, and she didn't like it because I wouldn't admit it. At school, she said, they gave you credit for trying. She brought home some little hen scratches with "Good!" written on the paper, and gave me a hard look, as if to say, "You paid a hundred dollars for that. What are you going to do about it?"

A cloud was gathering on my horizon. Could it be possible that my children were not adapted to progressive methods? But I didn't follow my sister's advice. I still held onto the book, and dipped into its pages occasionally. One of the rules said, "Don't sympathize with children when they are hurt. Get them into the habit of announcing it in a commonplace tone." One day Rodney's great-aunt, a strict Presbyterian, came to call. Rodney fell off his velocipede and skinned his knee. "Poor Rodney," said his aunt, sympathetically. He thought she was being sarcastic. "You fool," he said angrily.

"See," said his aunt, "I just laugh when little boys say things like that."

"You darn fool!" he cried, now mad as a hatter.

"I still laugh," said his aunt, bravely.

"You damn fool! Now let's see you laugh!" said Rodney.

It was no use asking my mother for advice. She considered the children paragons of virtue. A little high-spirited, perhaps, but what of it? That was because when she came to visit, the children were little angels. They ran to get her Shetland shawl for her, placed a hassock under her feet, and played endless games of dominoes, which they hated, with every evidence of enthusiasm. This was so that she would tell them stories.

Every afternoon at five, they washed their faces and hands, brushed their hair, and knocked on her door. When she said, "You may come in," they tiptoed in and ranged themselves on the floor around her rocking chair. Then she would hand out small pieces of Baker's chocolate.

"Tell about the girl whose feet bled, and the little girl who stole," they would burst out eagerly.

"Well," my mother would begin, "there was a little girl whose mother forbade her to go barefooted. But she *disobeyed her mother!*" Dramatic pause while the children appropriately registered horror. "She took off her shoes and stockings and placed them under a rock.

Before her lay a field of deep grass and clover. It felt cool and soft on her feet as she walked through it. On the other side she found a brook. She went in wading. She followed the brook for a way, tossing pebbles and watching the tiny fish dart in and out. After a time, she noticed the sun was getting low and she started back. When she arrived at the field she could hardly believe her eyes. In her absence it had been *mowed*. Where there had been soft grass, there was now only harsh stubble. By the time she had reached the other side, her feet were gashed and bleeding. She was unable to get her shoes on. She returned home, crying bitterly, sadder and wiser. She knew now that *children who do not mind their mothers always get hurt.*"

Here would come a brief interlude during which my mother solicitously wiped streaming eyes and dealt out more chocolate. This would be followed by the story of the little girl who borrowed a turquoise ring from a classmate at school and *lost* it. She was accused of *theft!* Her own family turned against her. Years later, it was found wedged in a crack at the back of a bureau drawer. But it was *too late. Never a borrower or a lender be.*

If time allowed, there was the harrowing tale of the boy who skated on the river after he had been told not to. One night he was seen just at dusk, skating along with swift strokes. As he rounded the bend, there was a terrible cracking. He was never seen again. "He was never seen again!" the children would whisper awestruck as they tiptoed out. These spine-chillers supplied the children's normal craving for ghastliness. The morals went in one ear and out the other.

It was when I followed the book's advice about sex instruction that I completely lost confidence in it. Rodney had inquired about the origin of kittens. I drew him to my side. In hushed tones I began the story of the flowers and pollen. His face got red. We were both embarrassed. Doggedly I went on to animals. "O.K.," he said suddenly, anxious to put me out of my misery. I rose and put my hand on his shoulder. "We won't tell anybody about this, will we?" I asked chummily. He gave me an understanding look. "Oh, no!" he said. "It's too dirty!"

The day Rodney came in and said he felt I ought to know that he'd set the barn on fire, I felt the end of progressive methods was near. He explained that he'd got very annoyed when I'd forbidden him to play with matches. He said he'd thought and thought about it, and had finally gone out to the barn and set all the newspapers on fire.

The end did come one fatal afternoon. In self-defense I had made two rules. The children were not allowed to ride their tricycles in the back door, around the kitchen table, and out again, when I was baking cookies. They'd wolf down the cookies, riding rapidly out with their spoils as they came off the assembly line, and I'd have an empty table to show for two hours' work. They were also forbidden to ride tricycles over my feet when I was reading.

"I wouldn't ride a tricycle over your feet while you were reading," I explained.

"We can't read," said the children, "and anyway we wouldn't let you."

That afternoon I was reading on the porch. I'd been baking and I was tired. Rodney not only slammed the door every time he rode in and out of the front door, but twice he ran over my toes. The other children were jumping in the yard on pogo sticks.

"Please, Rodney, you're disturbing Mother while she's reading. Please shut the door softly."

He slammed it.

"Stop that!" I said sharply.

He slammed it, and the top of my head nearly came off.

"If you do that again," I said, hardly believing my own ears, "I'll spank you."

He did it again.

I put down my book. He got off his tricycle and took my hand. We went up stairs, followed by the sad, horrified gazes of the pogo-stickers. He took his little pants down, and I took the hairbrush. I spanked him. Large tears rolled down his face silently. I began to stutter, but he looked at me sympathetically.

"I don't see what else you could do," he said.

We went downstairs and I began to read again. Pretty soon he appeared in front of me.

"You know those twenty-two little cakes you made for tonight for company?"

"Yes," I said.

"Well," he said, "I think I ought to tell you so you can spank me again if you want to. I was so mad at you I ate them."

Hand in hand we went upstairs again. After the children went to bed that night I heard him say, "If you'll give me a nickel I'll show you my black-and-blue marks."

"Well, you've had a busy year," my husband said on the last day of school. "How have the children really been making out?"

We called them in, and they stood before us, four little potential leaders.

"Well," I asked them, "what is the most important thing you've learned at school, children?"

They thought, and thought, and thought. Finally Barbara said dreamily, "You have to back out of the presence of kings."

"Where do we go from here?" said my husband.

"I guess my father was right," I said, after a little. "He said the only thing to do with children under ten was to keep 'em in a barrel and feed 'em through the bunghole."

We sent Barbara and Louise to Briarcliff. John and Rodney went to Harvey.

"We are *not* interested in the fact that Rodney has taken a dislike to Alcibiades," wrote Mr. Carter, Headmaster of Harvey. "He may *not* change history courses. This is *not* a progressive school."

"If you don't mind," said my husband, "I think I'll frame that and hang it in the living room."

I'LL GIVE YOU A NICKEL IF
YOU'LL WALK

MY WRISTS hurt," said Barbara.

"My ankles hurt," said Johnny.

"Come here and let me see," I said. I was putting books in book boxes. We were moving that afternoon. "*How* do they hurt," I asked as I examined their wrists and ankles. "I don't see anything wrong."

"They wouldn't hurt if we could have some cookies," said Barbara.

"You frauds! Go out in the kitchen and get some cookies, then."

"Bring me some," said Louise. She was lying on the couch.

"No we won't! No we won't!" said the children. "Doesn't she have to go out and get them herself? She's three!"

"I don't want to go out and get them," said Louise, "my legs are tired."

"Oh, get the cookies for her and then go out and play while I finish packing," I said, "or you'll drive me out of my mind."

I was glad we were moving. It seemed as if somebody had been sick every day we lived in the Ossining house. Measles, chickenpox, flu; and Rodney had fallen down into the cellar of the old barn and had to have five stitches in his face.

The little house on the hill in Scarborough was going to be wonderful. The hill was so steep, the driveway washed out in great gullies when it rained, so everybody would have to walk up and down. But that didn't matter. From the porch you could look off across the Hudson deep into orange hills. Around the porch was a rickety old railing smothered in honeysuckle. At the corner was a ginkgo tree that sighed at night and waved its arms gently across the windows. There were white birches to swing on, and there was a window cut in the roof of the children's room. They could lie in bed and look up at the stars.

"Can we ride over on the van?" the children asked after lunch, when the movers came.

114

"Yes," I said.

Louise didn't want to. She rode with me. She was tired.

Everybody was tired three hours later when the vans had been unloaded. The children looked white and I put them to bed.

"See," I said to Rodney, "how pretty the room looks. I let you have the Chinese picture. I thought you'd like it."

"I'm afraid of the Chinese picture," said Rodney. "The Chinese lady has long sharp nails."

The children ate their suppers of cocoa and toast when I brought them up, but when I went downstairs they called me. They said their throats hurt.

"I'm going to call the doctor," I said to my husband. "I think there is something the matter with them. Maybe I shouldn't have let them ride over with the moving men."

"Why do you always blame yourself for everything that happens to the children?" he said. "They're probably just tired out with the excitement of moving."

"I worry," I said, "because if I do everything right, nothing will happen to them. I just thought maybe they were too tired to have ridden over with the moving men."

I couldn't get our regular doctor. It was the Saturday before Labor Day, and he was off on a week-end holiday. I tried some other doctors. They were away, too, but I kept trying.

"I think you're just tired out yourself, and worried over nothing," said my husband as he heard me telephoning. "Why don't you let it go and see how they are in the morning?"

"I don't know," I said. "I just have a feeling they're coming down with something."

The doctor came about nine that evening. He asked if they'd had all the children's diseases. They had. He asked if they had been away from home lately. I said they hadn't. Except that I had taken them up to a lake above Peekskill, swimming, the previous Sunday. But we hadn't stayed long because there was a little boy with a runny nose who hung around. The doctor said if they were coming down with colds caught from the boy they would have been sick before this. He said their throats were a little red but he just

thought they were tired and excited. He said to call him in the morning if they weren't better.

In the morning they were fine. There was a gray squirrel who lived
on the roof who had looked right in the window. Then Louise fell
out of bed. I heard them all laughing.

"Hurry up," I said, "your cereal's ready."

"Louise won't get up," said Rodney. "She's lying on the floor, gig-
gling."

"You tell her to get up quick," I said, "or I'll come up and get her."

"She won't," he called. "Every time she gets up, her feet go right
out from under her."

I heard roars of laughter.

"Take her hand," I called, "and stop acting silly."

In a moment, they came down. They couldn't do anything with
Louise, they said. She had the giggles. I went up. Louise was lying
across the bed.

"Now we have lots to do and see in the new house," I said, "and
we can't have any lazybones. Take my hand and we'll go down and
get breakfast."

Louise said she wanted to stay with the squirrel. She wanted her
breakfast on a tray so she could give the squirrel some. Barbara took
her breakfast up. She said Louise was acting crazy. She dropped
her toast and she said she couldn't eat her cereal. So Barbara fed it
to her.

"Do you suppose there is something the matter with her?" I said
to my husband. "Ought I to call the doctor again?"

"Lord, no. Leave her in bed if she wants to stay there. You've got
enough to do and one less kid tagging around till you get straightened
out will be a godsend. She just wants a little attention."

The other children seemed fine. They made a little house for the
dog out back of the kitchen. They found an old sleigh in the barn
loft and played sleigh ride in it. They swung on the birches. They
said they were afraid of the ginkgo tree at first, in the night. They had
thought it was robbers. But when they realized it was the tap-tap of

the leaves, they liked it. They rode their velocipedes around the porch. They found a hummingbird's nest.

Louise was fine, too, when I went up later. She said when she grew up she was going to be a squirrel tamer. I asked her if she didn't want to come down and sit on a pillow in the sun, but she said she didn't.

When I went down I stood on the porch and looked out across the Hudson. As I stood there, I had a strange feeling. I went back upstairs as if something was pulling me. I went to Louise's crib and threw back the bedclothes. I swung her over to the side and took her hand.

"I'll give you a nickel if you'll walk," I said.

"I hurt my ankle," she said. "I can't."

I looked at her ankle. It was swollen.

"Is it sore when I touch it?"

"Yes," she said.

I called up the doctor.

"I know you think I'm silly, but I wish you'd come over," I said. He did think I was silly. He said if she turned her ankle when she fell out of bed, rest was all that was needed. But if I insisted, he would come over about seven.

I told my husband about it at dinner.

"I don't know what's the matter with you, worrying like this over nothing," he said.

"It's only that I couldn't stand it," I said, "if anything happened to the children."

"When you have children, you're vulnerable," he said. "Why should you be immune to trouble when nobody else is? You always think you can make everything come out all right if you only try hard enough. All you can do is the best you can and then it's out of your jurisdiction."

"But it isn't fair when things happen to children," I said.

"Who said it was? After all, you can't be Mrs. God," said my husband. "What's got you all upset? The kids all look great, and the only trouble is Louise turned her ankle."

"I don't know," I said. "All day I've had a strange feeling."

Just then the doctor came.

"You finish your dinner," said my husband. "You're all tired out with moving. Now stop worrying."

They went upstairs, and I thought how silly I'd been. I heard my husband and the doctor and Louise laughing. I stopped worrying. The long windows were open onto the porch and I looked out across the river at the sunset. I thought how lucky we were. The kids, a good job, the little house on the hill—everything the way we wanted it. I finished my salad and started on my dessert. The sun was getting lower now, a red ball of flame. I hoped my husband would come down before it disappeared.

Suddenly, a thought stabbed me. *They had been gone a long time.* There was no more laughing. Just low voices, talking, talking. I sat there. I couldn't move. "I'll give you a nickel if you'll walk." She *couldn't!* I thought of what my father used to say: "I don't want mercy. All I want is justice." That didn't make any sense. The sun dropped below the horizon. Before we're born, I thought, we don't have any body. When we're dead, we leave it. The clay the potter shapes. All shapes and sizes. There's nothing really but the spirit. How can anything hurt us if we *don't let it!*

I heard them coming downstairs, talking quietly. The doctor's voice. "Shall I tell her? The shock——"

They came into the dining room.

"Of course," began the doctor, haltingly, "we aren't sure——"

"Who is the best specialist on infantile paralysis in New York?" I said.

They looked at each other.

"Well," said the doctor, "you might call Dr. George Draper."

"The other children?"

"The others, too."

My husband stood looking out of the window. I felt queer. As if a burden had been lifted from me. What if this thing did maim the body? It didn't have to wound the spirit. I didn't have to fight something I couldn't conquer. I wasn't afraid.

"You accept it?" said my husband, turning and looking at me.

"On my own terms," I said. "I refuse to allow it to assume the proportions of a Great Sorrow. Crosses are made, not born."

"I don't see how you're going to keep it from creeping up on you," he said.

"By not crying over it. Not sentimentalizing it. Making it commonplace."

Dr. George Draper came a few hours later and he was fine. We all sat around and talked sensibly. He told us some interesting things. He said infantile paralysis was a strange disease. For some reason it seemed to strike at the huskiest, healthiest, handsomest member of a family. He had seen it hundreds of times. This was not a professional reflection. Just an odd fact. Where several members of a family had it, too, the disease struck hardest at the one with the darkest complexion, usually the type with a mole on his cheek. There was no reason. It just happened so. Barbara and John would get off lightly, he said. They had slight redness of the throat but no paralysis evident. Rodney had signs of paralysis, but we might try serum.

"And Louise?"

"At present she has only the use of her left arm," he said. "Prognosis for life is fair."

This was a shock.

"But she doesn't seem sick," I said faintly.

"She isn't very sick," he said, "but you can't breathe when paralysis reaches your lungs."

I didn't say anything.

"It helps if she keeps her courage up," he said. "I would let her do whatever she wants."

Before he had gone two nurses came. They talked in whispers.

"If you don't mind, I wish you'd talk out loud," I said. "I don't feel equal to being sad."

"Perhaps you don't realize," said one of them, "how serious this is."

Louise called downstairs.

"I want a cap pistol to scare the squirrel," she said. "With a lot of caps."

"The stores are open late tonight," I said to my husband. "Will you get her one?"

"I won't take the responsibility," said the nurse. "Her breath comes hard."

"You don't have to," I said, "I will."

I didn't feel strange any more. I felt things were going to come out all right.

I went out and sat on the front steps and watched the stars. She'd live. She *had* to live. But I knew something the doctor hadn't said. I knew she'd be lame. I thought of all the lame people I had seen. I saw a slow caravan of the lame, the halt, and the blind crossing the sky. Their faces were sad. They were a race apart. Nobody expected them or helped them to be gay. People around them spoke in hushed tones. Why should people say, "It's awful to be lame"? Why not "It's damn tiresome"? Why should the physical put a mark upon the soul? I thought of a time I'd sprained my ankle and walked with crutches. I felt very proud. People came up and talked to me. Asked what had happened. That wasn't bad. People treated me like that because it was *temporary*. Well, this would be *long temporary*. It could be worked the same. It would make people mad. They wouldn't like to have their vicarious sentimentalizing taken away from them. It would be a shock. Paralysis would be a damn nuisance. And that was all.

My husband got home with the cap pistol. I took it upstairs.

The nurse came out tiptoeing. "She's breathing easier now."

"Can I get up tomorrow?" said Louise.

"Maybe," I said.

"Can I have my cap pistol?"

"You'll have to load it for her," I said to the nurse.

"I think you're crazy," she said.

"I don't see how you can be like this," said my husband, "when you think what's ahead."

"The squirrel's gone away," said Louise. "He's gone to bed."

I wheeled her crib under the little window.

"Look, there's the Big Dipper. And the Milky Way. They're a long way off."

"I bet if I try hard enough I can hit them," said Louise.

"I bet you can."

Long after midnight, as I lay sleepless, I could hear her. Shooting, shooting, shooting at the stars.

FANNIE BRICE AND THE DEN
OF LIONS

*I*T WAS the year Wilson limped sick and beaten from the White House, and Harding and Laddie Boy romped in. It was down with labor and let a man make a decent profit. It was Sacco-Vanzetti and the Red Hunt. It was normalcy, the Legion, the Rotary Club, Main Street, Woman's Suffrage, and bathtub gin. It was the year ninety thousand people paid $1,626,580 to see Dempsey knock out Carpentier in the fourth at Boyle's Thirty Acres. It was 1921.

Idealism was out. Realism was in. The world had wearied of going forward with uplifted eyes. Too much ticklee, him bust.

In Scarborough, the pseudo-Utopia where we were living, there was a rift within the lute. The Utopians had split into rival camps. The money-grubbers were tangling with the intelligentsia.

I was in the forefront of the battle, though my status was questionable. As my husband was an officer of the National City Bank, with a salary of $10,000 a year, we were regarded by the intelligentsia as money-grubbers; by the rich as small potatoes.

Scarborough was originally a railroad station. When Mr. Frank A. Vanderlip, a liberal-minded financial expert from the west, came to New York to assume the presidency of the National City Bank, he stopped off there and bought the Helen Gould Shepard estate. Mrs. Vanderlip turned thumbs down on it in spite of the fact that it had solid-gold faucets and a solid-gold coal hod. Undaunted, Mr. Vanderlip turned it into the Sleepy Hollow Country Club and bought "Beechwood." Here he and Mrs. Vanderlip produced six children, built a school, and whipped up a community where the lion gamboled with the lamb and the sheep lay down with the goats.

It was the Promised Land. The burning question was: to whom had it been promised? The intelligentsia or the money-grubbers? Mr. Vanderlip, ignoring the pulling and hauling, went hopefully forward on the theory that there was no great gulf between the bright and the rich; eventually the bright would be rich and the rich wouldn't have got rich if they hadn't been bright.

Community activities were practically ceaseless. There was something for everyone: a gymnasium class; an amateur theater group; folk singing; a swimming pool; an Economic Forum. Thus did Mr. Vanderlip make war on the great American sport of spectatorism.

I joined everything.

My husband was skeptical. He said these activities were just modern editions of the Browning Club and the Ladies Aid. He was surprised at me. He suggested it would be a better world if I stayed at home and minded the children. I told him he was blind. It was a noble experiment, and I was proud to do my bit toward its success. Besides, it was better for the children for a mother to have outside interests. Nobody could be uglier and meaner to children by four o'clock in the afternoon than a mother who had stayed at home with them. It wasn't as if they really needed me. The three older children had completely recovered from infantile paralysis. And Louise was a doughty soul. She could hold her own with anybody, despite crutches and braces.

Hostilities between the bright and the rich were temporarily suspended during the gymnasium class. Both joined cheerfully in a common battle to ward off ills the all-too-human flesh is heir to. The gymnasium class was rugged. We were no effete group of gentle reducers. We went in for dumbbells, Indian clubs, and a basketball team. We thought we were pretty good until the team played Ossining. Then we found the world had moved since ten years before, when most of us went to college. Two of us, I and the girl who played opposite me, got our heads split open. After that, the umpire said she wouldn't umpire any more. So I picked up *The Education of Henry Adams* that I'd brought with me, and the other girl took her copy of the *Sheik*, and we went home.

"What price democracy?" said my husband, grinning at my bandaged head from behind *The Saturday Evening Post*.

"When I was a girl," I said, "they didn't throw you against radiators and gouge you with rings."

"And did you give your opponent a little talk on fair play?" asked my husband. "And from then on it was a brighter, happier world?"

"No," I said, "I knocked her against the radiator and split *her* head open."

"Well, well," said my husband. "You and Mr. Vanderlip don't seem to be making much headway. I remember when cooking in paper bags was going to save the world."

"I'd rather do something," I said, "than just sit around playing 'The Swan' on the phonograph and reading the *Post.*"

"It was a nice sunset," he said. "And it was lucky I was here. It seems Rodney threw eggs at the Stamford bus driver. The bus driver complained. The police were here."

"What did Rodney say?" I asked.

"He said, 'Don't worry. I wouldn't have thrown them if they'd been any good.' They thought that was pretty funny till they went to get on their motorcycle and found Rodney had been busy with a hairpin, letting the air out of the tires."

"But I couldn't have stopped him if I *hadn't* been playing basketball," I said.

"I didn't say you could," said my husband. "I just thought you'd be interested."

He refused to go to meetings of the Economic Forum because he said somebody ought to be home in case the police came. I thought this was mean, because I was secretary. I helped plan the program and introduce the speakers. The object of the forum was to foster genteel debate.

"It will provoke thought," I told my husband.

"It will provoke more than that if you don't can those controversial subjects you've laid out," he said. "It'll end up in a riot."

Mr. Vanderlip, a tall, stooped man with a leonine head of white hair, led off the first meeting of the forum with a subject he'd been thinking about for a long time: the wisdom of levying heavy inheritance taxes. He was a convincing speaker. He said it was unwise for a man to leave great sums to his children who had not had the foresight to earn it and would not know how to conserve it. He thought it was better for children to start from scratch and earn their own living.

This speech proved a bombshell. It appeared that up to that moment Mr. Vanderlip had not seen fit to broach the notion to his own family. They were surprised, to put it mildly. The money-grubbers received it in dour silence. Could it be that Mr. Vanderlip was a traitor to his class, a *socialist?* The intelligentsia were too smart to applaud openly. Though Dr. John Kingsbury, Secretary of the Milbank Memorial Fund, and Mr. Harry L. Hopkins, Assistant Director of the Association for Improving the Condition of the Poor, were seen smiling broadly.

But it gave the forum a lift. Everybody showed up for ex-Commissioner Frederic C. Howe's talk on immigration, for fear they'd miss something. Mr. Howe's theme was "The Melting Pot." He said the millions of foreigners being assimilated would be the making of America. It would enrich her culture and supply new blood. This was the year after Sacco and Vanzetti were arrested and Mitchell Palmer, the Fighting Quaker, had rounded up six thousand Reds in a bolshevik hunt. He was roundly hissed.

"It's about time we put a stop to these foreigners pouring in," somebody shouted. "America for the Americans!"

"You're locking the stable door after the horse is gone," said the ex-Commissioner. "The America you're talking about no longer exists."

"You're a radical," someone yelled.

The fight was on.

"We had a frank discussion," said Mr. Vanderlip, mopping his brow after the meeting had disbanded. "But both sides seemed rather intolerant."

Intolerant hardly described the attitude of the Utopians at the next meeting when Mr. Vanderlip spoke on conditions in Germany. Hell broke loose.

"I think here in America we are being shortsighted," said Mr. Vanderlip. "We have helped impose hopeless sums in reparations upon Germany and then boycotted her goods. She has no gold; she has no securities; if she can't sell goods, she can't pay. The result will be bankruptcy and revolution."

Mr. Maurice Leon, who had arranged loans for France of thirty-five million dollars, sprang to his feet. Mr. Vanderlip had been his friend for many years. Could it be, he demanded with tears in his eyes, that Mr. Vanderlip was pro-German? Mr. Vanderlip said heatedly he was not pro-German but he believed in facing facts. Mr. Leon pointed out that France had been despoiled and that not one foot of German soil had been invaded.

"Aren't we entitled to reparations?" he cried.

The audience cheered Mr. Leon.

"The hell with the Huns!" somebody shouted.

My husband grinned maliciously when I told him about it. "'Oh to be in Arcady,'" he said, "'in Arcady, in Arcady, Oh to be in Arcady when all the leaves are merry.'" He predicted that the coming lecture by Professor Westermann, which I had arranged so hopefully, would be the payoff.

It was not only the payoff; it put an end to the forum.

"Professor Westermann helped draw the boundaries at Versailles," I told the audience. "He can give you the real low-down."

Professor Westermann set up his maps and blackboard.

"We tried to give each country a river, some farm land, an industry, and a defensible frontier, as you see," he said, "with due regard to national unity. But we didn't please anybody. I don't think it will last."

Neither the intelligentsia nor the money-grubbers welcomed this sour news. The forum disbanded. Mr. Vanderlip was discouraged.

"It seems," he said, "nobody wants to hear the truth."

"They never did," said my husband, when I repeated this to him. "They're like me. They want to be amused."

Of course, my husband's life *wasn't* very amusing. It never occurred to me that he was hinting that it was my fault. I just thought how truly he had spoken when he said people *in general* wanted to be amused.

That was probably why the Beechwood Players were still going strong. But there again the intelligentsia were at odds with the bourgeois-capitalist world. I was on the Play Committee, where the battle raged fiercest.

The Players gave six plays a year, with three-night runs. They had started with three one-act plays but had graduated to full-length dramas. During the confusion resulting from the change-over from short plays to long ones, the intelligentsia had, for a brief moment, got the upper hand. Mr. Tom Cleland, an artist who designed covers for "slick" magazines, had put on a Chinese play. He adapted it, painted all the scenery, designed the costumes, and played the principal part. Artistically it was a gorgeous thing. The trouble was, nobody came to see it but Mr. Barett Clark, dramatic editor of *Drama Magazine*, who lived in Briarcliff. Mr. Cleland stubbornly maintained it was Art. Mr. Louis Westermann, whose firm illustrated the Sears Roebuck catalogue, said if nobody came to see it, it wasn't art; just as when, if you shouted and there was nobody there to hear it, there wasn't any sound. Mr. Westermann was for popular revivals.

At this point, the Players achieved real distinction by giving a first performance of Lulu Vollmer's *Sun-up*. Miss Vollmer was then an unknown ticket taker in a southern movie house, who had sent her manuscript to the committee in the crazy hope that they might produce it. This play pleased the simple-minded bankers and brokers and got under the wire as "folk drama" with the intelligentsia. More, it was bought by a Broadway producer and had a long run.

The rift was now healed. Filled with sweetness and light, everybody compromised next on a fantasy. Mr. Cleland consented to play the lead, a tin peddler.

"I wonder why I am so attractive to women?" was Mr. Cleland's opening line. Then after a moment's pause, "It must be the shine on the new tin."

This was received rapturously by the audience and resulted in Mr. Cleland's giving up taking the train to work from Scarborough after that, and using the Ossining station.

Desperately, we turned to bitter realism. We put on a dank thing called *Black Waters*, in which Rose Hobart played the lead. The hero, who had to carry her in dripping after a suicide attempt, sprained his back. She was very pretty and the consensus was that he insisted on too many rehearsals. He said he could have made it if he hadn't had to carry her understudy in the last play. She was pretty too, and repeated practice had loosened his muscles.

We had counted on a dash of incest in the play to put it over, but it was to the word "bastard" that it owed its success. When the word "bastard" rang through the auditorium, Mrs. Walter B. Mahony, Nicholas Murray Butler's sister, got up and stalked out. We were horror-struck. Should the play be abandoned?

"No," said Mr. Westermann firmly. "The play is made. If we are smart we'll hire a couple of other Confederate soldiers to stamp out every night when the word 'bastard' is said."

It wasn't necessary. The aisles were jammed.

Scouts from the Theatre Guild and New York agents besieged us. I didn't want to miss a trick so I signed up for acting. With the help of a ninety-eight-dollar dress from Russeks' I played the lead in *Julia Counts Three* with such success that I got cards to report to Max Gordon and the Harris office.

My husband said he'd leave home if I did. I thought that was a great joke. His talking tough like that. Of course, I had no intention of reporting, anyway. At thirty-three I knew I was too old to learn to be an actress. I never suspected that my husband was getting to the end of his rope. I thought he was sore because of an unfortunate experience he had had with the Players. At my urging, he had played a small part with Paul Hunt, a "regular," in a curtain raiser. They were both tall, thin, and pale and wore black suits and black horn-rimmed spectacles. On their entrance someone in the audience cried, "Here come the Frank E. Campbell boys." Frank E. Campbell was New York's busiest undertaker. My husband declared acting was just a pernicious form of exhibitionism; there was nothing uplifting about the Players.

As the Players seemed to be going from bad to worse anyway, I turned to the National League of Women Voters. This was Mrs. Vanderlip's contribution to the civic consciousness of the Utopians. She was a tower of strength in organizing it. She wanted me to hold office in the Westchester branch. Mrs. Franklin D. Roosevelt was a guest at the tea when my elevation was suggested.

"We expect great things of you," said Mrs. Roosevelt to me. "It is to women the world must look."

"I can't do *too* much work away from home," I told Mrs. Roosevelt. "I have four children."

"I have five," said Mrs. Roosevelt.

"Don't you find the children get to acting like the dickens if you're away too much?" I asked anxiously.

No, said Mrs. Roosevelt, she didn't.

It was because I had to do quite a little running around for the League of Women Voters that we sold the Marmon and got the Holmes. The Holmes was an air-cooler like the Franklin. It was comfortable to ride in, but the pistons had a disconcerting habit of dropping out. On cold mornings it wouldn't start, and I would let it roll down our hill in gear. Sometimes it started suddenly and I would go roaring right down the hill across Briarcliff Road, through the fence, into the aqueduct. Before you could crank it, you had to lift the radiator hood up. It lifted from the front and poised over your head like the sword of Damocles. Then, to get a good grip on the crank, you had to put one leg inside the front bumper. Once when I was cranking it, the hood came down and broke my nose.

"Why don't you stay at home?" growled my husband.

"I will," I said, "if you'll let me have another baby."

Utopia as a community proposition seemed to be flubbing out. But that didn't mean we couldn't have our own private Utopia; work it out as a family project.

"My God, I'll go crazy if we have any more children," said my husband. "I never wanted kids, anyway. You never asked me."

I was terribly discouraged. I didn't know which way to turn. I felt as if my usefulness had come to an end. I asked him if there wasn't something at the bank I could help him with. He said no. Leave his business alone.

I thought of what fun we'd had working together in the early days; of the essay I'd helped him write for the American Institute of Banking that had taken the prize. I'd been so proud when he'd suggested I work on the dummy for the magazine the National City Bank got out for South American consumption.

I had gone over to the library and done a lot of research. I found the Germans had entrenched themselves in South America. They came, brought their families, spoke the language, and sold goods which lasted. The Americans showed up with an air of patronage, spoke no language but their own, and tried to sell fur coats in summer and bathing suits in winter. I clinched the moral with an anecdote I found:

"What do you use for fuel?" asked someone of a South American engineer.

"Sometimes coal; more often wood; but always the catalogues of the American manufacturers printed in a language we do not understand."

My husband drew a picture of the two continents for the cover, and we called it *The Americas.*

"How'd they like it?" I asked my husband.

"Fine," he said. "I heard one of the vice-presidents getting a big hand for writing it. I forgot to put my initials on it."

We just laughed. It was all part of getting along. Maybe success wasn't such fun after all. Maybe people had the best times when they were struggling.

"Don't you have any more interesting jobs like the magazine?" I asked wistfully.

"Hell, no," he said. "Everything's different at the bank now that Mr. Vanderlip's gone."

He spoke shortly. I thought he was annoyed with me. I never guessed he was worried.

Mr. Vanderlip had left the bank shortly after his return from the European survey.

"How're things?" the ship news reporters who met him at the pier had asked.

"Terrible," said Mr. Vanderlip.

Stocks dropped ten points. The story was that the Board of Directors had said the least Mr. Vanderlip could have done was to tip them off so they could have sold short. Shortly after, Mr. Vanderlip resigned.

"Utopia's lost its sponsor," I was thinking one day a few weeks later, when I heard a step on the walk. I glanced at the clock. There is no more terrifying sound than your husband's footsteps at four P. M. It means he's lost his job.

"It's Charlie Mitchell," said my husband grimly. "The new president. I got the ax along with thirty-three others. We got two hours to clear out. Even Gus, the head bookkeeper, who's been there sixteen years. Wholesale house cleaning."

"But you're an officer," I said.

"So were a lot of others," said my husband.

"But I never heard of firing anyone unless he was drunk for a week," I said, "or stole."

My husband sat down and put his head in his hands.

"God," he said. "Just as you get something built up, somebody kicks it down again."

I mustn't let him see how badly I feel, I thought. That would only make him more miserable.

"What do you care for those double-crossers?" I said. "You've done a good job. And you've had wonderful experience. You'll find something you like a lot better than the National City Bank. You always said you wanted to be a surgeon. I could get a job and we could find some cheap little place somewhere. You could go to medical school. That job was a bore anyway."

"Well, for God's sake! You'd think a man could get a little sympathy from his own wife when he's lost one swell job he's worked his heart out over. But no. It's just 'the job was never any good.' And now I've got to throw ten years' banking into the ash can and go to medical school!"

It was then I realized that human beings have no way of communicating with each other. I mustn't cry, I thought. If I start I'll never stop.

"If I were a doctor, anyway, you'd want to diagnose the diseases, make the calls, and perform all the operations!" went on my husband.

"I'll tell you what," I said. "I'll make you up a batch of prospectuses. You'll get a job!"

The prospectuses were wonderful. They told who he was and the experience he'd had. For reference he had nearly every bank president in New York.

"How'd they go?" I asked the next night.

"Like hotcakes," said my husband wearily. "Make me up another batch."

While he was peddling the prospectuses around New York I saw an article in the paper about Harvey Firestone. Mr. Firestone had a wonderful idea for reorganizing his tire company. He was going to cut out all the red tape, interoffice communications, and chair warmers. He was going to have a live-wire organization. I could see it just the way Mr. Firestone did. I sat down and wrote a letter in my husband's name, outlining what he could do to help. Two days later we got a wire from Mr. Firestone that he was coming to New York to interview my husband.

When my husband met him, he looked hard at him. "You are not the person who wrote that letter," said Mr. Firestone.

"Hell," said my husband when he got home. "You can't live somebody else's life for him. Let me alone."

I looked at him and thought of the bills mounting. He looked so discouraged.

"You'll kill me," I said, "but there's an ad in the paper for men to sell Cities Service stock on commission. It's for some man named Henry L. Doherty."

"O.K.," he said. "I'm sorry. You'd have been a whole lot better off if you'd never married me."

"I told you once love had nothing to do with prosperity."

"It's just that it's a strain to live with someone so infernally brave," he said.

"Think nothing of it," I said. "I'm a New Englander. It's the granite in me."

It was the next day that I took the children to the Vanderlip pool, swimming, and somebody bet Rodney he couldn't hold his breath longest under water. I didn't know anything about it till the Japanese attendant touched my arm.

"Why your little boy, he lie at bottom of pool so long for?" he asked.

After three people worked over him for two hours Rodney came to. He was pretty mad because the boy he made the bet with had gone home.

In fact, he was so mad that at first he said he wasn't going to the Beyers' party that afternoon. But he weakened when somebody told him they were going to have spun sugar with the ice cream. It might have been all right if he'd stuck to the spun sugar instead of concentrating on the grapevine. When I went to get him he was green. He laid all before him just as we got to our kitchen door.

"Check," he said. "I ate eighty-one grapes and eighty-one came up."

He felt so much better that after supper he went over to take Mr. Easton, a neighbor, to task about his dog. He thought Mr. Easton oughn't to tie him to a stake. It was when he followed Mr. Easton into the garage to berate him further that he slipped on the tin Mr. Easton kept under his car to catch oil and cut his knee.

I washed it with green soap and dioxygen and put a bandage on. It healed all right. A week later the other leg began to swell.

"I don't think it's anything," said the doctor. But I did. I remembered the red *Textbook on Nursing* we had in the house when I was little. I was forbidden to read it, but I had smuggled it out to the barn and read every word.

"You can always diagnose blood poisoning," said the *Textbook on Nursing*, "by that anxious look."

"I didn't think," said Rodney to me as I walked along beside him as he was being wheeled to the operating room, "you'd let this happen to me."

My heart turned over. I'd let everything happen to everyone. And I'd been so strong. So sure of myself. *My* life was going to be perfect. What was it my husband said? "You can't be Mrs. God." No more I could. I turned away as Rodney waved a small white hand to me from the operating room. I didn't want him to see me crying. That was August. It was December and fifteen more trips to the operating room before he was home. It was now two children who couldn't walk. And we owed my husband's aunt $3000.

I thought, "I mustn't think. I mustn't feel. If I do I'll go crazy."

So I played the drunk in the revival of *Seven Days* by the Beechwood Players. Everybody said I was wonderful.

"I'm going to get a job," I said to my husband that night. I didn't ask him. I told him.

He shrugged his shoulders. "For better or worse, but you can't take worse," he said.

"I don't see any sense in taking worse," I said, "if you don't have to. What difference does it make who earns the money? If we're together it can still be Utopia."

"If I died," he said, "you'd just regard it as another way to develop your character."

That hit home. But you were what you were. You couldn't be any different.

I got two jobs. From eight to three every day I was secretary to the Director of the Scarborough School. From three till eleven at night I was secretary to the Director of the Beechwood Players. With the free tuition the Vanderlips gave the children (who had returned to the fold) I was earning $4800.

Everybody thought I was wonderful. I went home at noon and night to carry the two children who couldn't walk out onto the porch or up to bed. Everything was done according to a schedule. I made lists and checked things off every half-hour. I was afraid I might give out, so the Director of the Players let me have two nights off a week so I could take up acrobatic dancing with Mrs. Carter-Waddell, sister-in-law of Rollin Kirby, the cartoonist. She'd had a harder time than I had but she was going strong, so she was more than a teacher, she was an inspiration. Jack Carter—now Jacques Cartier, the famous dancer—and I could do the best leaps. But I was rotten on the back bend. "Relax!" Mrs. Waddell would cry. But I couldn't.

Then my husband got a job with the Guaranty Trust.

"Believe it or not," he said. "Five thousand dollars!"

"Hurrah," I said. "With what I'm making, we're in the money. You can play golf at the Sleepy Hollow Club and we can send the children to camp."

"Listen," he said. "I've got a job and from now on I'm going to support this family. You're going to have a rest."

"I don't want a rest," I said. I didn't take one either. I added a part in *The Small Timers* to my repertoire, and went out between the acts and took tickets.

When I got home from the final performance, my husband was sitting up for me.

"I'm moving into the Yale Club," he said. "I'll give you two thirds of what I make."

I sat dumb. I felt as if I were whirling through space. I was a *failure*. I thought back twelve years when we started out. I thought, "*Too many things happened.*"

"I'm tired of being something on a list," my husband said. "Something that didn't get attended to."

"I'll give up the jobs—" I started.

"Living with you and those kids," my husband said, "is like living with Fannie Brice in a den of lions."

And I thought, "*I bet it was like that.*" There was no use saying anything. It was all over. But I *did* everything, I thought. The meals were always on time. I never ran up bills. I was always cheerful. Maybe I did too much. It was too late to undo it.

"Let's not go over everything and cry and scream," I said. "Let's not destroy the past."

I didn't cry till he went upstairs. Then I didn't cry about anything sensible. I cried because when Johnny went racing down the field at the Yale Bowl to make a touchdown, his father wouldn't be there beside me. Johnny would be so disappointed.

I never believed in divorce, but I saw one thing clearly. You are divorced when somebody doesn't want to live with you any more.

"He may see the children at times and places agreeable to the plaintiff," it said in the divorce papers, "and he hereby agrees to deliver to said plaintiff, as long as she shall live, applications for tickets to the Harvard-Yale football game."

Maybe it *was* like living with Fannie Brice and a den of lions. But not for anything was I going to sit on the ten-yard line.

It was a couple of days after that I ran across the derivation of the word "Utopia." It was, I found, from the Greek "No Place."

HARD GUY OF F SECTION

"WHY SHOULDN'T we make a million dollars?" I said to Harold. Harold was my second husband.

"Let's not and say we did," said Harold. "After all, last year we paid an income tax on twenty-six thousand dollars."

"But when you married me you told me you wanted to do big things," I said. "You said you were just teeming with ambition."

Harold said big things, yes. But ambition was tricky. You had to be careful not to overdo it. He said he didn't want to get like John D. Rockefeller with lines in his face and no hair. "If you use up all your ambition making money," he said, "you haven't got any left to spend it. Then where are you?" I was sure by fast footwork he would always be able to avoid this disaster. He had devoted the greater part of his thirty-six years to cultivating the fine art of spending.

I was fascinated with Harold the moment I laid eyes on him. He was wearing a lighted Christmas tree on his head. It was at a masquerade at Philipse Manor. He was sitting head in hands, glowering ferociously beneath the twinkling candles and the star of Bethlehem.

"There," I said to myself, "is a man who has a problem to be solved."

As we fox-trotted around to the strains of "The Japanese Sandman," he told me that he had just returned from five years' service with the British army, where he was known as the Hard Guy of F Section. In 1915, annoyed with a sticky spark plug on his Rochet-Schneider, he tried to enlist in the Foreign Legion. The Foreign Legion passed him up because he didn't have his birth certificate with him and had no prison record. He took the train to Toronto. The Canadian Air Force turned him down because he was a doddering old man of twenty-six, too old by a year to be crazy enough to fly those crazy crates. As he walked dejectedly along King Street in Toronto he saw a papier-mâché horse in a window. "Why walk to Berlin," said the slogan slanting across its belly, "when you can ride?" He walked in, enlisted in the Cavalry Machine Gun Section of the Royal Canadian Dragoons, and as Machine Gunner No. 550333 swore allegiance to the British king.

After riding lead horse in a mobile Vickers unit at the front for four years, he found his father's wholesale rose business, and a masquerade at Philipse Manor, rather boring.

I was gone completely when I saw him in his British uniform on a plunging strawberry roan in the Memorial Day Parade. He chose a strawberry roan because he'd had a strawberry roan shot out from under him at Amiens.

I was a little leery about introducing him to the children. Their father hadn't been gone very long. But when he bounced Rodney off the ceiling they warmed up immediately; and when he showed them his spurs with the ace of hearts, diamonds, clubs, and spades inlaid in silver and gold, their hearts were won, especially when they found out it was the nickel he'd used in place of a rowel (so as not to hurt the horse) that made them jingle. He was a little surprised, I think, to find that while he had been playing with Rodney, the others had scratched their initials on the door of his new red Studebaker phaeton. But he didn't show it. "How about all going for a ride?" he urged. The children swarmed in over the fenders and radiator without opening the door. "Where did you dig up this little band of hell-cats?" he asked pleasantly. I explained to him that they were allowed to do that because it didn't matter what happened to our old Ford.

Harold's motto was "Let's go places and do things." We did. When I got home from work, he'd be waiting for me. We'd hit every high spot in New York. I saw where he got his reputation for being "wild." When my first husband entered a restaurant, the headwaiter always bowed from the waist. When Harold entered, the headwaiter rushed for the manager to warn him that hell was probably going to break loose. It usually did. His particular specialty, after four Scotches, was a sword dance, executed with drumsticks and his trousers rolled up over his knees.

I was crazy over him. I always had a weakness for big men with black hair and blue eyes. Besides, he was romantic, charming, spoiled, irresponsible, generous—a Robin Hood in plus fours.

He sat on a bench outside the office where I worked at the Scarborough School till I promised to marry him. "If you don't say yes," he said, "I'll lose you your job. Marry me and see the world."

In 1924, a year later, we were married.

"Are you sure you are acting wisely?" my mother wrote.

I wasn't. But I was tired of acting wisely. My sister pronounced Harold "fascinating" and predicted the marriage would be a success. My friends had doubts.

"Don't forget there are just as many of my friends sorry for me marrying you with those four kids," said Harold, "as there are yours sorry for you."

I was shocked. I had always pictured us as a prize.

"Sure you don't really mind the kids?" I asked anxiously.

"I love them," he said. "They're part of you."

"And you don't mind my white hair?"

My hair had turned white the year the children had infantile paralysis. He kissed me.

"I think it's wonderful."

I thought, "I bet he can take it." But when we took a little run around the shore drive at Newport before the wedding ceremony, and he drove his new Studebaker through the surf, I wondered if I could. Harold wanted to have all our friends at the wedding, but I didn't. I was afraid that when I said, "As long as ye both shall live" and "Till death do us part," they'd be thinking, "We heard you the first time." I insisted Harold wear his British uniform with all the medals. This wedding was going to be the way I wanted it.

"It's lucky your uniform still fits," I remarked as we drove along. "You may have to wear it again. Germany'll never stand that rotten Versailles Treaty. I wouldn't blame her if she stood up on her hind legs."

Harold said how did I get that way about Germany. What America and Britain should really have done was burn Berlin to the ground and hang the Kaiser. I said I tried to be *liberal*. If I'd known he had such stuffy, old-fashioned, narrow-minded ideas I'd never have married him. But it wasn't too late.

"Stop the car," I said. "I'll get out right here."

Harold said keep my shirt on. He said I thought everybody who disagreed with me about anything was wrong. I kept quiet because that was what I did think. By the time we'd got to the rectory I'd calmed down.

The minister was fine. As we stood in his little library before his desk, I could see Harold in his uniform reflected in the mirror on the wall. "With this ring I thee wed," said the minister. "With this ring I thee wed," repeated Harold. He looked at me blankly. "Good grief, I've forgotten the ring," he said. I got my little old secondhand ring out of my purse and we were married with it. When we got to the hotel, Harold said, "Hell, I don't know whether I've got any money." I spent most of our wedding night unraveling his checkbook. "Don't bother your pretty little head about that," he urged. "If any checks bounce back, Father'll pay them. Look. See what I've got for you." It was a diamond wrist watch. "I was going to give it to you to wear at the wedding," he said. "But after the way you stuck up for the Huns I was sore at you."

I laughed. Life with Harold would be fun, I decided. But complicated.

The children were mad as hatters because we didn't take them on our wedding trip.

"Would like to join you," they wired from camp. "Have very few friends left."

I wanted to let them because I don't like honeymoons. It is very trying to go on trips with people you don't know very well. You say, "Shall we play tennis?" and the person you're having the honeymoon with says, "Yes," just to be polite, when he doesn't want to at all. He says, "Let's walk over to the coast-guard station," and you say, "That would be lovely," when your new shoes are killing you and you wish you could go in the car. But Harold said it was unconventional to take children on a honeymoon; they'd better weather it out at camp. I said, "But it was unconventional to get sent to jail in Amiens for being drunk and disorderly and absent without leave." He said that was different. That was just because he wanted to get transferred to the tank corps.

I thought I'd never get him home from the honeymoon. I had to get the house ready for the children. He'd lie on the beach for hours talking about the old inns in England where he'd sat drinking ale while he was training. The old oak beams and paneling stained with the smoke of centuries were wonderful, he said. He would sit there for hours dreaming of the days When Knighthood Was in Flower. He kept saying we must do big things but he didn't seem to want to get started. He said he didn't care if we never got back to Westchester. Nantucket was a fine place.

It was on the way home that he said something that surprised me completely—he didn't want me to work any more.

"I don't want my wife," he said, "to be at somebody else's beck and call."

"But that's just what my first—" I began without thinking.

"What?" he said.

"Nothing," I said.

Getting married twice, I saw, was going to be hard. There were so many things that had to be left unsaid.

"It's only that I'm not happy unless I'm working," I said after a while, squeezing his arm. "You want me to be happy, don't you?"

I felt like a skunk using underhand methods like that. It was positively feminine. But I'd made up my mind not to make the same mistakes twice. I was going to be smart.

"Of course I want you to be happy, darling," he said solicitously. "I'll tell you what I'll do. I'll get Father to let you keep the greenhouse books."

I hated keeping books like poison, but it was better than sitting around doing nothing. And I was glad to work in an inconspicuous place. I planned to have another baby immediately. The four children were mine. I was sure Harold would want a son.

"Why in Sam Hill *should* he want a son?" asked my sister.

"Well, if he doesn't," I said, "he ought to."

In 1925 Frankie was born. Harold gave all the men at the greenhouses ten-dollar gold pieces and went on a fishing trip. In two weeks I was back keeping books again. There were plenty of people to run the house and take care of the children. Money flowed like water. There was more where that came from. We'd bought a Pierce Arrow for $3600 and on our way home from New York seen a Wills

St. Claire roadster in Yonkers we liked, and plunked down $1400 cash. Then we had a Chevy sedan and the station wagon. Rose, the children's nurse, had an Essex, and Ed, the chauffeur, had a Ford.

In spite of the dour predictions of my friends, I thought happily, everything was working out fine. Except that I wished Harold would help me correct the children. All he did was laugh at them. As their own father sent them lavish presents, this left me as the only bad news. I didn't realize how they had come to regard me till one morning at breakfast. We'd all been to a movie the night before. In it, a death ray of frightful mien mowed down cities and civilians, leaving ruin and devastation in its wake. As I came down the stairs in the morning, I heard sounds of merry laughter. The children were throwing biscuits. Harold was throwing them back at them. The bottom stair creaked as I stepped on it.

"Sh," said Barbara. "Here comes the death ray!"

There was a dead silence. I was horrified. But I was glad Harold and the children got on so well. That was important.

It was lucky Harold had a big income because we were expensive. Barbara and John had to have their teeth straightened. Louise had to have a couple of operations so she could walk better. Rodney kept having recurrences of his old leg trouble. Every time he got hit in the leg, an abscess would form and have to be lanced. One afternoon we brought him home from the hospital in the back of the Studebaker only to hear that Louise was lying on the curbstone a quarter of a mile away with her leg broken. She had been coasting in a wagon and hit a telegraph pole. She had refused to budge till we came.

"Darn that wagon," said Louise, when we reached her. "In the catalogue it had brakes on it. But don't worry," she added with streaming eyes, "it wasn't my good leg."

All these things cost money. Harold would show me socks he'd bought that were just what he wanted. Later a bill would come in for thirty-six dollars for three pairs. He never asked the price. He considered that a form of haggling. It took all his income, my salary as bookkeeper, and the checks the children's father sent to keep us going. That's why I said to Harold, "Let's make a million dollars!" Times were good. And I could see we might need it. "Let's build a big green-house of our own," I said. "Let's hit the jackpot!"

"How can we build a place of our own when we haven't got a cent of capital?" said Harold.

"You've figured out funnier things than that," I said. "Concentrate!"

I knew the Piersons were good thinker-uppers. Harold's father had made half a million financing the Klaxon horn. True, it had gone in silver mines in Mexico, in lime quarries in Dover, and in a photographic-paper plant. But he'd made it. Harold himself had made the first color movies ever produced. He'd had a moving-picture company with Ethel Clayton and Warner Oland as leads, as far back as 1911. He'd have been all right if he hadn't produced *John Bunyan.* And everybody said colored movies had no future, so he and his father sold out to Wurlitzer.

Harold evolved a plan. It was certainly sporting. He dove into its execution heart and soul. He loved a gamble.

First, we selected twenty acres of land in Millwood which belonged to the Lord High Executioner of Briarcliff, Mr. Henry Law. Millwood was a whistle stop on the "Put." The land looked terrible, but Harold had found out that the new Bear Mountain Parkway would cross it. We offered Mr. Law the privilege of kicking in the twenty acres for a third mortgage in a company which we incorporated under the name of Pierson Rose Plantation.

"But that's nothing but swamp," said Mr. Law.

"You can't grow anything there but muskrats or goldfish," said Harold's uncle.

"Beggars mustn't be choosers," we said, dropping our eyes modestly.

Mr. Law finally graciously consented to put it in the pot for a third mortgage of twenty thousand. It was highway robbery on his part, but we were no angels.

Then Harold went to the greenhouse people. A six-hundred-foot greenhouse would cost $75,000. He offered them $30,000 cash, and a second mortgage for $45,000. They bit. Now all we had to do was find the $30,000.

"I think we really ought to get forty thousand," I said. "We will need the extra ten for a road, boilerhouse, and icebox, plus expenses till it gets going."

The banks, needless to say, turned us down flat. So did a lot of other people. But we kept working. Then we heard about two men on West Thirty-third Street in New York who were bulging with money. We went to see them. Sure. They'd lend us $40,000. But they wanted a fee of $5000. That was easy. We just gave them a first mortgage for $45,000.

To cap the climax, we issued common stock. We owned one hundred per cent of it. This stock was put in escrow against the mortgages. As we paid off on the mortgages, the stock was released. What everybody overlooked was the fact that whether it was in escrow or not, we had complete control of the company.

"Don't you think you ought to have a lawyer?" Harold's father asked. We didn't. We didn't know any lawyer who could grasp the setup, it was so complicated. Sometimes I could hardly grasp it myself. But Harold assured me it was a honey.

Everybody else had lawyers. Two or three of them. When we met to conclude the deal it looked like a meeting of the New York Bar Association.

Finally, all the papers were signed. Everybody shook hands but Mr. Law, who was looking out the window.

"My God," he said. "I've just realized. The Piersons haven't put up a red cent. They've got us to set them up in business to the tune of one hundred and ten thousand dollars."

Everybody turned on us like snakes.

"Is this true?" one of the lawyers asked.

"Sure," said Harold.

"Where are you going to get the ten thousand dollars' worth of plants to plant the greenhouse?" asked Harold's father and uncle, who had wanted to be present at the meeting.

The truth was we'd forgotten all about them. Harold rallied quickly.

"We thought you'd give them to us," he said brightly.

The two guys who lent us the $40,000 beckoned to us to come out in the hall.

"You people have got something. If you have any more bright ideas, get in touch with us," they said.

We went home jubilant. We'd agreed to pay back on the mortgages at the rate of $2500 every three months. That ought to be easy.

"Now all we have to do is sit tight," said Harold. But I was going high, wide, and handsome by this time. There was a house with wonderful lines right opposite the location of the new greenhouse. It had five acres and an old red barn.

"Let's rent it," I said to Harold.

"But it's got no improvements," he said.

"You're not the only high financier in the family," I said. "Listen to this. We're paying two hundred dollars a month where we are. We'll tell Mr. Law we'll spend the equivalent of that in fixing it up in lieu of rent. Besides that, we'll make him give us an option to buy it."

Mr. Law was interested but, after his experience on the greenhouse, hardly effusive. However, he had the lease drawn up, and we signed it. He said he would sign it as soon as the engineers surveyed the property. He included an option to buy at $10,000.

I got permission from the people living there to go in, and found a Dutch oven, a Dutch door, and an old milk room with a cement-covered brick floor. I was wild over it. We had an architect draw up plans for remodeling. The children could hardly wait to take possession of the barn with its old cattle stanchions.

The girders for the new greenhouse were rising. Harold was having the time of his life. He loved building things. It was exciting.

We planned to move into the house just as it was and fix it over under our own supervision. It had no heat or bathroom, but it had a privy and a pump in the kitchen.

A month before we were ready to move in, I went over to see Mr. Law. It was a Saturday morning.

"Sit down," he said.

I sat.

Mr. Tuttle, his partner, stepped forward.

"You're smart," he said. "But sometimes people can be too smart."

"What's the trouble?" I asked.

"I'm not letting you have the house," said Mr. Law. "We've just seen the engineers. The new Parkway runs across in front of the greenhouse and within twenty feet of the house. That property is one of the finest properties in Westchester County."

"You mean you're not going to sign the lease after you *gave your word?*" I said.

Mr. Law moved uncomfortably. Mr. Tuttle was shaking his head at him.

"I think that is the dirtiest trick I ever heard of," I said.

"I don't want to go back on my word. I'll still sell you the house for ten thousand dollars," said Mr. Law.

"O.K.," I said.

"But the ten thousand has to be every cent cash."

"O.K.," I said.

"And it has to be in my hands before twelve o'clock tonight," he said.

It was eleven o'clock on a Saturday.

"You'll get ten thousand dollars before twelve o'clock tonight if it kills me," I said.

I called my sister. I knew she'd help us out in a pinch. But I couldn't get her. I thought of wiring my mother. She'd gladly lend us a couple of bonds if she knew a "home" was at stake. But time was of the essence. Harold's father kicked in a certified check for $2500. By this time, it was twelve, and the banks had closed.

"What we need," said Harold, "is a miracle."

"What we need is seventy-five hundred dollars cash," I said.

We called everyone. Harold's uncle said he would give it to us but if he did he wouldn't give us the plants for the greenhouse.

"Forget it, then," I said.

We had the cars appraised but we couldn't raise over $5000. Time was fleeting.

"Let's go down to Ossining and see who we see," said Harold.

"Take us," yelled the children.

"Pile in," said Harold.

I hadn't combed my hair or washed my face or eaten since morning. I thought if Henry Law beat us on that one it would kill me. He'd *given his word*. I'd counted on it. Well, he'd keep it.

We took the children into Rice's drugstore and bought them sodas. "Now you go back to the car," I said to them. Harold and I stood on the sidewalk and watched the Saturday-night shoppers. The clock struck ten. I could see the children peering out of the car anxiously. They wanted that barn.

"We've got about as much chance of picking up seventy-five hundred *cash* or its equivalent before twelve o'clock as a Negro has of turning white," said Harold.

"Hi," said somebody. It was Jake Myers. Jake did odd jobs around Ossining, wrecking and selling secondhand junk.

"What are you two so down in the mouth for?" said Jake.

"We're looking for seventy-five hundred dollars."

"Wait a minute," he said. Harold looked at me. I looked at Harold. Before we could speak, he came back leading by the hand an old man with a beard.

"He's from up beyond Brewster. I sold some junk for him. He showed me his bankbook. I happened to remember he had just seventy-five hundred dollars. He's looking for a good mortgage."

"Has he got the bankbook on him?"

"Ya," said the man.

"You want to do business?"

"Ya," said the man.

"He's crazy," I said to Jake.

"What do you care? He's got seventy-five hundred dollars," said Jake.

"Give me the bankbook," I said to the man. He handed it over.

I held it up high. "We've got it! We've got it!" I called to the children.

"Hooray!" they cheered.

I telephoned Mr. Law.

"We've got the ten thousand. We're coming right over."

"I'll leave the deed with the maid," groaned Mr. Law. "She'll give it to you. I'm going to bed."

"Don't you want to *see the money?*" I asked.

"No. I'll take your word," he said.

I was so happy I went crazy. I bought a little green piano for the

children. Harold bought two police dogs. We traded the Pierce for a
Packard straight eight.

Two days later we moved in. Before the furniture was unloaded I
went over to a near-by farmer's and bought two hundred and fifty
chickens to put in the red barn. Just as the sun was setting, the children all took baths in a little tin tub out back of the house. It was
perfect.

As it got darker, a mist, a good-smelling mist, came up. Harold put
his arm around me and we walked across the drive to the old red
barn. Nixie and Gunner, the two police dogs, nuzzled us and we could
hear the chickens getting settled in their nests. From the distance
the greenhouse—*our* greenhouse—winked at us with its thousand
twinkling eyes.

"Happy?" I asked Harold.

He squeezed me tight. "You bet."

"Even if we don't make a million dollars, it's good," I said. "It's
ours. Or will be—when we've paid off a little matter of a hundred
and twenty thousand dollars."

"Don't give it a thought," said Harold.

We didn't. It was 1926. The Era of Wonderful Nonsense was in
full swing.

THE CRUISE OF THE FIDGET

*T*HE *Fidget* was our yacht. It wasn't really a yacht, but that's what Harold's uncle called it. He said if he'd known we were going to be such fools as to buy a yacht he'd never have endorsed our note at the bank for $10,000.

We bought the *Fidget* to defeat Sunday. It was a thirty-seven-foot power boat with a six-foot beam and a self-bailing cockpit. It was painted black. The license numbers ran 16927 on one side of the bow and 72961 on the other. That was to fool the coast guard, because it had belonged to a bootlegger.

My idea was that when we got to the Pause that Depresses about four P. M. Sunday we would be whirling merrily over the Sound and not notice it. It would be expensive but worth it.

We tried renting a boat first but we had hard luck with it. We rented the *Wild Duck*, a cabin cruiser. We saw the ad and went down to the boat yard at Stamford. The *Wild Duck* was all covered up with sailcloth. It didn't look very wild to me. It looked tubby.

"Will it really do ten knots?" I asked the man at the boat yard.

"Hell, no, lucky if it does five. Lucky the motor don't conk on you entirely," he said. Then he lost interest. "I drove first load o' garbage ever dumped in this spit o' land," he went on dreamily. "Off horse was no good, but nigh horse she was a daisy."

We tried to lure him on to tell us more about the *Wild Duck* but he wouldn't.

"When the Owner comes," he said darkly, "he'll tell you plenty."

The Owner drove up in a battered old station wagon, wearing a wild rose in the buttonhole of his sixty-dollar white linen suit. He turned out to be pretty snooty.

"You will want a bilge pump, of course," he said, wheeling like a cavalryman on my husband. Harold had a far-off look in his eyes that indicated he was off the Bahamas giving cards and spades to Lipton.

"Oh, no," he said absently, "we won't need one."

148

"You will," said the Owner, looking at him disgustedly, "and I will supply it."

We thanked him.

"You will want awnings, of course," he went on firmly. We knew the answer.

"Of course," we chimed blithely.

"Then you," said the Owner, "can supply them."

"What is this, a game?" said my husband.

"I shall have to have references," said the Owner. "I wouldn't rent the *Wild Duck* to *anyone*."

"You've got insurance, haven't you?" asked my husband.

"It's a feeling a man has for his boat," said the Owner, beating his chest. "You wouldn't understand it. Did you bring the check with you?"

Harold handed him the check.

"I see it's not certified," said the Owner, turning it over several times. "In that case I won't have the charter party till Wednesday."

"A party! That's darned nice," said Harold, coming to. He was raised on the Hudson.

"A charter party is the lease form," said the Owner coldly.

When it arrived, we found we had the *Wild Duck* F.O.B. Luden's, Stamford, and it cost plenty to launch it. We bribed the launchers to take it around and moor it in Greenwich.

The next day was Sunday. We loaded the children into the car with baskets of lunch and bathing suits. When we got to Greenwich it was dead low tide. We oozed out to the *Wild Duck*, which was lying dispiritedly on its side. The sun beat down relentlessly.

"We can polish the brightwork till the tide comes in," I suggested. I produced the polish and we polished and polished.

"And whose idea was this boat anyway?" said Harold at four precisely. We were burned bright red, and apparently Greenwich is the last place in the geography the tide comes into.

We oozed back through the mud and went home. Before we got home a terrific thunderstorm came up. About eleven that night we got a phone call from the Owner.

"The *Wild Duck* broke up on the rocks. You didn't moor it properly," he said. "I should never have let you have it anyway. I am returning the check."

"Thank heaven," said everybody.

But I wasn't discouraged. I got *Motor Boat* and *Yachting* and I combed the ads in *The New York Times* and I found the *Fidget*. For $750 she was ours.

"The motor ain't so hot," said the man at the boat yard at Portchester, "could do with a little tinkering."

It was a four-cylinder Palmer.

"Let's let Ed put it in shape," said Harold. Ed was our chauffeur.

I was horrified. "Half the fun," I assured him, "is working on your boat yourself."

"If the other half isn't any better than that, count me out," he said.

The motor took quite a lot of tinkering. When we finally got it going, the only original part left was the flywheel. There was a good deal of mahogany and copper to be polished.

Everybody got to dreading Sunday.

"Keep your courage up. We'll have it in the water before long," I assured them. I described our trips across the Sound with the salt breeze blowing through our hair, the cool salt spray arching from our bows, and egged them on to paint it. "The *Fidget* can do sixteen knots. We'll zip over the Sound," I told them.

It looked pretty when we got it in the water at Portchester. It was long and slim and sinister. We bought three hundred feet of anchor rope and a new anchor.

"My gosh, are you going to anchor in the middle of the Atlantic?" asked the man at the boat yard. But my husband said he thought we should have plenty. It was a good idea as it turned out later. We bought a little gasoline stove and lots of cans of things. The children got quite pepped up about it.

The next Sunday, we left Millwood with sweaters and coats and blankets and supplies enough for Peary. The tide was high and when we got near the shore the children shouted. It was going to be wonderful. We rowed out to the *Fidget* and stowed our duffle. Then we rowed back and forth for two hours with can after can of gasoline.

Finally I pulled up the anchor, and the children helped me coil the rope.

Then Harold turned over the engine. Not a peep. He turned it over again. After the first hour, I took turns with him. The tide slowly went out. The sun rose higher and higher in the heavens. At last we slogged through the mud back to shore.

"Now," said my husband, "are you willing to have Ed fix it?"

"Well, it wouldn't do any harm to have him look at it," I admitted weakly, "but you always tell everyone you're a born mechanic."

Ed allowed as how it was the damndest bunch of junk he ever saw but he'd do what he could with it.

Ed fixed the *Fidget* and the *Fidget* fixed Sundays. The children went right out after breakfast Sundays and disappeared for fear they would have to go out in it. They didn't play the radio or fight or whimper. Sundays were fine.

"What I want to do with the *Fidget* now," I said to Harold, "is take a trip in it. I see that Eugene O'Neill is reviving *The Emperor Jones* at Provincetown. Maybe we could actually see him and congratulate him."

"If we get to Provincetown in the *Fidget*," said my husband, "he should do the congratulating."

The children said count them out.

"I think you must have taken leave of your senses," my mother wrote, "to take a trip in that boat when you have five little children."

"We have been advised," the greenhouse people sent word, "that you are contemplating a dangerous sea trip. Will you let us know at once as it vitally affects the $100,000 insurance policy we are carrying on your life."

"Let's take Ed," said my husband.

But I didn't want to take Ed. I wanted it to be romantic.

"I'm surprised you want to take Ed," I said to my husband, "when to hear you tell it, you practically took Peronne singlehanded." We didn't take Ed.

We set out from Portchester about five o'clock in the afternoon of August first. There was a brisk east wind blowing, and the Sound was choppy. Off Stamford, the motor went dead. The *Fidget* settled comfortably into the trough of the waves, slapping back and forth sideways. Harold started spinning the flywheel. The motor was located right at the entrance to the cabin, with no headroom. Harold cranked. The *Fidget* threw him against one side of the cabin. He cranked again and it threw him against the other. Large welts rose on his forehead and his ears looked as if he'd been in a prize fight.

Suddenly, there was the comforting roar of a motor. But it wasn't ours. It was Vincent Astor's. A long racy craft with Vincent Astor at the wheel, in a double-breasted blue jacket, flew by us. As we watched, a jet-black cloud of smoke issued from her exhaust. Harold sprang angrily to his feet.

"He's giving us the razzberry," he said, "and I don't blame him. If I had an ax I'd chop this bunch of junk to pieces."

"There's no use grousing," I said. "After all, the John Paul Jones you're descended from didn't have the foresight to go into the fur business."

He started cranking again, but it was dark when we got started.

I was pilot.

"What are those lights?" I kept asking. There seemed to be lights in every direction. The mail-order map described the lighthouses and their signals, but cars on shore can do the same thing when they want to. I was afraid we'd end up on the Post Road.

"I think we ought to anchor pretty soon," I said. We cruised along awhile, and I saw several small boats outlined in the lights from the houses.

"We must be just off Milford. That's thirty miles on our way. Drop anchor," I said. Harold dropped it.

I decided to sleep on deck. It was a lovely evening.

"How different everything feels just a few miles out on the water," I said dreamily. I had a sense of the great open spaces. It was just as I thought it would be.

When I awoke I was surprised. We had anchored right outside the boathouse at Portchester.

"Let's go ashore and get a good breakfast at the lunch wagon," said Harold hopefully. But I wouldn't. I cooked it all on the gasoline stove and we set out again.

The Palmer did all right after it got its second wind. Only it shook the boat from stem to stern, and the gasoline fumes were so strong even gulls flew away from us.

"I wish we had bought a yawl," I said, "with an auxiliary motor."

I didn't want to tell Harold, but I didn't know whether I could stand a week of it.

In the middle of the morning, we really reached Milford and put in for gasoline. We'd used twenty-two gallons. About the middle of the afternoon we saw a city.

"What is it?" asked Harold. I consulted the map for all kinds of signs, but the map seemed pretty sketchy.

"It's New Haven," I said finally.

"O.K.," said Harold. "We'll spend the night there. I could do with a little shut-eye."

I *thought* it was New Haven, but I had never approached New Haven any way but along Route 1, and it looked kind of funny. We zinged into the harbor hell-bent for election.

"Which side of this red buoy?" asked Harold suddenly.

I looked at the map of New Haven harbor. There wasn't any red buoy. I turned desperately to the index.

"Which side?" he yelled.

"Right," I said. I had to say something.

There was a grinding crash and our propeller dangled listlessly.

"There," said Harold, "now you've done it."

A trim little motorboat whizzed out from shore and threw us a rope. It was a marine ambulance chaser.

"You hit the only rock in New London harbor," the skipper said. He towed us over to the New London Ship and Engine Company. Our crankshaft was bent. It would take them three days to fix it and it would be seventy-five dollars.

"We better run up the Thames a little and see how the motor is acting," said Harold when we got under way again. It was breezy and he didn't want it to quit outside. He said we'd stop and start a few times.

It would have been all right if I hadn't kept getting mixed up with reverse.

"If you're going to put it in reverse," said Harold, "haul up on the dink rope. Otherwise it slacks and winds around the propeller."

I kept thinking I wasn't putting it in reverse. When the rope wound around the propeller, Harold had to dive over with the potato knife in his teeth and cut it loose. Then we had to rig up a new rope. It was cold, and after it happened three times he got pretty mad.

"Let's get the hell out of here even if I do get my head bashed in cranking the Palmer. It's better than drowning with a knife in your teeth," he said.

Off Point Judith we ran into a storm. Seventy-five-foot tugs were laying to. We went right through it, though, because we had a self-bailing cockpit. That night we anchored in Buzzards Bay.

The wind and tide were with us in the morning, and we went through the Canal like a bat out of hell. But about halfway to Provincetown the motor quit and it was almost dark when we got it going again.

"Now for God's sake take the flashlight, and read up on Provincetown light and get us inside it," said my husband. "If we miss Provincetown, the next stop's Portugal."

As we neared Provincetown a terrific wind came up. I kept thinking I saw Provincetown light and then I didn't. But I didn't tell Harold. I was afraid he would get discouraged. Fortunately, outside Provincetown we picked up a Portuguese quahog dragger homeward bound.

"Follow the dragger," I screamed to Harold above the wind. The dragger was making about twelve knots and we were making sixteen. We would shoot up on her starboard bow and she would veer away from us. Then we would dart back and shoot up on her leeward side. The Portuguese got pretty mad.

"What are you trying to do, sink us?" they yelled. But something had gone funny with the Palmer, and we couldn't cut our speed.

Suddenly, the water got quiet and lights from shore shot out at us.

"Christ Almighty," shouted the men on the dragger, "look out what you're doing!"

"Shut her off," I yelled to Harold. We were shooting through the whole Provincetown fishing fleet lying at anchor dark as pitch.

We dropped anchor right where we were and, without taking off our clothes, fell into a deep sleep. When we woke up, the sun was setting and the *Fidget* was lying about half a mile out from shore on her side. The tide had gone out.

"Get up," I said to Harold, "or we'll miss Eugene O'Neill and *The Emperor Jones.*"

I put on my knickerbockers and slung my sneakers and stockings around my neck. My feet were bleeding from mussel shells when we got to shore. I got my sneakers on so we could enter the theater respectably, but during the performance I took them off and couldn't get them on again.

"Come on," said Harold, as we emerged from the theater, "let's get back to the boat."

I knew he was in no mood for Eugene O'Neill. But he was pretty tired of tongue sandwiches.

"Let's stop in this little ice-cream place and have some ice cream," I said.

There was only one other customer in the store. He had on old dirty white ducks and no necktie. He was sitting at a little oilcloth-topped table attacking a double scoop of vanilla. It was Eugene O'Neill.

"Look," I said to Harold. He took me by the arm and dragged me out of the store. "You cannot congratulate Eugene O'Neill," said Harold, "in knickerbockers and bare feet."

When we got to the beach, we saw the *Fidget* bobbing gaily at anchor half a mile away. We stripped and tied our clothes around our necks and swam and swam and swam. The tide had come in.

Next morning we set out for Boston. I thought I knew Boston Harbor, but it had changed.

"I thought you were born and brought up in this backwash of civilization," said Harold bitterly as we narrowly missed two ledges of rock. "I thought it was the backbone of the country and never changed."

He got so mad he wouldn't get out of the way of ocean liners and big freighters. He said it said in the book we had the right of way. I said we knew we did, but the liners didn't. What good would it do if we were right when all people found were a few floating fragments? When we crossed right under a freighter's nose I went down into the cabin and shut my eyes and stopped my ears so I couldn't hear the terrific blast from the boat whistle. Harold got quite cheerful.

"If you've had enough," he said, "we might as well start for the Cape Cod Canal."

It was almost dusk when we got to the Canal, and I never saw so many lights in my life. We cruised up and down trying to get our bearings. Then a fog came up.

"We better make a run for it before it gets so foggy we can't see where we're going," I said. "That must be the entrance between the red and green light."

We shot for the center full speed and came within a hairbreadth of crashing into a high stone wall.

"We'll anchor, and you and I will take turns blowing our little foghorn," Harold said.

He began paying out rope.

"Seems to take all we've got," he said. "I never realized the shore of Plymouth Bay went off so deep."

The fog was pea soup by now. We couldn't see our hands before our face. All around us, on every side, boats were whistling, horns were blowing. I blew the foghorn for a while. Then Harold blew it. Then we fell asleep.

When I waked up I saw a black wall in front of me. The wall was moving. It was a freighter brushing by. We had anchored spang in the channel of the Cape Cod Canal.

We stopped in at Wickford to see my sister, and nobody ever forgot our visit. Something happened to the motor right off the bathing beach and it let go with seven quarts of coal-black oil. Nobody in Wickford could go in bathing for two weeks.

When we ran into New Haven Harbor we could hardly find a place to anchor. The New York Yacht Club was there. As our sinister black craft slithered swiftly in and out among the naval "four hundred" it attracted a good deal of earnest attention.

"The *Fidget* looks pretty crummy alongside the *Corsair*," said Harold. "But why the binoculars? Do they think we're pirates?"

I had no sooner started cooking dinner than people from the big yachts started shouting to us.

"Hi, how's everything?" they yelled.

"Fine," we yelled back.

"Imagine. Those guys are human," said Harold.

Two slick mahogany launches from two of the finest yachts shot out and circled around us. One of them pulled up alongside.

"How about two cases of Golden Wedding?" said the skipper. "Money no object."

"Listen," said Harold to me. "Let's get the hell out of here."

It was when we got off Stratford that we noticed the awful calm. The sea was translucent and great schools of fish drifted by. The sky was black. Overhead white clouds of gulls circled, darting at the schools of fish. It had been hot, but now a sharp coolness pierced the air. We ran like a hare to get in shelter of the breakwater, but before we got there the storm broke. The rain came down in sheets, and the wind blew so we couldn't stand up against it. The water poured into the cockpit from every direction. But the little Palmer chugged along. Finally, a rainbow came out.

When we made Portchester it was almost midnight. We were dirty and soaked to the skin. We telephoned for Ed to drive over for us in the Packard.

"I hope you won't hold this trip against me," I said to Harold, as we sank back luxuriously against the cushions. "After all, you always said you liked roughing it."

He put his arm around me. " 'I went to sea as a bold A.B.,' " he chanted. " 'But I thought as I got on board. An admiral's berth would do for me. As for Charlie Beresford.' "

"You'd make a lovely admiral. The uniform would match your eyes."

He kissed me. "I had a wonderful time, honest," he said. "I wouldn't have missed it for the world."

I almost believed him.

The ad we put in *The New Yorker* cost thirty-five dollars:

FIDGET

CASH   **$1200**   CASH

Take less? Dun't esk!

SERIOUSLY this is the finest little cruiser that the Coast Guard
    ever put its spotlight on.

RAKISH as a Pirate; 36 ft. long; narrow; black as your hat. 60
    h.p. motor drives her 16 m.p.h. as we seafaring folk have it.
    Sleeps two.

TOOK a whirl in her up the Cape last summer and Man howdy,
    you should have seen her leap those rollers off Point Judith.
    Nothing passed us but ocean liners.

FIVE years ago the hull cost $3000—mahogany trim, copper
    rivets, all that sort of thing.

BUT the awnings are simply terrible. We mean they're awful.
    Don't say we didn't warn you.

REASONS for selling. We've got to pay some bills.
    You can see the *Fidget* at Chester Martin's boat yard at Port-
    chester. Ask Martin about her. He's one of those guys who
    were born honest. Or write or wire H.C.P. (Care of *The New
    Yorker*.)

I had included "TOILET if you must know!" but *The New Yorker*
editors evidently thought you mustn't. However, they fixed the ad up
great with anchors all around it. Earnest Elmo Calkins wired from
Washington for permission to use it before the National Advertising
Men's Convention as the best ad of the year.

Nobody answered it. The *Fidget* languished, unasked about, in
Chester Martin's boat yard.

"But I wouldn't worry," said Martin. "Somebody'll be along. Don't
forget there's one born every minute."

THERE WAS NO MORE WHERE
THAT CAME FROM

*H*ow does the water taste?" asked Rodney, rushing in as we were eating breakfast.

We all took deep swigs.

"Fine," we said.

"That's funny," he said, "because the Portuguese are washing their feet in the spring."

Everybody got up hastily and rushed out to strafe the Portuguese. We had no other water supply than that piped from the spring by gravity.

The truth was, the rehabilitation of our farmhouse was not going forward according to a schedule.

We'd started out great guns. Scorning our original modest plans for remodeling, we'd sent posthaste for a Mr. Harvey Stevenson. We'd heard he was the last word in young architects and very dynamic.

We couldn't wait for him to draw up plans. We got the men over from the greenhouse and tore the porch off. We replaced the modern windows with twelve-over-twelves. The children and I manned crowbars and dug out four concealed fireplaces. Louise and I axed the cement off the milk room's lovely uneven brick floor. We all got together and hauled a huge beam out of the brook behind the house and set it above the Dutch oven for a mantel. Not that we couldn't have afforded to have someone do this work for us. But every good New Englander knows that happiness is not complete without an element of suffering.

Ed, the chauffeur, was not enthusiastic over our efforts.

"You cough up ten thousand good simoleons for this joint," he said. "Then you work yourself dizzy making it into a log hut."

"Simoleons grow on trees these days," said Harold. "There's plenty more where those came from."

But Mr. Frank A. Vanderlip didn't seem to think so. He thought the country was heading for disaster, and he was drawing in his horns. He telephoned me that he was closing down his private greenhouses unless I cared to run them. I could have them for nothing if I would supply flowers for his house.

I thought he was crazy but I was willing to take advantage of it. I'd been lost since I'd given up keeping the greenhouse books.

"I'll grow miscellaneous stuff," I said to Harold. "I can make a nice piece of change."

I bought a copy of Fritz Bahr's *Commercial Horticulture* and studied it till it was dog-eared. If some dumb German could grow African daisies and vincas and calceolarias, I could. I borrowed Larry, the Italian, from our greenhouses.

"We grow everything everybody grow. We grow more. We grow better," said Larry enthusiastically. "Very import'. No quest'."

We did grow more and we did grow better. We grew so much I had to open a store in Dobbs Ferry.

"You're spreading yourselves out too thin," said Harold's uncle. "You're overextended."

We didn't listen to him because Harvey Stevenson had come through with the plans for our functional farmhouse and we were excited over them.

"We'll make the house express the personality of the owners," Mr. Stevenson said. "We'll make it jazz antique."

The only really authentic part of the house was the ell. The rest was commonplace. The trick was to re-create a glorious if nonexistent past.

We paneled the ell in wormy chestnut and painted the door to the little winding staircase dusty pink.

We "antiqued" the white paint in the hall with raw sienna, swabbing it on with a pair of B.V.D.'s. We designed a pair of pewter sconces which only cost sixty-eight dollars and looked great. We papered the hall in French provincial. Mr. Stevenson didn't wholly approve of this. The design was "too busy," he said, though the color was nice.

We went to town on the dining room. We dug up a wallpaper with old red clipper ships. For fun, we painted the woodwork red. Mr. Stevenson said it was "too exciting," that so much red would induce quarreling and indigestion. So we got a bucket of whitewash and an old shirt and tamed it down. We made cupboards of pecky cypress, pegged and adzed out by hand.

"Now we need something definitely intriguing to put in the cupboards," said Mr. Stevenson.

I shot down to Rich and Fischer's in the Packard and for $385 picked up a set of Red Tower spode.

Even the bathrooms were functional. I specified three washbowls.

"Then," I argued, "the children can't honestly say they have 'no place' to wash their hands."

"Where did you ever find such a marvelous old house in such a remarkable state of preservation?" asked our friends.

"We really ought to get busy on the heat and water systems," I said to Harold.

By this time, winter was almost upon us. It was getting cold. I figured to abandon the privy by the time the wild geese were flying south.

So Harold and Ed buried some mysterious contraption known as a septic tank in the back yard, and piped water into the house by gravity. It would do "temporarily," Harold said.

"Why bother with a makeshift thing like that?" I demanded. "And what about heat?"

"I've put off telling you because it's so silly," said Harold. "But we're short of cash."

I couldn't believe it till I went over the books. Each new venture we'd embarked on had tied up money. We were, as Harold's uncle said, overextended. Of course, there was no money coming in from the new greenhouse; we'd agreed not to draw any till it was paid for. But Harold's income from his father's business should have been ample to pay the bills. To my amazement I saw he hadn't drawn anything. There'd been no deposits for three months.

"What on earth's happened?" I asked Harold.

Harold said the rose business was bad. Prices were dropping. The market was glutted with roses pouring in from the new million-dollar ranges in the west. His father had all he could do to meet payrolls. He was up against it.

I didn't have time to stop and worry over how we were going to live on nothing. I thought the trouble was just temporary, anyway.

"It's cold," I said to Harold. "We've got to have heat, cash or no cash. Why don't we get some secondhand pipe and radiators on credit and get Lyndhurst?" Lyndhurst was the greenhouse engineer.

Things were humming along for us when Lyndhurst quit. He went home one night to find his wife in the arms of another man. Being a man of action, Lyndhurst acted. He socked his wife in the eye, knocked the other guy downstairs, threw all the furniture out of the window, and made a bonfire out of it. Just for good measure he dug up the garden.

"I ain't got the heart to go on with the piping," he said next morning. "I'm shipping on a tug."

The new greenhouse engineer we hired had no "faculty" with pipes. Ed, the chauffeur, who was now doubling as greenhouse truck driver, finished the job after hours. But he had to hook up one second-hand radiator at a time because fittings cost money.

"If I could just lay my hands on some cash," moaned Harold.

To our amazement, Johnny and Barbara spoke up. "We bet we could make some money if you'd let us," they said.

"For heaven's sake, how?" I asked.

"Selling plants. Down by the road."

It seems they hadn't told us, but, the Sunday before, they'd taken pitchers of ice water down to the road, displayed them attractively on a table, and sold out at two cents a glass. Louise was awful, though, they said. She'd charged five cents for a saucer of water for a dog. Dogs couldn't help being thirsty. You shouldn't charge dogs anything. But she said business was business. The people didn't seem to mind. Everybody asked what was in the greenhouse. They wanted plants.

"Why don't you have Ed bring over a load of ferns from the Vanderlip greenhouses," said Harold. "It can't do any harm."

We didn't think it would really amount to anything. But it would please the kids. A few hours later we looked out the window. There was a line of cars stretched out along the road a mile long.

"It must be an accident," I said to Harold.

We rushed down.

"Get us some more plants quick!" shouted the children, when they saw us coming. "We're cleaned out!"

By night they'd sold three truckloads and taken in $275.

"It's a gold mine!" declared Harold. "Our problems are solved."

Harold was apt to grasp at a straw under the delusion that it was a magic wand. I knew that it would take more than a few roadside sales to balance our lopsided budget. But the money would help till his father's business picked up.

The children were brimming over with plans.

"Next Sunday make some hermits and lemonade and I bet we can sell them," they urged. "The people were hungry. They wanted eggs when they saw the chickens. They had great rolls of bills. They just wanted to spend them. We charged them ten cents to look at Frankie in his baby yard, and a quarter to look at the police pups. They'd buy anything."

I wished they had bought the police pups. We had fifteen of varied sizes. Gunner and Nixie had been very prolific.

It's a crazy idea, I thought, but the cash would help. It would keep the children busy, and take our minds off our troubles.

I made the hermits and lemonade. Harold knocked together a stand for the plants. When the crowds came through the following Sunday we were ready. By six in the afternoon we were cleaned out. The children were right. People were on a spending spree. They'd grabbed up ferns, begonias, hermits, and police pups indiscriminately. Louise in a money-mad moment had even been persuaded to put a price of fifty cents on Smut, her pet kitten.

"School's out in another week. We'll make a fortune," said the children. "We'll sell stuff every day in the week, not just Sundays."

"We'll clean up," said Harold. "We'll build a roadstand."

We called it The Flower Tub. It was built like a tub, with gay window boxes and striped awnings. The top was planted with evergreens. Harold and I and the children and Ed and the men from the greenhouses built the tables and chairs. As an anchor to leeward, I insisted we install gas pumps.

"That little Tub's going to save the day," said Harold, surveying it proudly.

"Wishful thinking," I thought. Still—if we made it the finest roadstand in the county—it might—it just might . . .

I made hermits in droves and lemonade in buckets for the grand opening. We were swamped. But people weren't satisfied with hermits and lemonade. They wanted meals. So we took down the Red Tower spode from the house and got a stove on credit. Harold said he'd be chef—he could broil steaks to the queen's taste. He'd always longed to be chef in a diner. To the children's delight, he insisted on wearing a big white apron and chef's hat made of newspapers. John and Barbara waited on table. They looked so dignified and serious for fourteen-year-olds that the customers never guessed they retired to the kitchen every half-hour for a knockdown drag-out over the tips. Rodney was supposed to tend the gas pumps. Unless actively pumping gas, however, he retired to a tepee he had constructed of burlap bags and lost himself in the delights of Jules Verne's *Off on a Comet*. It was necessary for a customer to enter the tepee and snatch the book out of his hands in order to get service. As Louise walked with crutches, she rated the plushy job of cashier. She sat up on a high stool, proud as a peacock of her responsibilities. She could make change like an old-timer. You'd never have known she was only eleven if she hadn't kept Speckles, her little downy yellow pet chicken, parked on the cash register. Frankie continued to draw big crowds in his baby yard. Rose, the maid, had to tell people that at two, Frankie's diet didn't include candy and peanuts. I roasted and baked. I made ice cream and froze it.

There was one bad angle to the layout. The Tub had no sink. The children had to run up to the house with dirty dishes, and back with clean ones.

"Don't get discouraged, Ma," they pleaded. "We don't mind it."

They would stagger up the rough bank from the Tub to the house with great trays of spode amid the cheers of the customers. Rose and

I would slam through them. When we'd finished a batch I would ring a bell, and the children would dash up and get them.

We charged $1.25 a dozen for little cupcakes and twenty-five cents a plate for homemade strawberry ice cream. Nobody kicked. When we ran short of ice cream and I had to freeze another mess in a hurry, customers came up and helped me turn the crank. They even helped with the dishes.

Once when I was rushing down from the house with two newly roasted chickens that a man in a Dusenberg had ordered, Gunner and Nixie grabbed them. The man thrust a ten-dollar bill into my hand.

"It's worth it to watch this three-ring circus," he said.

When Rodney charged five dollars for a cactus I'd bought for ten cents, the customer wouldn't let me refund the money.

"I've had five dollars' worth of fun," she said. "Forget it."

"Pretty soon the children will be back at school," I assured the customers. "We'll get a regular chef. Things will be on an even keel."

"Don't change anything!" they said. "We live cooped up in apartments bored to death. A crazy place like this is a godsend."

"I want my sister to see it," I told Harold. I thought it might cheer her up. A year before, her husband had died suddenly, leaving her alone with her two little daughters in a big house in Yonkers. Against everybody's advice she'd accepted a demanding position as confidential secretary to a busy New York lawyer. She'd had pneumonia three times and been warned to be careful. "You've got plenty to do with," I'd told her. "Why risk your health?" But she said she was better off to have her mind occupied. Besides, she'd made very definite plans for the children's education and social life and she was going to make sure she'd be in a position to carry them out. "Everybody always gets poorer and poorer as they get older," said my sister. "I'm not going to."

I was freezing ice cream when she came. The two little girls had on smocked print dresses just alike, and big straw sailors. My sister was wearing a smart linen suit and gillies. I felt like a truck driver in my old dungarees. My sister said it didn't cheer her up to see us. It made her tired.

"For heaven's sake," she said to me, "what's the matter with you? You've always got some new great scheme to set the world on fire and in six months you're back picking oakum. Here you married one of the richest, best-looking, most fascinating men around New York and you've got him behind a cookstove frying hamburg."

"Oh, I wasn't one of the richest," said Harold glowing modestly.

"You've got a martyr complex, that's what you've got," went on my sister. "Hasn't she, Harold?"

Harold said it did seem sometimes as if I enjoyed doing things the hard way. He said he could have borrowed ten thousand dollars from his uncle, but I wouldn't let him. I said I wanted us to be independent.

"Borrow the ten thousand and buy stocks," urged my sister. "I'm making money in the stock market, so it must be easy."

I was blue after she went. Her children looked so fresh and pretty. Mine looked tired. There she was—prosperous, well dressed, with an established social position—just as she'd planned. Here was I still freezing ice cream and dreaming of greatness just as I'd been twenty-five years before in Cohasset.

"Hurry up with the ice cream, Ma," yelled Barbara.

My sister had certainly got a darn sight farther along the highroad to destiny than I had, I thought, as I ground the crank furiously. But she was wrong about one thing. I didn't mess things up on purpose. I didn't enjoy being a martyr. We'd be on the inside looking out again before you knew it. I'd just have to get up earlier in the morning, and work harder.

Every Sunday night we all gathered in the library about midnight to count the money. I had to sit with my feet in a pan of salt water, they were so swollen.

Each week Harold said, "Next week we can build a sink and enlarge the Tub," but we couldn't. All the money we took in had to go to our creditors.

But whatever we'd taken in, the children said, "Next week we'll do better." And we did. It got so I was making hermits and little chocolate cupcakes by the thousands. Saturdays and Sundays I made forty quarts of ice cream. We were disposing of the whole contents of the Vanderlip greenhouses, so I closed the Dobbs Ferry store.

Harold, the week we took in $1400 said, "I think we've got things licked!"

I knew we hadn't. But I didn't say anything. Everybody had worked so hard I couldn't bear to take the heart out of them. How could we have things licked? We had no income but that from the Tub. It would be closed in winter. There was no telling when Harold could draw any money again. His father was still in trouble. My only consolation was that the Pierson Rose Plantation, our big new greenhouse, was doing fine. Even if prices were low, the income was jumping because we produced more roses. We'd paid off $25,000 of our $110,000 indebtedness. Our *future* was safe, if we could only hang on till we got the Plantation free and clear.

But the fame of the fabulous Tub spread to the greenhouse people. They got uneasy. They called a directors' meeting. Were we, they asked anxiously, paying strict attention to business?

We certainly were. At Pierson Plantation we were growing a deep red rose called Mrs. F. R. Pierson. It was a big seller at Christmas. In 1926 Harold's uncle had got two dollars apiece for "extra-special" Pierson. Extra specials were roses with very long stems.

We aimed to hit the Christmas market with at least ten thousand extra-special Piersons. That would knock the greenhouse people for a loop.

"But don't forget we're taking a hell of a chance," said Harold. "We can't cut any roses for four months before Christmas if we want those extra-specials. Then if we don't hit Christmas right on the nose, it's curtains."

"O.K.," I said. "But I think you ought to know. No matter if the whole shebang blows up in our face, I won't compromise on the kids' education. I'm going to send John to Andover next fall if it kills everyone."

Harold said he didn't see how we *could* send Johnny to Andover. We didn't have a thin dime. My first husband wasn't able to contribute; he was out of a job.

"I'll apply for a scholarship," I told Harold. Johnny was a plugger; he had a good record.

The summer was almost over when the good word came. Johnny

was to leave a week after the Tub closed for the winter. The children were wild with excitement. They planned a whopping send-off.

Johnny had arranged to drive up with Billy Winters, a scout brother who had an old Model T. Billy, a frail, determined boy of sixteen, in torn sweater and knickerbockers, was going to Vermont to "seek his fortune farming," so he told us. He'd let John off on the way.

"Maybe Billy'll get to be President," said the children hopefully. "Coolidge did."

"So he did," said Harold.

Noon was the hour set for the momentous departure. At one, Billy sent word he couldn't get the Ford started. It was after dark and chilly when he and his old jalopy finally chugged up. We all rushed out, the children dragging a hamper which they had prepared in the best British tradition. It contained everything but dried pemmican. They were a little hazy as to where Andover was. While Harold stowed the luggage, Johnny waited, very small and erect and dignified.

"Climb in," said Billy finally.

Johnny climbed in. We all stood huddled beside the ancient Ford.

"Well," said the children, peering in at the two white faces.

"Well," said Johnny.

"Well, write," they said.

Johnny turned to Rodney.

"You can have my stamps," he said.

The children looked at each other. Johnny! Giving away his stamps! Why he never let anybody so much as look at his things. Slowly, they realized. Johnny was different. He was going away to school. He was lost. Nothing would ever be the same again. The Ford lunged forward. Johnny waved. We waved back till he was out of sight. Then, silently, with tears streaming down our faces, we went back into the house.

It seemed lonesome with Johnny gone and the Tub closed. Only Frank was home, the other three children were away at school all day. Then I got a letter from a cousin in Portland saying my mother was having short fainting spells. Nothing to be done, the doctor said. At seventy-six such things were to be expected. I mourned to think of her alone in a tiny north room in a boardinghouse. But she refused to let us so much as provide cream, instead of milk, for her coffee; or see that she got *The Boston Transcript*. She wanted to be independent. It was her own fault that she had only ten dollars a week, she wrote. "Be faithful over a few things and thou shalt be ruler over many things." Well, she hadn't been faithful over a few things. Why should anyone else have to suffer for her mistakes? Of course, the days did seem long sometimes. She'd be grateful if I'd send her my mending. And would I look in the little right-hand drawer in the secretary and see if there wasn't a paper with directions for a game of solitaire? It *should* be there. Right under the game of cribbage. It was thoughtful of Harold to add that postscript to my last letter saying *he* wanted her to come and live with us, too. But she was better off where she was. She didn't want to be a burden to anybody. She ought not to be allowed to go out alone, I thought. Supposing she had a fainting spell when she was crossing the street? But as she said, she "always disliked being restricted." She must get "a breath of fresh air," rain or shine. Every time I saw the telegraph boy coming down the street on his bicycle I had a sinking feeling in the pit of my stomach. If she didn't write on her "regular days" I was worried sick. But if I called her long distance she said "Good-by" almost before I'd said "Hello," because she was fine and it was a wicked waste of money to call five hundred miles long distance just to inquire for an old lady "who'd outlived her usefulness." A penny saved was a penny earned, and I was to remember it.

I missed having Harold around to laugh off my apprehensions. But he was spending every waking hour at the greenhouse.

"I'd mulch those roses with caviar and spray them with Scotch if it would help any," said Harold. "We've got to make a killing at Christmas."

A week before Christmas we stood up on the benches and looked over the greenhouse. It was a forest of great swelling crimson buds.

Four days before Christmas we began cutting. Heaps and heaps of long-stemmed Pierson piled up on the packing benches. Yet the acre of roses didn't look as if they'd been touched. The icebox was jammed. 10,000, the packer marked up on the sheet above the bench.

15,000! 20,000! Every rose perfect. The packer was swamped. Everybody had to pitch in and help. The children knocked together boxes and lined them. Rose chopped ice. Harold and Ed helped with the packing. I put on a pair of knickerbockers and shuttled back and forth between Millwood and New York in the Dodge delivery truck. The police picked me up on the Parkway.

"Only pleasure vehicles allowed," they said.

"It's a pleasure," I said, "to deliver these roses."

They let me through.

We finished Christmas Eve about eleven.

"Come on," we said to the men, "we'll celebrate. The children have been busy trimming the tree. We'll all have some red wine and cakes."

"We're too dirty," said the men, but we wouldn't listen to them.

The functional farmhouse looked like a Christmas card as we tramped up through the snow. I poured wine into the little crystal glasses and we all raised them.

"Good luck," we said.

"Good luck," said the men.

"I'm going to call up the wholesaler," said Harold. "Listen, this is going to be good."

We all gathered round.

"Pierson talking," said Harold. "Merry Christmas."

"What's merry about it?" asked the wholesaler. We could hear him. He talked loud.

"How's the market?" said Harold.

"Shot to hell!" said the wholesaler. "You busted it. When the buyers saw those boxes piling in from Pierson Rose Plantation they sat tight. They knew they could name their own poison. Got fifty cents apiece for the first five thousand. About ten thousand'll go to the dump."

Harold hung up slowly. Nobody said anything. I filled up the glasses again.

"What can you do?" said the men. "Better luck next time."

But there wasn't any next time. The plants had been forced so hard they got black spot. We just squeezed out the $2500 for the quarterly payment.

"If you're late on the next $2500 payment," said the greenhouse people, "the place is ours."

"We must be dumb as hell to get ourselves in a spot like this," said Harold despairingly. "Everybody else is sitting on top of the world."

"Press where you see my white plume shine," I told him. "We'll put up a fight."

We got Harold's uncle to take a $2500 second mortgage on the house. I took a stenographer's job with the poet, Florence Kiper Frank. We ate hamburg till it came out our ears. The chickens roosted on the Packard straight eight.

But the bills mounted. And there was no money accumulating toward the quarterly payment. The black spot got so bad the whole place had to be pruned.

I went to the next directors' meeting with Harold.

"Don't forget that when you forgot to register your old mortgages we could have taken advantage of you but we didn't," I told them. "We played along."

"If you *should* lose Pierson Rose Plantation you would really be better off," said their lawyer blandly. "You've got too much on your hands."

I would have hit him if Harold hadn't stopped me. I went home quietly but I began to have crying fits. My friends said I ought to be psychoanalyzed.

Dr. L. Pierce Clarke was the best psychoanalyst, everybody said. He had a sanitarium for violent cases out in the country, where they did big things like weaving, and an office on the East Side for people like me who just had "problems." Every day he had fresh orchids on his desk.

I was "unadjusted," Dr. Clarke said. An hour a day would fix me.

I lay on a couch talking and he sat back and listened, smoking a big black cigar.

I would talk and talk and then I'd stop suddenly to see if he'd gone to sleep. He'd start slightly but he always made the right answers.

He made me talk about why I wanted to have nine children. I didn't know why I wanted to; I just did.

We switched to money. He asked me if I thought money was important. I told him I didn't see anything wrong with money. I liked spending it.

Then he asked me about the greenhouse. Whose idea was it? If Harold was crazy about it, why didn't he fight for it? If we lost it, wouldn't we be better off?

I sprang to my feet.

"But I thought you were going to build me up so I could *fight* for the greenhouse!" I cried.

"I was going to make you see that environment is nothing. True happiness lies within. I was going to fix you so you could be happy *without* the greenhouse," he said.

"But I don't *want* to be happy without the greenhouse," I fairly screamed.

He bowed deeply. Then he could do nothing for me, he said.

As long as nobody could help me, I saw I might as well give up having crying fits. I went back to the greenhouse and cleaned the boiler pit.

Harold interrupted me to say that the greenhouse people had just called up. They wanted their money or else.

"Let's go down to Ossining," he said, "and see Joe Greene."

Joe Greene was Harold's father's lawyer. He wore a high starched wing collar and looked like Otis Skinner. He was a gentleman of the old school.

"They're just trying to kick us when we're down," I said. "They know we can pay when the crop comes in. It's dishonest, that's what it is."

"Not dishonest," said Mr. Greene. "Just business."

He knew we could pull out of it if they'd give us a little time, he said. So did they. But we'd built up a wonderful investment—the greenhouse in full production—the Tub—the house that would make a fine inn when the Parkway came through. Too good an invest-ment. That was the trouble.

"When you have something good, somebody else always wants it," said Mr. Greene. "That's when you have to watch your step. They want it and they're in a position to take it. I don't see what you can do."

I started to cry, I was so mad.

"If you wish," said Mr. Greene, "I'll call them up."

We couldn't tell how things were going by what he said.

"They say they intend to take it. But they realize you're up against it. They are therefore willing to retain Harold as manager. What do you say?"

Harold looked at me. I could feel my face growing red.

"It's a living," said Mr. Greene.

Harold grabbed the telephone.

"I'll see you in hell before I'll manage that greenhouse for you," said Harold. "Take it and be damned!"

Mr. Greene's eyes shone. "That," he said, "was what I hoped you'd say. You're young. You can start again."

When word got round we'd lost the Pierson Rose Plantation, our creditors descended on us like a flock of vultures. It was pay or else. Harold's uncle took the Tub and the house. I let Larry, the Italian, have the Vanderlip greenhouses. We sold the chickens and the cars and the little green piano.

Our liabilities were $72,000.

Our assets were some old furniture, a secondhand Erskine, and five assorted children.

"Are we downhearted?" said Harold. "*Yes!*"

THE CONNECTICUT YANKEE, AND
THE MARMOLA AD

WHAT would you rather do than anything else in the world?" I asked Harold.

"Hell," he said, "seeing we're flat broke, with five little hostages to fortune draped round our necks, isn't that question a trifle academic?"

I explained that my psychoanalyst said if you are doing something you dislike, you subconsciously court failure. I told him he must secretly have hated the rose business or we wouldn't have wound up with a list of judgments against us a mile long in *The New York Times.*

"This is an Undesirable Situation," I said, "which calls for a New Approach."

Harold said was I telling him this was an undesirable situation. But he didn't see anything to do but get out and get under. Much as he disliked the prospect.

"God only knows what I can do," he said. "The only business I really know is rose-growing, and that's shot. I'll just have to scratch around for some job—any old job—that'll bring us in an assured income, and hope to heaven it won't be in an office."

"That's just what I mean," I told him. "It *must* be a job you like. If it isn't, your subconscious resentment will create the Will to Fail, which in turn will cause the New Situation to Deteriorate."

Harold said it sounded wacky to him. How was he supposed to go about it?

I said suppose we were all dead and he was absolutely free to do what he wanted.

"You're all dead?" he asked eagerly, entering into the spirit of the thing, I felt, a trifle too completely.

"I said 'supposing,'" I reminded him. "Life isn't as simple as all that. Never mind about our being dead. London Bridge is falling down. Which'll you have, pearls or diamonds?"

"I suppose you'd go up in the air a mile high," said Harold, "if I said aviation."

"We'll all go up in the air a mile high. Hooray! We're off," yelled the children.

"America's new frontier is in the sky," said Harold, picking up speed. "We'll stake out our quarter section."

"Now you're getting into the spirit of the thing," I said. "Let's go!"

We all jumped into the car and made the rounds of the airports. The children, who had read about the airports in Germany and Russia, were a little disappointed. In 1929, American airports were mostly cow pastures surrounded by high-tension wires. We were all pepped up when we came to the Bridgeport airport, a large bumpy field down by the shore at Stratford, Connecticut. It was operated by the Curtiss Flying Service. Curtiss had built a hangar and a small office. There was a full-time instructor on duty. In the hangar were three planes—two Jennies with OX5 motors, and a Curtiss Robin. In spite of the fact that the field had been going only six months, there were five students.

We hopped out and went across the street to see the Sikorsky factory, where Igor Sikorsky, the White Russian, was building amphibians. They had two planes at once on the assembly line.

"We're just in under the wire," said Harold. "They're right on the verge of mass production."

We waited breathless while Harold went into the Curtiss office. I knew by the grin on his face when he came out he'd hit bingo.

"Mechanic's job at thirty-five dollars," he said. "I told 'em I was the best God-damn mechanic in the British army. I will be before they can find out different."

We drove around till we ran across an old deserted mansion with paneling and a Dutch oven right on the bank of the Housatonic. It was just a stone's throw from the airport and the Sikorsky factory. We could have it for a song, the owner said, if he didn't have to do anything to it.

"But what could he do?" I asked. "It's perfect."

"Oh, I suppose some people might kick because the plaster's bust-ing off the walls," said Harold. "And it hasn't been painted since 1860."

"Who cares for plaster and paint," I said, "when they've got a view of the river?"

The kids were crazy about it because it was so near the airport. They were glad vacation was just beginning.

A week later we swarmed into Stratford with an Erskine full of children and police dogs, a washbasket and broom fastened to the radiator. By night we'd arranged two vanloads of furniture and I fixed supper on the porch overlooking the river. Out on the Sound a lighthouse blinked; little oyster boats chugged homeward; overhead planes droned.

"This is the life," said everybody.

If Mother could only come for a visit, I thought, how she would enjoy it. She loved the water. She'd seemed better lately, my cousin wrote. Perhaps the trip wouldn't be too much if we went up and got her. I'd write and let her decide.

When Harold got home from work the first night, he was so excited he could hardly eat his supper. A Danish engineer named Svend Olesen had come into the shop. This guy had worked with Sikorsky on the S35, the $100,000 airplane with which René Fonck was to have blazed the trail to Paris. It had caught fire and Lindbergh had beaten him to it. Now he'd designed a low-wing monoplane. It was light, and fast as hell. It had only a twenty-six-foot wingspread. It would be cheap to operate, too. Everyman's Plane! One hundred miles for a dollar. He was building it in a friend's cellar.

"But no, of course!" said Harold. "You wouldn't! It's no use asking you."

"Wouldn't what?" I asked.

"Wouldn't consider our lending him a thousand dollars. He's busted. For a thousand dollars we could get in on the ground floor. He'd incorporate and we could have a half interest in his company."

"But we haven't got a thousand cents," I said, "let alone a thousand dollars."

I was upset. I'd secretly determined not to embark on any more chimerical schemes to make a fortune. I'd thought we'd forge ahead slowly but surely.

"There!" said Harold sighing. "I said you wouldn't! I figured it was all bluff about doing what I wanted."

Upset as I was, I grinned inwardly. I had to admire Harold's technique. He was past master at getting what he wanted.

"How can you be so mean, Ma?" asked the children. "The first thing you know we'll be in another undesirable situation. Don't you worry, Pa. We can earn it."

"But you kids have never done anything but work at the Tub," I said. "Rodney and John aren't sixteen anyway, so they can't get jobs."

John said he'd washed dishes and collected laundry bills to pay for his meals at Andover. John was tall and husky but he looked frail compared to Rodney. He'd worked hard for his eighty-eight average. I thought he ought to have a rest. Rodney at fourteen was six feet two and weighed two hundred, but was apt to be playful. I didn't think anybody'd take him. Barbara was a trifle on the haughty side, though she could work like a demon when she wanted. "Don't you wish we had a mother who wore a satin negligee trimmed with marabou instead of one who's always getting arrested for speeding?" she'd asked Harold, shortly after we were married. Harold said he did and he didn't. He was adroit at walking a tightrope. Barbara's liking for luxurious things had somewhat abated after a harrowing experience she had shortly after. Upon the arrival of the new $3600 Pierce Arrow we bought, she'd rushed out, jumped in, and sat down. A look of intense disappointment came over her face. "You don't feel any different sitting in a Pierce Arrow," she said sadly, "from what you do sitting in a Ford." This incident had radically altered her sense of values. But practical as she'd become, she'd never had to push her way through crowds. I couldn't see her fitting into a tough industrial city like Bridgeport. The whole thing sounded fantastic.

"I'm over sixteen," said Barbara firmly. "And the boys are so big everybody thinks they're twenty. Tomorrow morning you give us ten cents apiece for carfare, and put us up lunches. We'll show you."

Maybe they were right and I was wrong, I thought. Maybe I was losing my nerve as I got older. Thirty-five dollars a week for seven people was pretty slim pickings. If the plane *should* be a success . . .

"O.K.," I said. "Go to it."

I put up the lunches, and the children set out early the next morning. When they got home at night their eyes were shining. Barbara had landed a twelve-dollar-a-week salesgirl's job in Howland's department store. The boys had already started work in the Bridgeport rolling mill at twenty-two dollars a week. John's job was unloading freight cars. Rodney's was wheeling white-hot ingots in a little wagon. He'd gotten afire twice and had to be rolled in burlap; it was exciting. After supper they got pencils and paper. They had twelve weeks before they had to go back to school. They could make $672.

"Come on, Ma, snap into it," said the children. "You've got to get a job."

"But who'll look after Frankie?" I said.

Frankie was only four. He'd hardly left my side since Rose, the maid, had gone.

"Louise is twelve," said the children firmly. "She can tend Frankie. After all, she's a wonderful swimmer. They can play on the beach."

"Sure I can tend him," said Louise stoutly.

Louise had the build of a wrestler and the courage of a lion. I'd had her taught swimming at Briarcliff Pool by Eileen Riggin, the professional. Frankie was a freckle-faced, good-natured little tyke. I didn't doubt they'd make out.

"It's the chance of a life if we can raise the dough," urged Harold. "The stock market is up in G. If we get the plane licensed we can incorporate and issue stock. Half a dozen firms will fall over each other to underwrite it."

"I'm getting along in years for a stenographer's job," I said. "They don't pay much, anyway. But maybe I could get a job on the *Bridgeport Herald*. I'm a wow at truthtelling."

The *Bridgeport Herald* was a Sunday newspaper dedicated to the dissemination of the truth, no matter how unpleasant. Or, possibly, the unpleasanter the better. It had a very large circulation. This had been built up by strict adherence to the sound theory that to err is human and makes good copy. It's more fun to read about how a hitherto respected citizen got caught red-handed snitching a pair of rayon bloomers from the five-and-ten than to ponder glumly over what to do with our bumper wheat crop. And worth ten cents of anybody's money.

The *Herald* bobbed up all over the state, with its front page slightly lifted under the guise of the *Waterbury Herald,* or the *Meriden Herald.* But turn to page two. There, to brighten up your Sunday-morning pancakes and coffee, would be the bracing little item about the man whose truss slipped under such embarrassing circumstances. It was still the good old *Bridgeport Herald,* in there swinging, in spite of its false whiskers.

Nobody in Connecticut went to bed until the *Herald* appeared on the stands about one A. M. Sunday. There was a universal feeling that if your foot had slipped, even though your conscience might have been dragooned into insensibility and you had made your peace with God and your wife, your little peccadillo would not escape the eagle and definitely jaundiced eye of the *Bridgeport Herald.*

There was only one fly in the *Herald's* ointment.

The truth which cuts like a sword, makes men free, and never hurt anybody yet had to prevail without much advertising. Advertisers couldn't see the *Herald* for sour apples. The only advertisement of profitable size which graced the *Herald's* pages was the ad for Marmola. This, I found out later, was known as "Old Faithful." However, the *Herald* had only to run its little story about the drugstore cowboy in Meriden who was kidnaped by three girls in a coupé, made the grade nicely with the first, weakened on the second, reneged on the third, and so was thrown ignominiously out and made to walk home, complete with names, dates, and places, for subscriptions to come pouring in from all over. The item incidentally would end on a high moral tone, such as, "This will teach drugstore cowboys to be more careful whose coupés they get into," or "Let this be a lesson to you."

The *Herald* staff was composed of old U.P. and A.P. reporters who at the age of sixty or seventy were glad to indulge their pent-up passion for telling all, along with their unpent-up passion for lapping up double Scotches.

"What could you write about for the *Herald*?" asked Harold, doubtfully.

"They haven't got any aviation page," I said. "I could write the truth about aviation. Provided I didn't have to go up in a plane. I can't lean out of a second-story window without fainting."

"Oh, you won't have to *go up* in planes," said the children. "You'll just *write about* them." They were crazy to have me get the job. It might pay enough so Harold could take flying lessons. "Then he could demonstrate the *Connecticut Yankee*," they said.

They'd named the low wing the *Connecticut Yankee*.

"Write up a sample page and I'll take it to the editor," said Harold. "Editors always hate women."

"All right," I said. "Here goes for the truth, the whole truth, and let's see your lawyer prove it's libel."

"That's the old fight, Ma," said the children.

I ought to be able to swing a newspaper job, I thought. My sister was doing a swell job as society feature writer on a big metropolitan daily. She'd suddenly decided that horseback riding would be good for her health, and a change of schools good for her daughters. So she'd picked out a city with a bang-up school and good bridle paths, moved in, and snatched one of the best newspaper jobs in the East right out from under everybody's noses. She was in the money.

Fortunately, the truth about aviation turned out to be appropriately appalling. I paid a visit to a company which had bought the rights to manufacture the British Avian, a little wooden plane with a Cirrus motor, and struck pay dirt. Money had poured in from investors—before it transpired that the U. S. wouldn't license wooden planes. The manufacturer had tried to solve his problem by substituting metal wherever wood was called for, thus unbalancing stresses and strains. The result of a year's work, during which several hundred thousand dollars had gone down the drain, had been dragged to the airport under cover of night. When flown it had, as I recall, major defects and a too-low ceiling.

From here I jumped to a two-million-dollar outfit which was trying to manufacture a French plane. I found the whole crew on the floor, gazing at blueprints and scratching their heads.

"We don't know where the hell we're at," said the foreman. French measurements were approximate, it seemed. One centimeter might mean 1 c. plus or 1 c. minus. "But you can bet your boots it don't mean one centimeter," said the foreman. "Them Froggies build planes by eye. Specifications don't mean nothing to them."

Everybody seemed to be trying so hard I hated to write the truth about it. But the fate of the *Connecticut Yankee* was at stake. And Harold was wild to begin his flying lessons.

He took the sample page over to the editor of the *Herald* during lunch hour. He came home in high spirits.

"He says it's damn good," said Harold. "He'll use it. Unless you look like Zip the Famous Whatisit he'll run your picture at the top of the page. But if you get one little fact wrong he'll break your neck. It might cost thousands. And don't come near him; he hates women. If the page is lousy you'll know it. He'll slap that big Marmola ad right in the middle. That means you're fired."

"How much will he pay?"

"Twenty-five dollars for the drool and fifteen for expenses."

"Sign up for your flying lessons," I told him.

"Your first job," said Harold, "is to report your emotions when you fly over Bridgeport with the mayor at three this afternoon in the Curtiss Condor, the new sixteen-passenger plane."

"But you said I didn't have to go up in planes!" I said. "I won't do it."

"It's too late now. You're elected," said Harold.

At three, the mayor, a large fat man, and I stood greenly waiting. He was as scared as I was. As there were no steps to the plane and the door was about four feet from the ground, the mayor and I took some boosting.

"Contact!"

After a minute I tore my gaze from a strut where it had been glued and glanced at the mayor. He was wanly struggling to open a window. I gave him a sickly smile and then sank to the bottom of the plane and lay flat on my stomach.

Several centuries passed. There were a series of bumps. Then quiet.

The mayor and I emerged tottering. Harold rushed up to say the *Herald* had left word they would write the story of our trip, as it took a disinterested onlooker to do justice to the pictures their photographer took of me and the mayor being boosted.

Harold started his flying lessons; work on the *Connecticut Yankee* progressed apace; I roamed from one end of Connecticut to the other, digging up dirt for the *Herald*. Mechanics who left cotter pins out of wheels which came off in mid-air; pilots who got drunk; inventors who'd staked everything on a plane with retractable wings which retracted but failed to unretract again. I felt sorry for the victims, but my work was laid out. If I rated the Marmola ad, all was over.

When Louise got tired of tending Frankie, I took him with me. He enjoyed looking in factory windows at the planes. Once we stopped outside an office.

"Look," he said pointing to a woman writing at a typewriter. "They've got a mother in there."

This gave me an awful shock. Was that what "mother" meant to Frankie? I wondered if I was doing right by the children.

We all took turns at the housework. Sundays, the girls and I pitched in early. Louise was so strong she would work rings around Barbara and me, in spite of her crutches. Her specialty was scrubbing floors. When we'd finished, Harold would take the whole family out driving. We were glad to sit back and rest.

One Sunday Harold and the boys had forty-two shirts in the wash. I ran them through the washing machine and hung them out. Louise and Barbara ironed them. Harold said we'd done so fine he'd let us have a picnic on the beach. This was a terrific compliment because he hated picnics. On our way home from the beach, we heard the fire siren.

"Don't say I never did anything for you," said Harold. "I'm going to break another lifelong rule. I'm going to let you go to the fire."

I'd always been used to piling the kids into the car and taking off whenever I heard a fire siren, but Harold had put a stop to it. I wished I'd been driving when the hook and ladder whizzed by us. We tore along, dodging traffic.

"It must be near our house," said Harold as we turned into South Street, the street we lived on.

"Oh boy, it looks like a good one," I said excitedly as I saw the great billows of smoke rising and the crowd running.

It was a good one, all right. Half the back of our house was burned away before the firemen got it under control. Louise and Barbara had left the electric iron on.

"We seem to go up one step and back three," I said dejectedly as I picked the charred remnants of Frankie's kiddie car out of the burning embers.

"We're on the home stretch," said Harold. "This is no time to get gloomy."

I didn't. When it appeared that our combined resources wouldn't provide for the old rebuilt Velie motor they needed to power the plane, I started a welding school with Ole.

We rented some loft space in an old rickety factory down Seaview Avenue. Then we rented ten welding outfits. Ole got some pieces of duralumin and other metals. I put an ad in the *Bridgeport Herald.*

WANTED: Men with the ambition and vision to learn airplane welding. Great future. Experienced instructor. Class limited. Enroll now.

By Sunday twenty-seven had signed up. Ole worked on the plane days and taught nights. I drummed up customers.

September came. Barbara and Louise registered at the Stratford High School. Reluctantly John set out for Andover; Rodney for Exeter. Rodney had been granted a scholarship, too.

"You've all done a swell job," I said. "We're proud of you."

"It'll seem awful dull," said the boys, "after the rolling mill." They made us promise to wire them when the *Connecticut Yankee* came through.

It seemed so quiet without the boys I was overjoyed when my mother wrote me she was coming for a visit. "She's so frail we don't feel she should travel alone," wrote my cousin. "But she's bound she's going to. She says it's 'too much trouble' for you to come up and get her." I wished now she could have come when we had the Millwood house and the cars and servants. "I've written my page ahead so she doesn't need to know I'm working," I told Harold. "I don't want her to know things aren't so good."

Harold and I and the girls and Frankie met her at the station. Harold took her arm.

"That can't be Grandma," cried Barbara. "She looks so little."

She did look little. It brought the tears to my eyes.

"Harold called me 'Mother,'" she said to me afterward. "You don't know how good it sounded. I've been away from my own so long."

She only stayed a week. We tried to get her to stay longer, but she wouldn't. She said it would be "too much" for me. I don't think we fooled her for a minute. She knew just how sketchy our finances were. It was a bright October morning when I took her to the station.

"I wish it could be October always," I said. "I dread the winter."

She put her hand on my arm. "I know," she said. "Mothers always know. I wish I were in a position to help you."

"Why should you help me?" I said, the tears raining down my face. "You did everything. You denied yourself so I could go to college. And now I——"

I couldn't go on. She touched my cheek with her hand.

"Don't cry," she said. "It's not like you. I shan't see you again. I don't want to remember you crying." The conductor took her arm and helped her up the car steps. At the top she turned and waved. "Good-by," she said. "Good-by."

The train pulled slowly out. I stood there waving long after the train had gone.

"I felt awful to think we couldn't do more for your mother," said Harold when I got back.

"She didn't want anything done for her," I said.

"Well, then, to think I couldn't do more for her daughter."

"Don't worry," I said. "If I can only hang onto my job three weeks longer, everything will be all right."

I was nervous because the editor of the *Herald* kept digging up stunts for me to do. He wanted me to fly to Long Island with Ralph Wilson, a daredevil test pilot, and be the first person to land at the Bridgeport airport after dark. I was glad I didn't, because the watchman forgot to turn on the new lights and the plane crashed, though Wilson was saved. The editor wasn't glad though. He said it would have made a good story. He was pretty disgusted at my refusal to go up in a trick plane which flew apart spectacularly in mid-air and dropped through a roof onto somebody's dining table. A blow-by-blow description of dropping into dinner via the roof, he said, would have been both entertaining and novel.

Another bone he had to pick with me was about Sikorsky. I couldn't get to first base with the White Russians. The editor said he had heard there was a wonderful story in Sikorsky's test pilot, Sergievsky. But all I could find out was that he had ten thousand flying hours and could barrel-roll an amphibian. The editor claimed Sergievsky fought his way out of Russia with the crown jewels in one hand and a Turkish scimitar in the other. He said the least I could do was to find out how the White Russians smuggled the jeweled icons they had in their little Orthodox Church in Stratford out of Red Russia. He said I wasn't as keen on the truth as I was on the Russians.

The truth was the Russians were building a little experimental amphibian, called the S39, with two Cirrus motors. But they wanted it kept quiet. They promised they would notify me so I could be present at the test flight if I'd play along with them. As our house in Stratford was only a hop, skip, and jump from the Sikorsky plant I figured it would be hard for the Russians to double-cross me. I thought maybe if I humored them I could get some information out of them.

While I was waiting for the big news to break I concentrated on little truths such as how a mechanic left a pin out of the steering-gear assembly on a Curtiss Robin and the pilot found himself flying along with the stick in his hand and nowhere to go with it.

"You might take it a little easy on Curtiss," said Harold. "After all, I'm working for them."

"Thank the Lord the *Connecticut Yankee*'s going to be tested next week," I said. "Between one thing and another I can't call my soul my own."

The *Connecticut Yankee* was hauled up to Hartford on October 28, to be tested the next morning.

She looked so trim and neat as Lieutenant Generous, the State Inspector, taxied her out onto the field, my heart bounded. I tried to fight down the old optimism, but I couldn't. We'd make a fortune! As we watched, Olesen came up to us.

"I've got two sets of financial big shots coming over from New York tomorrow if she's O.K.," he said. "Harold can fly her. They say if she's licensed they can float a stock issue of a million dollars!"

We held our breaths while Generous climbed into the cockpit and climbed out again. The cockpit was so small his parachute crowded him. He threw it on the ground.

"I like the feel of this little bug," he said. "The hell with the parachute. I've got confidence in it."

He climbed in again and gave her the gun. She took off like a breeze. Up, up, up she went. He circled and circled. Then he brought her in. She came in about ninety miles an hour but smooth as silk.

"Too fast," said Generous, "but that can be corrected. We'll give her 4004 for a license number. You can quote me that she flies as well as any ship I ever flew and better than most."

We almost went crazy. It was too good to be true.

"Remember," said Harold, slapping me on the back. "You said I'd succeed if I did what I wanted. I said you were wacky. Who's loony now?"

We sent wires to the boys: "*Connecticut Yankee* came through with flying colors."

I bought a bottle of sherry and mushrooms and a steak three inches thick for supper. Olesen ate with us. We took a night off from the welding school.

It was while we were eating that we heard the sound of strange motors.

"The S39," I cried. We all raced for the airport.

Just as we got there I made out the shape of the little amphibian over the swamp in the dusk. Suddenly one motor putt-putted, then quit entirely. The plane dipped and wavered. The other motor couldn't hold it. There was a terrific crash.

I rushed over and joined the jabbering, gesticulating Russians. Miraculously, nobody had been killed.

They held up their hands appealingly.

"Please no, please, please," they said. "If you don't tell, no one will ever know. It is dark and there is no one at the airport. Already in Russia and now here we have so much trouble. By mistakes we learn. Tomorrow we start over again."

"We're set," said Harold. "There's no need of kicking somebody when they're down."

When I got back to the house there was a call from the editor.

"I don't know why I bother with such tripe on a day like this," he said, "but I hear the Russians ran into a little trouble with the amphibian they're building."

"Did they?" I asked innocently.

"You know God-damn well they did," said the editor ungraciously. "Now snap into it."

I hung up. Nuts, I thought.

"It seems too good to be true," Olesen was saying. "Our troubles are over. With the stock market the way it is, we might do better than a million dollars. I can't help feeling sorry for the Russians."

But I was thinking.

"What do you suppose the editor meant by 'on a day like this'?" I asked. "That's a funny expression."

Just then I heard a voice calling, "Extry! Extry!"

"I'm going to get one," I said to Harold.

We all stood under the hall light reading it.

"Biggest Stock Crash in History. October 29 will long be remembered," the lead story started.

It was all we could do to keep Olesen from taking an ax and going up to Hartford and smashing the *Connecticut Yankee.*

I wasn't surprised when I looked at the *Herald* Sunday. There, spang in the middle of my page, was the Marmola ad.

"Well," said Harold, "I may as well tell you. Curtiss says the bottom's shot out of their business. After next week they won't need me."

Later in the afternoon, Ole came around to say that nobody showed up at the welding school.

"This has all the aspects," said Harold, "of an Undesirable Situation. What New Approach do you suggest?"

I didn't have any. I felt heart sorry for him. I knew the little *Connecticut Yankee* meant everything to him—adventure, romance, success.

"I shouldn't have dragged you and the kids into this thing," he went on. "But I thought sure I could make a go of it."

"Still love us?" I said. "The five hostages and the ball and chain?"

He put his arms around me and kissed me. "That's why I feel so damn bad."

"What have the Russians got that we haven't got?" I said. "By mistakes we learn. Tomorrow we start over again."

EVERYTHING'S GOING TO BE
DIFFERENT ON CAPE COD

*T*HERE was a roar of gunfire. Rodney crashed backwards through the front door of the Pochet house, clutching his double-barreled shotgun.

"Don't get excited," he said, angrily waving away would-be rescuers. "I just put in a double load to see if I couldn't get one of those ducks."

"It's time somebody got excited," I said. "After all, yesterday you shot my hat off just as I was getting into the Willys-Knight."

"But, Ma, he didn't hit you," protested the children. "And nobody ever liked that hat."

"It's not the hat I'm worrying about," I said. "It's Rodney. He can't seem to adjust himself to Cape Cod."

As a matter of fact, Rodney could never seem to adjust himself to anything. There were those so unfeeling as to suggest that he didn't try. But of course you always run across old fuddy-duddies who just don't like being hit by flying glass or getting a load of buckshot in the seat of the pants. Rodney had a high I. Q., but he didn't know his own strength. And despite the fact that, at fifteen, he was six feet two and weighed two hundred and twenty-five, he constantly labored under the delusion that people were picking on him. His first question on entering a room was likely to be whether somebody wouldn't like their puss smacked. He was always surprised to find that they wouldn't. He would have been amazed to know they would have as soon tangled with Attila the Hun. (This prejudice didn't apply to women, who fell willing victims to his melting brown eyes and impudent grin.) He regarded himself as the peace-lovingest guy who ever lived, and his battle with life as purely defensive.

But it wasn't just Rodney who couldn't adjust himself to Cape Cod. It was all of us, with the possible exception of Frankie. He was that *rara avis*—a contented child.

Yet the move to the Cape had been made only after careful consideration. We'd even called in my sister to advise when, after my mother's death, I'd received my share of her estate, twelve thousand dollars.

"Why don't you buy a mink coat and all take a trip around the world?" asked my sister. "You've never bought yourself anything more dynamic than an iron dishcloth. You've always spent every cent you had on houses, or the children, or business. Why don't you just relax for once, and have a good time?"

I didn't say anything. I was thinking of how my mother had saved and scrimped the last ten years of her life to leave us every nickel. I knew my sister was investing hers carefully. I couldn't just blow mine in on idle pleasure.

"I think a farm's the answer," said Harold. "Back to the land."

"It's all we can do to keep him from buying the 'Oh Boy,'" I said. "'Oh Boy, you will go crazy when you see this nifty farm on the Eastern Shore of Maryland with mule, harness, and four fertile acres we are offering for only $1200. Old house with slave quarters. Anyone can see there is a terrific romance connected with this old house albeit repairs are needed. Act quick or some fortunate buyer will beat you to it. Terms to responsible parties.'"

"That lets you out," said my sister. "Heaven knows you aren't responsible."

"My theory is that life has gotten too complicated," said Harold. "Too many gadgets. All a man really needs is a woman, three square meals a day, and a roof over his head. People existed before they ever heard of General Motors."

"You're a fine one to talk, in that hundred-and-fifty-dollar Abercrombie and Fitch tweed suit," said my sister. "Personally I'd rather have lobster Newburgh at the Ritz than skin mules."

"I think Harold is right about the simple life," I said, "but I don't think he quite visualizes the 'Oh Boy.' I think he sees himself in the bow of a canoe, coming home from duck hunting with Ol' Jasper and Joe Faithful manning the paddles and Miss Lizzie callin' to Sukey to make it a long one with plenty of mint because she can see the Massa roundin' the bend from where she's standin' under the white Corinthian columns, an' he-all pretty dawgone tahd. I'm afraid when he gets to showing neighboring planters the slave quarters with Old Lil and her daughter struggling with the hams and hickory, it'll turn out to be me and Louise blacked up. I'm for the good earth, but I'm too old to learn to card wool."

"If that's the way you feel," said Harold, "the farm is out. But what would you say to a little ice-cream store down on Cape Cod? Ben Thompson who runs the drugstore where I get cigarettes has been telling about a place we could get for only five thousand dollars. He's made a big success of the place he's running. I'd take his word. He goes down to the Cape summers. He says it's great. Fog, honey-suckle, bayberry; quaint lovable characters. Peace and security. No more running around in circles."

After the two trains going nowhere we'd taken, it sounded fine. I remembered the summers I'd spent at Chatham when I was young. I could just see the fishing fleet coming around the bar at sunset; the decoy ducks hanging in the gun room; taste the blueberry ice cream and tangy wild-beach-plum jelly.

"What do you want to go down on that Godforsaken sandspit for?" asked my sister. "Those quaint lovable characters sold their land at war prices to the city suckers in the Cape Cod boom of 1926 and hung onto every sou. When the boom blew up, they took their land back again. They're tight as ticks. They've got plenty stowed away in the old horsehair sofa, but they'll never part with it. You won't make any money."

"We wouldn't expect to make money," said Harold. "Just a living. Maybe thirty-five or forty a week. Where could I do any better than that anyhow? My father and uncle are on their uppers. The rose business is down and out. I think the Cape's the answer. We'd be living a normal life in God's country. It's better than the slums."

"What could be drearier than a normal life?" asked my sister. "Don't forget that the week before you married Louise you rode a cab horse down Broadway with a chorus girl in the cab. I'm not re-proaching. I'm just reminding."

"People can change," I said. I thought the little store on Cape Cod sounded wonderful.

"If they can, why don't they?" asked my sister. "I never saw anybody that did."

I knew Harold hadn't, really. He was incurably romantic.

"Harold's thinking of the Cape in terms of whales, clipper ships, and privateers," I said. "We'll probably have trouble to keep him from buying a cutlass, rubber boots with tassels, and a spyglass."

Louise said that sounded fine to her. Get her a wooden leg and she'd play Long John Silver.

But it was the little white cottages set in scrub oak and scrub pine beside the oyster-shell roads, I was thinking of. The fresh, salty smell of the ocean. The sighing Cape wind.

We wouldn't have to worry about the children's schooling, I reflected. John was all set at Andover. Rodney was still hanging on by his teeth at Exeter. "Rodney could make a really outstanding record," wrote his adviser, "if he could just be persuaded to go to classes." Maybe Barbara could get a scholarship at Sea Pines in Brewster. Frankie and Louise would love a village school.

"But what will you do all those endless days and nights in winter?" pursued my sister.

"We'll sit on our tails and take it easy!" said Harold.

I wondered. We never had. I thought he probably just said that to put an end to the argument.

As we crossed the Barnstable bridge the night we moved down, Frankie roused himself from the back seat.

"I'm going to brush my teeth every day after we pass the canal," he said. "Everything's going to be different on Cape Cod."

"Smell the clam flats," I said ecstatically.

"Look at the old one-track railroad," said the children. "See the windmills."

"I feel ten years younger already. It'll be a new life," said Harold.

"You don't think we're being escapists?" I asked anxiously. He said he didn't.

It was twelve o'clock at night when we reached the Snow Inn, but Louise was so excited at the prospect of a new life that she insisted on staying up and washing her stockings.

As I'd assured everyone that the Cape was warm as toast in March, due to the proximity of the Gulf Stream, the family was a little put out when they awoke next morning to find it snowing. Our home, a weatherbeaten captain's house above the sand dunes, shivered and shook in the teeth of a wintry wind straight from Portugal. On the beach below, the breaking waves dashed high. Frankie said he wished he'd brought a clothesline so he could find Barbara and play wreck of the Hesperus. She'd be perfect for the captain's daughter because she had blue eyes. At noon our furniture hadn't arrived yet, but every fifteen minutes some courier would dash up and give us news of its progress: "Seen a van with a furrin' license down by Barnstable"; "Seen a feller said he seen a van with a furrin' license comin' through Dennis." When it finally showed up we were so cold we were glad to help unload.

"We'll have a little music to cheer us up," I said brightly, snapping on the radio.

"This is the Genial Oil Man of the Boston Fish Pier," said a lugubrious voice, "calling the Captain of the *Sally Ann*. Calling the Captain of the *Sally Ann*. Tell him someone is dead at home. Tell him someone is dead at home."

Barbara and Louise burst into tears.

I felt pretty sunk myself. The Cape brought back memories. Fourth of July at our house in Chatham; my father setting his beard on fire leaning down to see why the giant bomb he'd lighted didn't go off; my sister at the helm of Captain Bassett's catboat when we sailed outside the bar; my mother building tiny shell castles in the sand. I tried not to think about my mother because I couldn't bear it. But I couldn't get that last day out of my mind. The telegram: "Your mother has fallen and struck her head." The dreadful, endless ride to Portland. "You'll find your mother in the little back room on the third floor," the landlady said. "Look out for the stairs. They're pretty steep. Your mother didn't seem to mind them. But then she was never one to complain." What would my father say, I thought. "The best was none too good," he always said. The nurse opened the door. My mother lay there on the narrow cot bed, looking so pretty. She was half smiling, only her eyes were closed. I knelt by the bed and touched her small white hand. "It's warm, she's going to be all right!" I cried to Harold. "She's going to be fine!" The doctor touched me on the arm. "She's lain there just like that ever since we found her and brought her in," he said. "If you spoke to her she might know you. But then she would know she was dying. Are you strong enough to be kind?" Harold and the nurse and the doctor went out. I stayed there kneeling a long time. Then I went out and I didn't go back. "Isn't it wonderful," said my cousin after the funeral, "to think a woman your mother's age had so many friends?" I didn't answer. I hadn't seen anybody. I only saw that small white hand.

"Oh dear," I said. "Maybe we shouldn't have come down to the Cape in winter. It seems so far from home."

"Come on," said Harold. "Let the kids shove the furniture round. We'll go over to the village and take a look at the store."

We jumped into the car.

"Ben says the outside isn't much," said Harold as we bumped along the little winding Pochet road. "But the inside's a riot."

As Ben had made a success of his business, we'd bought sight unseen on his say-so. The Cape Cod bank had verified his figures on the store's gross income. Harold stopped at an old rickety wooden building opposite the cemetery in the center of town.

"There is our future, darling," he said, pointing dramatically.

"Where?" I asked. "I don't even see a sign."

"Don't crab," said Harold. "Wait till you see the inside. Ben says the summer people think it's priceless."

We got out and entered a large square room papered with fading roses. On the fountain, which was at the front, rested a box of dried-up cigars. Next it stood a homemade showcase full of mildewed chocolates. In the center of the store was a large fluted iron stove with the word "Ideal" molded on it. The stovepipe made four or five Rube Goldberg turns before it wormed its way outside. Two or three men in Sears Roebuck overalls and rubber boots (without tassels) were standing around the stove. Occasionally, one would open the door and spit inside. The "Ideal" would hiss menacingly. At the back of the store were several stalls made of shoulder-high pieces of wallboard. These, Harold said, must be "booths." In each booth was a marble-topped table and three bentwood chairs.

"If it's whimsical," I said, "I'm too old and feeble to grasp it. I was never one to dash over to Hoboken and hiss Christopher Morley. It strikes me as pure Tuckahoe."

"Ben says the trick is not to spend a cent on it," said Harold. "Leave everything the way it is. The owner fixed it up in 1910 and it hasn't been touched since. The summer people are mad about it; it's so amusing."

He tried to sound convincing. But I could see he was shaken.

"We are not amused," I said, in a feeble attempt to be humorous. But too much was at stake. It didn't go over.

Harold said oh, for God's sake, for once in my life, try to be sensible. It was no Schrafft's. But it did the business. He said if I couldn't stand it not to come near it. There was nothing for me to do there, anyway. He was going to keep on the two girls the owner had trained. As it was winter there was no business anyhow. Just a quahoger in for a plug of dark BL chewing tobacco; or the men from the French cable station in for papers. The gas pumps on the corner went with it, but in winter there was no traffic.

"All right," I said. "It's just that it doesn't look like *us*," I added doubtfully.

Harold said forget it. We'd come down to the Cape to be happy. We weren't going to let the business own us; we were going to own the business.

As long as there were no customers to speak of, Harold joined me and the children in the pursuit of happiness. He read *Adventure* while Barbara and I did the housework. Barbara wouldn't be able to enter the senior class at Sea Pines until September. After lunch, we all walked out to the coast-guard station. When Frankie and Louise got out of school at three, we all went riding. We drove to Provincetown. We drove to Hyannis. Then we drove to Provincetown again.

"Isn't it great to have no worries?" asked Harold as we gazed bleakly out over the ice-covered harbor.

"Yes," we answered bravely.

I started a hooked rug. It had a cottage and a cat and a boat and Rock of Ages Cleft for Me on it. In a week it was finished.

"I might as well be dead and buried," said Barbara. "I'll never meet anybody. It would be too bad if you found yourselves at fifty with a lot of middle-aged children on your hands."

Barbara was seventeen now and devastatingly pretty. She had a mild flat way of speaking with no emphasis on important words. Surprisingly pithy truths issued from her Cupid's-bow mouth, in spite of her dead-pan expression.

"Why don't you let Barbara and me go down with you and help tend store the day the girls are off?" I said to Harold. I thought it would be a diversion.

"All right," he said grudgingly. "If you two don't have any bright ideas about revamping it."

While he read *True Detective* Barbara and I passed the time trying to make sodas. It wasn't as easy as it looked. Barbara did pretty well, but when I turned on the fine soda stream the soda flew right up and hit me in the face. When I didn't the soda looked like dishwater.

At noon, Barbara said she'd go over to the station with Harold and get the papers. "I hope I won't be frightened," she said, "when I see the train."

While they were gone, Gene Snow, a native, came in for a chocolate frappé. I put the sirup, milk, and ice cream in the metal container. Then I shoved it under the mixer. The mixer tossed the ball of ice cream right into space. Automatically, I put out my hand and caught it. Before I thought, I tossed it back into the mixer.

Gene Snow gazed me at me fascinated.

"Pretty fancy," he said, "ain't yer?"

When Gene Snow went out I took a good look at the equipment. The pipe that led out to the soda compresser in the back room ran in an uncovered little groove cut in the floor. It was clear that if you didn't remember to step over it, it would break and soda would spurt to the ceiling. There was no warmer for the fudge and butterscotch sauce. There was no hot water to wash the glasses.

"We really ought to have a new fountain," I told Harold when he and Barbara came in.

"We'll *have* to," said Barbara. "I've been telling Pa the same thing."

"I warned you two if you belly-ached about the place," said Harold, "you couldn't come down here any more."

I kept quiet till five minutes later when I turned up on the busy end of a short circuit and realized how sketchy the wiring was. I'd made myself an orange freeze. When I shoved it on the mixer I got a terrific shock. I grabbed it off so fast I threw it right into Harold's face.

"We'll have to have this place rewired," I said angrily, "whether Ben Thompson likes it or not."

"Well, just state it calmly," said Harold wiping the sherbet out of his eye. "Don't dramatize it."

I could see by the dirty look he gave the mixer that he wanted to yank it out by the roots. But I could see by the set of his jaw he didn't intend to. I kept thinking how pretty a window box would look. And some petunias and zinnias out by the gas stand. The big windows were glary too. They'd be better for awnings. The tables and chairs were really awful. But I knew Harold was right. We didn't have enough capital to swing a remodeling job. We'd be in over our ears if we tried it. And money aside, we'd be fools to change the store if the summer people were crazy about it. Ben knew best.

We varied our trips to Provincetown and Hyannis with visits to old houses. We'd get out and look in the windows at the Dutch ovens and old paneling. The kitchens with pumps and low ceiling were wonderful, especially Joseph C. Lincoln's birthplace in Brewster. Since he made so much money he'd built himself a villa on the Bluffs at Chatham.

"I wish we didn't live in a decent house," said Louise, "so we could take an old one and fix it up."

After the drive we were always depressed. It was hard to gear ourselves down to the pursuit of happiness. And the Cape seemed so lonesome. It wasn't the gay Cape of my youth I'd remembered. Nor was there a whale or privateer in a carload. The summer influx was still months away.

"I'd trade thirty sea gulls in good condition," I told Barbara secretly, "for one glimpse of the spire of St. Patrick's Cathedral on Fifth Avenue at twilight."

"Cheer up," said Barbara hopefully. "When the boys get home for spring vacation, there'll be some excitement."

There was.

John arrived a little early and, surprisingly, not under his own steam. I'd been sustained by the thought of the bang-up job John was doing at Andover. Tall, husky, dark, handsome, industrious, John was my ewe lamb. In fact, he was practically perfect. His only fault was a slight tendency to smugness. This had been his undoing. Clothed in the majestic thought that he could do no wrong and if he did it was nobody's business but his own, he had paraded down to Shawsheen Manor to get advertisements for the *Phillipian* without bothering to ask permission, though he knew Shawsheen was outside the school limits. His majestic mien had rendered him neither invisible nor invulnerable. Two professors whom he met and greeted jauntily reported his dereliction. He was told to go home and stay there until recalled. He arrived heartbroken.

It was Rodney whose irrepressible energy lifted us out of the dumps and stepped up the quiet tenor of our lives to the peak voltage of manic depressives.

The first thing that happened was Rodney went out to start the pump, and the pump house burned down.

"But it wasn't Rodney's fault," protested the children. "It said in *Popular Science* that a match goes out when you throw it into a can of gasoline. The first one did but the second one didn't. Rodney's writing them a good stiff letter telling them they are wrong."

"Just the same, he needn't have stood there in the kitchen for fifteen minutes explaining the theory of the thing before he told us the pump house was afire and that was why he wanted a pitcher of water. And he needn't have offered to punch the fire warden's nose when he came to arrest us for having a fire without permission."

It was really my fault about the loon. It was I who suggested shooting out the car window. Rodney wanted to go duck hunting and it was raining pitchforks.

"You know where the shore runs right along the road between here and Chatham?" I asked Rodney. "Well, I could drive you along there and you could pick off the ducks from the Willys window."

Frankie and Louise and Barbara thought it sounded like fun, so they went along.

"Are you sure that's a duck?" I asked Rodney, as we cruised along the shore road and he took aim.

"It's lots bigger than a duck," said Louise. "I think it's a goose."

"Fire when ready, Gridley," I urged happily. "Roast goose sounds fine."

We drove down to the store to show it to Harold.

"How'd you like a nice roast goose for supper?" we shouted, waving it at him as he stood in the doorway. "Rodney shot it from the car window."

"You idiot, it's a loon," said Harold. "Don't you know it's against the law to shoot loons? Or to shoot from cars? Or to shoot anything without a license? I just mention it because that's the game warden's car back of you."

"Throw me the coal shovel," I yelled.

He threw it. We shot down the road toward Provincetown with the game warden in full pursuit.

"Keep your eyes glued to the rear window," I said to the children. "Tell me when I've lost him. We'll dash down a side road and bury it."

We roared down Route 6, with the throttle wide open. The children and the loon bounced around in the back like peas.

"We've lost him. O.K., *turn!*"

I veered into a side road on one wheel and brought up short against a cranberry bog. Two men working there were so frightened they ran and hid behind beach-plum bushes while I backed around. We shot out the side road a mile a minute just as the game warden turned in. He drew respectfully aside into the ditch as our juggernaut tore by and hurtled on toward Truro.

"There's a road. Turn!" yelled the children. We ripped around a corner right into a large barn, almost taking the pants off three men pitching hay. "Just passing through," said Rodney, tipping his hat politely as we shot out the other side.

We tried a road to the outside beach, but the coast guard was having drill. We tried the bay. Men were quahoging.

"And they say the Cape's deserted in winter," I said. "I'd just as soon try to bury a loon on the corner of Broadway and Forty-second Street."

We dashed desperately on toward Provincetown.

"I've got a plan," I said suddenly. I turned around, pushed the gas pedal down to the floor, and streaked it back for Orleans. When we reached our store I grabbed the loon and raced inside. "Give me an empty five-gallon ice-cream can," I yelled to Harold.

"Right here," said Harold, thrusting one into my hand. "I'm on my way over to the express company to ship these empties back to Hood."

I ripped open the canvas bag, grabbed off the can cover, and shoved the loon into the can.

"Ship it to Hood," I said to Harold. "Letter follows."

As Harold went out the door with the cans, the game warden came in. He searched the store. He searched the car. The corpus delicti had flown the coop.

"Doggone it," he said, sourly, sipping a lemon coke, "I'd like to know what you done with it."

I heard the whistle of the afternoon train.

"If you're referring to that loon which was swimming off Chatham about two hours ago," I said, "I have a hunch it's outside your jurisdiction."

Harold was furious. "For God's sake," he said, "why don't you and the children pipe down? Here I am trying to keep things on an even keel for once and no co-operation from anyone."

"You needn't act so darn superior," I said. "You know very well you're as bored as I am. You're just jealous."

Harold said he was darn glad he didn't have to have a three-ring circus going on in order to be happy. He was Captain of his Soul. But his tone didn't carry much conviction.

He said he was relieved when John, triumphantly recalled by a unanimous vote of the faculty, went back to Andover and Rodney to Exeter. He said he enjoyed "the quiet."

"Take them off, Pa," said Barbara. "We know you. Let's fix up the store. We know you want to just as much as we do. Be human. It's three months till Fourth of July, when the summer people come. We haven't got a living thing else to do. Let's go to it."

For a moment a wild gleam came into Harold's eye, then faded.

"Nope," he said. He wasn't going to. He was going to be sensible.

He had more granite in him than I did, I thought. I wondered how he could stand it.

I was about ready to jump into the Atlantic when I got a telegram from my sister saying: "Coming for a visit. Meet me at Hyannis." I didn't tell Harold she was coming. I saved it for a surprise.

"And you honestly haven't thrown that money down the manhole yet?" asked my sister as she got into the car. "Or killed yourself working? And you're living in a house with hot water laid on and central heating? I can't believe it. And you're happy?"

"Cape Cod is a marvelous place, simply marvelous," I said evasively. I figured that what she didn't know wouldn't hurt her. I hoped she didn't hear the children snickering.

"You'll die when you see the store," I said as we neared Orleans. "It's exactly as we found it. I wanted to make one or two minor changes but Harold wouldn't. We've made up our minds not to be foolish."

As we drew up to the store I noticed a number of cars parked outside. There was the sound of hammering. I burst in, followed by my sister and the children. Harold was in the middle of the store with a crowbar ripping things out by the roots. A bunch of quahogers in hip rubber boots were pushing the fountain around on rollers. "Better this way," they were shouting happily, "or this?"

Harold's face was covered with dirt and his hair was hanging over his forehead. His eyes were bright.

"Hello," he said absently to my sister.

He turned to me.

"Listen!" he said. "About two hours ago I heard that a new modern ice-cream store is going to open up opposite the post office.

We've got five thousand smackers invested in this joint. We've got to protect it. We'll fix this place up so it'll knock your eye out." He turned to my sister. "I hate to have you see it before it's fixed up," he said. "I'm going to panel the whole store in knotty pine. We'll get Vernon Smith, the artist, to do murals. We'll have him do Bill Ike, who cleans out privies, with his beard and rabbits; and Joe Gundry's boat *Quahaug* and his dink *Little Neck;* and the three churches at Truro. We'll throw out these junky tables and chairs and build booths. I can build 'em myself. We'll rewire the store and put in some decent showcases and a new fountain." He stopped for breath. "Of course," he said, "it'll take a little money."

"We don't really need to live in the house we're living in," I said. "The rent was more than we expected."

"We could take that little old Cape Cod cottage down in Barley Neck we looked at," said Louise. "And fix it over. It hasn't got any improvements. But it's got a pump in the yard."

"And the mantels are honeys," said Barbara. "We could put that Daniel Boone paper we saw in Hyannis on the living room and the Dickens paper on the dining room."

"As long as we've got water," I said, "the other improvements can wait."

"You work like hell on the house and I'll work like hell on the store. We'll make 'em the finest places on Cape Cod. What do you say?" cried Harold happily.

"Hooray!" we shouted.

"Officer, we're in again," said my sister. "Same old leopard. Same old spots."

GIT ALONG, LITTLE DOGIE

"THAT tall man sitting at the second table from the door says that when he bit into his hamburger sandwich there was a lighted cigarette in it," cried Barbara, bursting out into the kitchen.

I peered anxiously through the peephole in the door leading into the grill.

"Which man?" I asked, as if it made any difference.

"The one opposite the two swordfish," said Barbara. "Next to the scallops and French-fried."

"Tell him we're giving away lighted cigarettes with every hamburg," I said. "Where else could he get such service?"

It was eleven o'clock Saturday night and I had cooked eighteen orders of broiled live lobster, twenty-two steaks, and nineteen orders of scallops when Barbara had come out with the order for twenty hamburgs.

"Who is it?" I asked. "Gargantua?"

Barbara said no, it was four different parties.

"The place is packed," she added happily.

I toasted the rolls and laid them in neat rows on the upper shelf of the table. Then I started the hamburgers. I was so tired I must have inadvertently parked my lighted cigarette on one of them.

"Well, that's one more black mark they can chalk up against me," I said wearily. "For heaven's sake, remind Rodney he's not of age and not to serve any beer on pain of death. If he does someone'll call up the liquor board. Don't serve the bus driver beer when he stops or someone'll call up the selectmen."

From the moment I'd got the beer license and we'd added the Ship Ahoy Grill onto our streamlined ice-cream parlor we'd had trouble.

"You get the beer license and we'll build a restaurant," said Harold. "We'll have an honest-to-God night club."

"Orleans will scalp us," I said. "The town's always been dry. Besides, we aren't *sure* it would make any money."

Harold said we had to do something. The way things were going we couldn't make enough to buy a bucket of clams.

This was 1933. The depression had finally hit the Cape. Besides, several rival ice-cream "parlors" had opened up. What business there was had to be divided and subdivided.

We'd hoped the agency for the Western Union would solve our problems. The first night when Phoebe Atwood Taylor, author of the Asey Mayo mystery stories, came in and sent an eighty-word message to her publisher, beginning "Caloo, calay, oh frabjous day," we thought it was going to be a gold mine. After that there was nothing but collect messages from Still, the wholesale fish dealer in New York, saying "Don't ship any more clams."

"I can't charge those poor devils down in Truro and Eastham anything for those telegrams, let alone the delivery," said Harold. "Most of them live in huts. When they open the door and see me they look so down in the mouth it's all I can do to hand the message to them."

We figured that, counting gas for the Packard, every "Don't ship any more clams" message set us back two dollars. Of course, a Packard wasn't an economical form of transportation. But the Willys-Knight had given out and we'd selected the only car that had a spark of life in Harry Kent's automobile graveyard.

We were really relieved when the telegraph company took away the agency. They removed it because of a reporter from the *Globe* who was in a sweat to send a story to his paper about the damage done by a nor'easter. But customers kept coming in to the store. Harry Kent, the automobile tycoon, wanted a package of Bull Durham. Bill Maier, a budding author, wanted a pair of work gloves. I had to wait on them. Then Bill Ike, who cleaned out privies, came in for a coffee cone. He got to telling about how his business had fallen off since the depression, and I didn't like to interrupt him. As soon as I'd cooked Louise a couple of pork chops I'd promised her, I sent the message. But the reporter wrote a piece for the *Globe* about why I didn't wait on him quicker. They ran it on the first page. He even described the pair of dungarees that I looked as if I'd been "poured into." The Western Union saw it and felt I'd pulled them down nationally.

The Cape season was short at best—July 4 to Labor Day. The other ten months were dead.

In '30 we'd made money; in '31 we'd lost it; in '32 we'd gone in the hole right. It was only because my first husband was once more contributing that we'd been able to hang on.

"Our only hope is beer," Harold had said.

"The natives will never grant me a beer license," I said. "We're furriners."

"They'll figure we'll go bust," said Harold. "That would drive us out."

Our battle with the natives dated back a long time. They disapproved of the old fifty-dollar Model T I had bought for the boys. They were sure I was crazy when the boys quarreled so over who owned it that I bought them a second one. They weren't sure that Rodney, who wasn't old enough for a license, would restrict his activities to Pochet, where they had private roads. Then someone reported that while we were busy at the store, *Louise* was driving one of the Model T's around Pochet. I put a stop to that, but not before Louise lost control and went barging down over the field back of the house. As the top was down, she and the other occupants came within a hairbreadth of being scalped by the clothesline.

"There's no need to get into a stew," said Louise airily. "My crutch slipped off the brake. It could happen to anyone."

The natives despised me for letting Lonnie Chase, a shrewd old Yankee salt, soak me seventy-five dollars for painting our little sailboat. It was no good anyhow, they pointed out, after Rodney climbed the mast. When he rocked back and forth to see how near he could come to tipping it over, the seams split open. The next time we went down to go out sailing, somebody had stolen the centerboard and the ballast.

Another evidence of my lack of sanity was the fact that I was bound and determined that the boys should play football. At eleven o'clock every morning all summer I drove Harold and the boys to the beach. Harold then ran three miles up to the wreck and back with the boys to get them in shape for the fall season. Occasionally, I ran with them, dirty apron and all. Frankie ran halfway, rested, and joined us on the way back. The natives didn't blame the boys for kicking. It was "damn foolishness." The boys said if I hadn't wanted them to play football they would have been dying to. But they hated to be regimented.

"I've dreamed for years of your running the length of the field for a touchdown," I told them, "while I looked on proudly from my favored position on the fifty-yard line."

Sometimes the debate waxed so hot everybody on the beach could hear us. An added insult was when, toward the end of the season, I hired the coach of Middlebury College who coached the Orleans summer baseball team to give the boys workouts.

"Take so much out o' him trainin' those hellions," they claimed, "won't have enough git up an' git left in him to be worth his salt to Orleans."

We had our petty triumphs. One was the day the Genial Oil Man of the Boston Fish Pier referred to three of our family in the same broadcast: John, who had just received the DuPuy scholarship at Yale; me, who had got up a little brochure called "Who's Got Eight Dollars? Elmer Wants to Know," describing how Orleans could get a new high school for eight dollars if they'd get a PWA grant and follow my directions; Louise, who was at Washington with her high-school class and was calling on the President of the United States at the President's personal invitation. (She had written congratulating him on his election. He'd replied, urging her to come up and see him sometime.)

My stock fell again, however, when I broadcast for Harold.

I wouldn't have broadcast for Harold if I hadn't been so worried. Ever since we'd been on the Cape we'd hardly been away from each other two hours. Of course, when he went over to the bank in Chatham he always stopped in stores to sample their 3.2 "near" beer and ask the proprietors how business was going. But he didn't stay long.

I might not have thought so much about his being late from the bank that day if he hadn't promised to take Louise to her cornet lesson. When he didn't show up I walked over to the house to tell Louise. Rodney and Barbara were at the store, so I stayed home. About three hours later Charlotte Mayo drove up and said, "Barbara and Rodney are telling customers, 'Pa hasn't come home and Ma doesn't know where he is. Have you seen him?'"

"Good heavens," I said. "Tell them to stop it."

She came over to the house again about six. "I told them to stop," she said, "but they didn't. They called up the bank and asked the bank if they'd seen him and the bank went into a tailspin."

"I should think they would," I said, "considering the size of our loan with them."

"They asked if he deposited seventy-six dollars and the bank said yes and they said well, then he can't get very far because he hasn't any money. The bank said, '*Is he missing?*' and the children said yes, and the bank said if they could do anything to help they'd be glad to."

"The fatal fondness of the young for giving unasked-for information," I groaned. "But I can't imagine where he is. After all, there aren't many places on the Cape you *can* go in winter."

I thought I'd better ride over to the store with her. I was really getting worried.

At ten o'clock he still hadn't shown up, and quite a crowd had collected. Bill Corcoran of the *Standard Times* took me aside.

"If you want the police to broadcast for him," he said, "I can fix it."

"I honestly think you'd better," I said gratefully.

We closed the store and all went home and sat around the living room. Rodney sat down by the radio and began "fishing."

"If we only knew where he was," said Louise, "we'd know what attitude to take. If he's blotto and having a marvelous time, we could break out refreshments. But we ought to be howling like dogs if he's lying dead in a ditch."

"There's nowhere he can get blotto on Cape Cod," I said. "He doesn't know anyone."

"Hush!" said Rodney. "Here it comes!"

"Calling Harold C. Pierson, Packard sedan license M26–450. Calling Harold C. Pierson, Packard sedan license M26–450. Maine, Vermont, Massachusetts, Rhode Island, Connecticut, New York. Tell him someone is sick at home. Tell him someone is sick at home."

We snapped it off. Louise burst into tears.

"He was always so good to us," she sobbed. "And we've acted like Sancho."

"I kept saying 'Hurry up with the French-fried potatoes' because I thought the customer would give me a tip if I got the orders out fast," said Barbara quaveringly, "when he was doing the best he could."

"You wouldn't let him march in the American Legion parade!" said Rodney turning on me. "You were awful to him!"

Although Harold had now persuaded me that the Versailles Treaty wasn't half tough enough on the Germans, I still frowned upon parades. They were, I insisted, the rankest combination of nationalism and exhibitionism. Secretly, I adored them. But I wanted to be modern. Keep up with the times. I felt like a skunk when I thought how hurt Harold had been when I wouldn't shine his medals and mend the moth holes in his uniform. "Hell," he said, "you make anyone feel he was a criminal to have fought in the war."

We sat there wrapped in gloom.

"Let's go to bed," I said finally. "If he's only spared we'll try to make it up to him."

Next morning while we were eating breakfast Harold drove up like a tornado. He jumped out of the car, and I rushed to the door to meet him.

"Who's sick?" he cried.

"I am," I said, mad as a hatter to find him all in one piece and in such good spirits. "Where have you been?"

It seems he had stopped in a little store in Chatham where he knew the owner, to try out the 3.2. The owner served him heavy bootleg beer for a joke.

"That's the finest 3.2 I ever tasted," Harold had said. "Let's have another."

About four o'clock in the afternoon he groped his way through the forest of empty bottles out to the Packard and started home. Home, he recalled dimly, was Tarrytown, where he was born. He didn't remember going through New London or New Haven at all. He began to come to about Stamford. Then he thought he might as well go to his father's in Ossining and spend what was left of the night. As he started down the Parkway, a motorcycle cop stopped him.

"Are you Harold C. Pierson?"

"I think so," said Harold.

"Step on it. Somebody's sick at home."

He was tearing through Norwalk when another cop drew alongside. "Make it snappy, buddy," the cop called. "They need you down on the Cape."

Everybody was furious at me for broadcasting.

"Seems like a man can't git a few hours ter himself without somebody's gut ter broadcast and spile his fun," the Cape said. They all had short-wave receiving sets.

"Oh, I didn't care about *him*," I said. "You can pick up a good man any time. But a good secondhand Packard's hard to replace."

This raised my stock slightly. In New England repartee is highly esteemed.

A temporary truce was called when Barbara confounded everybody by marrying the cream of the native crop. Although her hand had been sought by numerous eligible young men among the summer population she had turned them down in favor of Howard Mayo, a dark and handsome young Massachusetts Aggie graduate who was profitably raising sixty thousand ducks and a hundred thousand chickens yearly on his ancestral acres bordering the Atlantic. She had met him when he came to the grill to deliver an order.

I was tickled pink. Howard was the salt of the earth—as solid, dependable, and American as Plymouth Rock.

At the astounding announcement of the engagement, Orleans hoisted the white flag. Everybody wanted to be invited to the wedding. Everybody was.

It was held in the little old white-painted Congregational church. The bridesmaids wore long old-fashioned gowns of colored calico, black lace mitts, and organdy calashes. Louise was maid of honor.

"If I fall flat," she said, "don't try to pick me up. I get laughing so hard when I fall down all my muscles relax." Frankie, in a little black-satin suit with white Eton collar, was ring bearer. He carried the ring on a little cushion that had always been in the drawer of the secretary. On a yellowed card attached to the cushion was written in my grandmother's careful script, "This cushion has been here ever since I can remember." She was born in 1826. "It was probably there," I told Barbara, "before there was any United States." The lace on it was a little worn, but Barbara thought it would be nice to have Frankie carry it. So everything might be in keeping, Barbara wore white dotted Swiss and carried a bunch of white home-grown chrysanthemums.

The day dawned bright and fair—one of those warm, sunny, dazzlingly bright October days you find only on the Cape. The boys drifted in about noon; they'd hitchhiked. The wedding was to be at five.

I made the bridesmaids' bouquets and helped trim the church with pine, and bright perennials from friends' gardens. I prepared doughnuts and cider for three hundred and fifty, downstairs in the parish room; I frosted angel cakes, and supervised the preparation of ice cream with pink sherbet hearts for the less hearty. At quarter of five, I was ready in my blue-velvet gown and matching toque. I was glad I'd kept my figure, I thought, as I looked in the glass; and the blue was so becoming with white hair. The children would be proud of me. As I descended the stairs, I thought the house seemed strangely quiet. I looked in one room after another. There was nobody there. I glanced outside. Not a car in sight. They had forgotten me.

I stood on the porch, looking out over the blue Atlantic. For the first time in my life, I realized I wasn't needed; life could go on without me. Like the queen bee, I'd fulfilled the mission for which I'd been put on earth. I'd produced the generation who would carry the torch. A tear rolled down my cheek and fell on the blue-velvet gown. It was hard to be an ex-torchbearer. It seemed just a minute ago Barbara had been a little curly-haired baby playing on the floor.

"What's the matter with me?" I asked myself angrily. "Indulging in self-pity like this."

But I couldn't help it. I felt old. Just then I heard a Ford chugging up the hill. It was Lewis Delano, a friend who had been sent to retrieve me. At the last minute John, who was head usher, had counted the people who should have been in the front pew. One was missing.

Everybody agreed it was the loveliest wedding Orleans ever had. Barbara looked ravishing. As she passed me I heard her say without changing her rapt expression, "Pa, don't you think it's about time to tell me the facts of life?"

At the house, about fifty people gathered for creamed chicken and Parker House rolls, and watched Barbara cut the cake.

It had been the wedding of my dreams, I thought as I watched her. The wedding I'd wanted and never had. Gay, original, different. Nothing banal or commonplace. As Barbara came downstairs in her traveling suit I whispered, "Where are you going?"

She whispered back, "Niagara Falls!"

It was while the spell of the wedding lasted that I got my beer license. The restaurant we built was in the shape of a ship. There was an upper and lower deck and two masts with sails. It was lighted by ship lanterns, and candles in tin sconces shaped like sea shells. The flickering yellow light from the candles contrasted beautifully with the deep-blue goblets on the trestle tables. We added a little kitchen with some simple equipment.

"Pierson's Ship Ahoy Grill," went up in electric lights.

It caught on like wildfire. Even the natives came. We got a little three-piece orchestra from New Bedford to play for dancing Friday and Saturday nights. They were three boys who'd been a success in vaudeville and were working in the mills until prosperity once more showed her face. The piano player could sing a beautiful soprano. His specialty was "Love in Bloom."

We had five in help besides the family. Harold and I were chefs. John was store manager. Rodney handled the gas and was general clean-up man. Louise washed dishes. Barbara was waitress. She wanted to help put our great venture over. Frankie watched over papers and magazines till suppertime. Then he and Louise went home.

The first Friday night we sold four barrels of beer and thirty-nine cases. People called up from all over the Cape to make reservations. It was then our troubles began.

An investigator arrived from the Board of Health. He'd had an anonymous telephone call that we threw the garbage down a hole in the floor in the kitchen instead of putting it into cans and taking it to the dump in the Packard. The truce was over.

The man was apologetic. "I knew it wasn't true," he said. "But where there's a complaint we have to investigate."

It seemed as if he came every day after that. He'd had a complaint we didn't have screens in the kitchen. The milk was short of butter-fat. The lobsters cooling on the back fence were "shorts." The steaming clams we used were "seeders." The complaints were always anonymous.

"By golly, if I knew who it was I'd fix them," I said angrily. "Here we are working our hearts out to try to pay our bills and somebody's knifing us. How can people be so mean?"

"Every small country place is the same," said Harold. "They resent outsiders coming in and doing business. We're furriners. They don't like us."

"We've got our last nickel invested in this dump," I said. "They'll never drive me out. I'm staying."

I had a narrow squeeze over the slot machines but I couldn't blame that on "Anonymous." It was my own fault. When the man came to check on the place for our amusement license there was a crowd playing.

"What are those slot machines doing here?" he asked.

"Making money," I said pleasantly. I didn't know there was a law against money machines. Every store on the Cape had one.

"You can't have these here," he said. "If the police see them you'll be out of luck."

"A policeman came through last week and saw them," I said. "He said sometimes people complained about slot machines being gambling, but he'd see they wouldn't bother me."

He didn't say any more, but an hour later the policeman and the captain roared up.

"What the hell did you want to tell that guy I said you could have those slot machines in here for?" said the cop.

"Well, you did," I said.

"You should have had sense enough to put them in the back room when he came," he said. "Keep them there from now on."

We did, but it was very inconvenient. The back room was really just a passageway between the store and the kitchen. Sometimes there were so many people playing the slot machines the waitresses would have to go around by the street to get their orders.

"I feel like Al Capone or something to have those in there if it isn't right," I said to Harold. "But, after all, the minister plays them." I realize now I was rationalizing. He was a Unitarian minister who had once read Santayana at a funeral and everybody thought it was the Bible, he read it so fine. I should have known his patronage was not tantamount to an endorsement by the frocked.

But if Anonymous didn't object to slot machines, he did call up the liquor board and say that we were allowing people to stand up and drink beer. It's a law in Massachusetts you have to sit at a table. We had to have an extra boy Friday and Saturday nights to push people down into chairs. The complaint that Rodney was serving beer was ridiculous because we had a bartender named Zeke, with no teeth, who cooked for the Goff "boys." The Goff boys were two oversized quahogers about fifty who lived in a ramshackle dump on the road to Eastham. They had a sign on it, "Goff's Ranch." They kept birds and dogs and cats and chickens in the ranch house. They could drink twenty-four bottles of beer without going "out back."

After Harold thought of putting on a floor show with the Goff boys doing folk dances in hip rubber boots, the place was mobbed. We brought all the chairs down from the American Legion rooms and pieced them out with upended beer boxes. Still there was a long line of people waiting who couldn't get in.

When the orchestra paused for station identification everybody played lotto. The winner got a round of free beers. We'd fill in with "Ida, the Wayward Sturgeon" or the "Debutante and the Horse" on the phonograph, till the orchestra got rested. Harold would do the hat-and-paper trick, and Roy Taylor, a seminative who "drove" for summer people, would play his accordion.

It wasn't a store, summer people said. It was an institution. It was an institution all right, the natives said. It was an insane asylum.

Our big moment came in mid-August when Joe Gundry's sister, Lady Bede Clifford, sailed up in her Rolls Royce.

"You better station Rodney outside," said Harold, "to keep the shadows of unbelievers from falling on her Indian chauffeur and footman."

Joe Gundry's brother John, who married a Biddle from Philadelphia, came out in the kitchen and grabbed me, kitchen apron and all, to join in the barn dance. While I was dancing, the telephone rang. It was Anonymous.

"You'll get into trouble *right* if you don't stop your customers singing!"

The customers were wild about singing. Next to the "Daring Young Man on the Flying Trapeze" their favorite was "The Last Roundup."

"Watch everything," I said to Harold. "I have a feeling, to quote Stalky, they're 'maturin' something unusual damn mean.'"

Saturday started out inauspiciously. Rodney went down the cellar to fix the hot-water heater. Coming up, he tripped and fell. He landed flat in a flock of lemon-meringue pies I'd set in the back room to cool. It wouldn't have been so bad if he hadn't knocked over a gallon jug of coffee sirup, dislodging the cork. In the afternoon Rodney knocked John's two front teeth out.

"It was my turn *not* to wait on a gas customer," said Rodney. "John wasn't fair about it."

"It would be nice," said Harold, "if Rodney didn't hit anything or anybody for about five minutes. As long as we haven't a 'special fund reserved for such contingencies'!"

"Every time something goes wrong, you have to dig up that old chestnut," I said. "All right he *did* throw the pitcher of cream through the portrait of the Founder at Andover. But the Andover authorities themselves admitted he was only acting in the line of duty."

Rodney had transferred from Exeter to Andover that year to be near John. It was the first in a long line of transfers.

Harold resented the cream throwing because it spoiled the Andover-Exeter football game. But it really hadn't been Rodney's fault. He was waiting on table when Hite, the guard, yelled for cream with his baked apple. Rodney wouldn't give it to him because he was in training. Hite came over and grabbed the pitcher of cream, and Rodney grabbed, too. It went through the portrait of the Founder. When he and Hite went outside to finish the argument Hite broke three bones in his hand knocking Rodney's teeth out. As the two of them were the best guards Andover had, it threw a wrench into the football game. Naturally I offered to pay for restoring the portrait, but Andover said they had "a special fund reserved for such contingencies."

"He wasn't acting in the line of duty at the rolling mills," pursued Harold, "when he hit Gus Hovack, the foreman, every Monday morning. How about that time he had to have three stitches taken in his forehead?"

"That was because Hovack had a hang-over and pushed everybody around on Mondays," I said. "If Rodney hadn't had a reason he wouldn't have hit John."

He *really* hit John to pay John back for a joke he'd played on him, the last week of school. When John went to Yale, Rodney transferred from Andover to Westminster. Two hundred-and-twenty-five-pounders can always get scholarships. As John ran the laundry at Yale, Rodney thriftily sent him his wash. The last week before school was out, John returned his wash. In it, he jestingly placed six empty beer bottles. (John had his moments.) Rodney was up against it. How to dispose of them? Westminster was strict. Desperate, he waited till all Westminster was at chapel Sunday morning. Then he placed the empty beer bottles on the Headmaster's front steps. Unfortunately, the Headmaster, who was confined to the house with a cold, was looking out the window.

"I admit Rodney had just cause for protest," said Harold, "but for God's sake why does he have to pick a day like this to revenge his injuries? Tell him to pipe down. We're swamped already and the day's young yet."

By six that night the grill was jammed. By eight we were feeding people at ice-cream tables in the store. At ten, people were still coming in for supper. I was cooking with one hand and washing dishes with the other when my legs went out from under me. I fell into a chair.

"Keep your courage up," said Harold. "It's two minutes of twelve."

The orchestra was playing the last bars of "Git Along, Little Dogie" and the crowd was singing. The orchestra put up their instruments and the crowd sang on.

John came rushing into the kitchen. "The police sergeant wants you!"

I went out, dirty apron and all.

"Do you know what day this is?" shouted the sergeant.

"No," I said.

"It's the Lord's Day."

"I lived in New York so long I didn't know the Lord had a day," I said.

"In Massachusetts," said the sergeant with dignity, "He not only has a day, He has a department."

"Do tell," I said politely. I could see we were in for something.

"You have disturbed the peace by allowing these people to sing on the Lord's Day," said the sergeant. "I shall report the matter to General Needham, Commissioner of Police and Public Safety, and you'll lose your amusement license."

"How did you happen to be outside here at one minute past twelve?" I asked.

"We received a complaint."

"Who from?"

"Anonymous."

"Oh, you did, did you?" I said. "Well I'll fix Anonymous. I'm fed up with him. It's the Lord's Day and there's a law against singing. But there's no law I've got to sell papers. I've got two hundred and seventy-six Sunday papers coming in at noon today. Try to buy one. I'm closing."

"Have it your own way," said the sergeant.

We did, too. Two hundred and seventy-six angry customers milled around begging for papers but we didn't open. The newspaper people called up and asked what I was going to do. I said, "Nothing."

"I paid for those two hundred and seventy-six papers," I said. "They're mine. If I want, I can throw them into the Atlantic Ocean." I turned from the phone.

"For once," I said to Harold, "we fixed this town."

Monday we got word that our amusement license was revoked.

We put up a sign on the store:

GENERAL NEEDHAM REFUSES LICENSE FOR ORCHESTRA—DANCING—RADIO
CLOSED!
UNTIL WE FIND OUT WHO THREW THE WRENCH IN THE GEARS!

The Boston papers sent down photographers and took our pictures, standing in front of the sign.

One of the papers reported:

The majestic dignity of the law must decide whether the questionable harmony of "Get Along, Little Dogie" emanating from the restaurant Ship Ahoy at Orleans on Cape Cod is sufficient cause to reject an application from the proprietor for an amusement license.

A sergeant of the state police in a report to General Daniel Needham stated that in the wee sma' hours of the morning, the peace and quietude of the Cape were shattered by the choral effects of inmates to render the song depicting the Valhalla of the cowboy.

Mrs. Louise Pierson, proprietor of the restaurant, vehemently stated:

"I throw out drunks, hire a deputy sheriff to keep order, and run a respectable place. 'Get Along, Little Dogie' is a beautiful song. *I'll sing it to General Needham myself!*"

I showed the paper to Harold.

"That's horrible," I said. "I couldn't have said that."

I found myself on the front page of all the Boston papers.

That afternoon I got a telegram from General Needham to come up and see him.

I entered his office to the tune of flashlight bulbs and passionate pleas that I sing loud enough so it could be heard through the key-hole.

The General turned out not to be old at all, as I'd imagined. In fact, turned out to be very good-looking.

I was in his office about an hour. When I got ready to leave, the General said, "The least we can do is look serious."

Next day my license arrived.

There was a picture of me in the Boston *American* entitled "The Winnah."

Anonymous was silenced. For the rest of the season there was SRO in our little night club.

TAKE A NUMBER FROM ONE TO TEN

As I WHEEZED into the yard in the Anna Mae, our 1926 Oldsmobile, after a day's work on the ERA in Hyannis, I saw the long, low yellow supercharged Auburn standing in front of our door.

My heart leaped up as it always does at the sight of a custom-built convertible. It looked like Good Times Are Here Again after the Anna Mae, symbol of our failure. "Maybe our worm has turned; maybe something good is going to happen," I thought instantly. I'd been low in my mind, since after two years' desperate struggling we'd lost the store. I rushed around to the kitchen door to question Louise.

"It's two men," she said excitedly. "They won't say what they want. I told them Pa was working on the Wilcox's stone wall and wouldn't be home for an hour, but they said they'd wait. One's tall and has a diamond stickpin that would knock your eye out. The other's short and dark and has dirty fingernails. He keeps spitting on the Oriental rug."

"Oh," I said, a trifle dashed. "But it's an off-the-Cape license. I've never seen that car before."

"I've seen it once or twice down by the station," said Louise, "about eight o'clock at night when the movies opened. It's got a nifty searchlight on it."

"Maybe it's somebody from Boston with a job for Harold," I said hopefully. "He answered a couple of ads. I hope it is. I figure even if the Anna Mae holds out a month more, so I can get back and forth from Hyannis, and Harold's back holds out so he can finish the wall, it'll be a month before we have money enough to get off the Cape."

"I wish we could go this minute," said Louise. "It breaks my heart to see somebody else in our store."

Even the land-office business we'd done in the night club hadn't offset past failure and the deepening depression. We'd made enough money to live on but we hadn't made a dent in our old bills.

"We're just taking it out of one pocket and putting it into the other," said Harold. "There's no use saying next year we'll do better.

We did the biggest business we can do with the place we've got. And we worked ourselves right off our feet. I know we've got our hearts and twelve thousand dollars sunk in the place. But we owe two thousand dollars, with no prospect of paying it. I don't see what we can do but sell. Then we could pay our bills and go back to New York and get jobs. There's no use our trying to get jobs here. There aren't even enough for the Cape Codders."

Barbara and I burst into tears.

"Vernon's murals," said I.

"The little tin sconces with the candles," said Barbara, ". . . the blue goblets . . . Pa doing the hat-and-paper trick . . . the orchestra playing 'Love in Bloom.'"

Were we getting the failure habit, I wondered. What was wrong with us? We had family, background, brains, ambition, and we weren't lazy. Were native Americans extinct, really, and didn't know it? Should we be put on reservations like the bison? Right next to Lo, the poor Indian?

"I know it's tough," said Harold. "But we can't get through the winter without asking for more credit. I may be a gambler but I'm no heel. I'm damned if I'll run up bills when I *know* I can't pay them. It isn't decent."

A couple of days later, when a Mrs. Flanders showed up with an offer of $2500 cash, we snapped at it. The real-estate dealers said we were lucky to get anyone to consider it. As far as price was concerned, it was 1934; a buyer's market.

"It'll pay off all our debts," said Harold. "And leave us five hundred dollars."

"I hate to see her clean up on us," I said. "But there's one satisfaction. She isn't a native. She doesn't know what she's got coming to her."

She wasn't a native but she was a shrewd trader. When word went around that the selectmen might not renew my beer license, Mrs. Flanders withdrew her offer of $2500. But she was still interested. If my beer license wasn't renewed we were licked right and she knew it. All she had to do was sit tight.

Harold talked to the selectmen about the beer license. They

hemmed and hawed. They'd granted several to natives. "They'd take it under consideration."

"I'm afraid it's no soap," said Harold. "We'd better take whatever she'll give."

In 1934 a business was a drug on the market. Buyers were non-existent.

Mrs. Flanders said she'd take over the Hood mortgage of $1000 and pay us $500 cash. The day the money was to be paid over, collectors from Boston newspapers we owed money to descended like vultures and flew away with $250. Mrs. Flanders' lawyer refused to part with the other $250. He said he'd keep it for contingent bills. We traded the Packard for a 1926 Olds and a little cash. Harold got a job building a stone wall and I got a fifteen-dollar-a-week stenographer's job on the ERA. It was December and pretty cold. We didn't have any coal, but we had fireplaces. When they turned off the light we used lamps.

"If we can save a hundred dollars out of our wages," said Harold, "we'll go back to New York and start again."

"It still tells in the papers about wild bands of boys and girls hitch-hiking on freight trains," said Louise. "And little white hands foraging in garbage cans."

"Don't worry about those," I said. "They're just left over from the last political campaign. Anyway, I'd rather go back to New York and take my place in the forage line than go 'on the town' on Cape Cod. You have to remember that Barbara's married and living here. It might tear her down socially to have her father and mother crushing rock."

If only something good would happen, I kept thinking every day. And now here was the supercharged Auburn.

It seemed hours before Harold got home.

"Pretty snazzy," he said as he burst in through the door. "Who's your friend?"

"Sh," we said. "They're in the library."

Harold went in and in a moment came out for me.

"The man wants to talk to both of us," he said.

The tall man rose as we entered, bowed low, and extended his hand. I noticed he had on a four-carat diamond ring and a platinum wrist watch as well as a diamond stickpin. The short man didn't get up.

"This is Frenchy," said the tall man. "Get up, you ape."

Frenchy got up and sat down again.

"I was wondering if you could use any money, Mrs. Pierson," said the tall man. He took out a roll of bills that would choke a horse. "I noticed your Olds doesn't seem to be hitting on all six. You ought to have a new car."

God moves in a mysterious way, I thought, looking at Frenchy. But I didn't say anything. I waited for the plot to unfold.

"I think I can put your husband in the way of making enough to pay your bills, buy you a fur coat, and stake you to a Cadillac. You'd like that?"

"What doing?" I asked.

"Now, that's what I'm going to talk to you about," said the tall man. "First I wanted to discuss a couple of little matters. Your rent is three months overdue. Right?"

I nodded.

"You have a loan with one of the small loan companies. Your eighth payment was due the tenth of last month. But you haven't paid it. Mrs. Pierson's first husband is no longer contributing. He's out of a job."

"How did you know that?" I asked.

"We make a thorough investigation before we make anyone a proposition. We don't like to step in where we aren't wanted. I happen to know just what bills are hanging over your head and who they're owed to."

He ripped twenty-dollar bill after twenty-dollar bill off the roll and threw them on the table.

"Count it," he said. "I think you'll find that'll take care of it."

"I think I know what you have in mind," said Harold. "I've seen you downtown. I don't think I'd be interested."

Our caller's face darkened slightly.

"It would be very unfortunate if the loan company were to find out what a tough spot you're in, and decided to take your furniture," he said. "It wouldn't help any if your pay was garnisheed."

"If you're threatening us—" I got up and started for the door.

"Frenchy!" said the tall man.

Frenchy went over and stood by the door.

"Show the lady your muscle."

Frenchy rolled up his sleeves and flexed his biceps, then rolled them down. As he returned to his seat he spat on the rug.

"I can't seem to keep Frenchy from spitting on rugs," said the tall man. "He isn't housebroken."

Harold started to get up but I motioned him back.

"Let's hear your proposition," I said.

"I'm glad you're taking this in the spirit it's meant," said the tall man. "I know what it means to be up against it. I was a ringer for Purdue. You see, the football team wasn't doing so good. Needed a shot of the old moxie. So they signed me up for an education. They promised to get some four-eyes to figure out my arithmetic and language lessons. I played guard. I thought I'd be in the money. But I got a black eye and my nose broken, and the bastards never came through with anything but room and meals. I said to myself then there must be some easier way of earning money than being kicked in the tail for it. I got wise."

He looked at Frenchy, who was dozing quietly.

"Open your eyes, you so-and-so," he said sharply. "Or I'll clip you one."

Frenchy smiled.

"Have you your pocketbook with you, Mrs. Pierson?" asked the Ringer pleasantly.

I went out and got it.

"Open it," he said.

I opened it.

"May I see your policy slips?"

"I haven't any policy slips," I said. "I don't know what they are."

"Play bridge?"

"Yes."

"Well, if you asked the other three ladies you are playing with to open their pocketbooks, you'd find two of them held policy slips. Our survey shows that fifty per cent of all women buy them. You buy a policy slip for as low as five or ten cents. If your number wins in the next drawing, you make several dollars."

"I don't believe anybody I know buys policy slips," I said.

"I'm afraid you're wrong," said the Ringer. "You're a little naïve. There's magic in numbers, Mrs. Pierson. Most women realize it."

"Where could anybody buy policy slips in Orleans?" I asked.

"At several places. It might surprise you if I told you. Now in each town on the lower Cape are several what we call 'writers'—the men who sell slips. They get twenty-five per cent of all money they take in and ten per cent of the winner's earning if one of their customers makes a hit. Now at present this business is in the hands of a Boston outfit who've held it for some time. We're newcomers. We intend to take over the business. There may be a little rough stuff if they put up a fight. That's why I wanted to talk to you. We want your husband for pickup man for the lower Cape. He's fine-looking. He's a gentleman. He has a place in the community. He'd be the last person suspected. You and he are in the habit of driving all over the Cape. We always like to talk freely to the wife so she won't worry if her husband's away at night. If she worried she might start talking. Talking is fatal. We think your husband can make around two hundred dollars a week without trouble. We've appointed our agents in the various towns. We're new, but we'll be known inside a week. We'll lead off in every town with a couple of hits. We'll give your husband protection. Maybe you've seen a laundry truck parked in front of the police barracks up the Cape. That's not a laundry truck. And we're not stingy. We'll give him a bodyguard, too. Sorry I can't give you Frenchy. Frenchy used to be one of the best writers we had—stationed in the State House in Boston. Things got a little hot around there and he's down here cooling off."

"You're wasting your—" began Harold, rising.

"Your husband could try it for twenty-four hours," said the Ringer. "I'd pay him twenty-five dollars. If he didn't care to go on, O.K. If he did, O.K. No skin off anybody's nose."

"I tell you—" started Harold.

"I'll talk to my husband," I said to the Ringer. "Come back in an hour."

They went out, leaving the money lying on the table.

"What's the matter with you," said Harold angrily, "have you gone crazy? What do you think I am?"

"Now calm down, calm down," I said. "He said you could try it for twenty-four hours. Why don't you? You were always crazy for adventure. You've been a small-town shopkeeper too long. All right, you find you don't like it. You tell me the low-down. I write a story about it. I can sell it anywhere. Real inside dope."

"So I should get shot so you can write a story about it?" said Harold. "Besides getting jail for life. Adventure! Hell, you don't know what you're talking about. Those birds would cut your heart out and eat it if something didn't go right."

"Bosh, they're just talking big to try to pull in suckers. All it is is just collecting a dollar or two from some hangers-on around the towns, and turning it in. You've been seeing too many movies. Who do you think they are, Al Capone?"

"I still say you don't know what you're talking about," he said. "This is the numbers racket. It's big and it's tough. I know how many people play it. They take thousands of dollars out of Cape Cod. This is no penny ante with Little Lord Fauntleroy. You're unconscious."

"Well, for heaven's sake, somebody that wears a diamond ring has got a tough hombre like you buffaloed," I said. "He probably wears rubbers and carries an umbrella when it rains. The whole thing's a big bluff. But it would be fun to find out how it works; a real thrill after this dreary drudgery. After all, they aren't going to shoot you the first night."

"I suppose that's true," said Harold. Then, "As a matter of fact, I wouldn't mind seeing how these beggars work it. They're certainly slick."

"And we'd have the twenty-five dollars plus what I get from the story."

"Forget the story," said Harold. "That's out. I don't mind admitting

I wouldn't like to see you shot down by strangers in cold blood—though there have been moments when I've toyed with the notion myself. In fact, I like you. Though, of course, I'm only breaking down like this because death seems imminent. If I live I don't expect you to take advantage of it. But I think I ought to warn you. You'll never get anyone as kind as I was—not with those five children and a furnace to tend."

I laughed. I didn't think he'd be in any real danger. I thought it was all a big joke.

It was seven o'clock when the Ringer and Frenchy showed up.

I scooped the money off the table and handed it to them.

"I'll be with you directly," said Harold. "I've decided to look it over."

"Remember this is yours, Mrs. Pierson," said the Ringer, waving the bills at me, "if he sticks with us."

After he'd gone I felt a little nervous.

"Do you suppose he'll be all right?" I said to Louise. "I never heard of these policy slips. I don't think there's much to it."

"Sure he will," said Louise. "Those men were just fourflushers."

I was glad to see Harold walking up the path, though, at eight the next morning. We rushed out to meet him.

"How was it? What was it like? What did you have to do?" we asked him.

"Give me some breakfast," he said. "You've fixed things right. I ought to have known better than to listen to you."

He wouldn't tell us a thing until he'd eaten breakfast. He let us stew.

Then he began:

The Ringer and he and Frenchy had driven to a tumbledown ducking camp on the shore of Hyannis. The place looked as if it had been going to rack and ruin for twenty years. There was an old broken-down dory halfway across the front step. There was no light at the windows. Frenchy put the Auburn in an old shed and closed the door, while the Ringer knocked on the door of the camp with a peculiar rhythm. The door opened onto what looked like a prosperous business office. There were men sorting slips, making entries in books, and working at calculating machines. There were piles of money lying around.

"Meet the gang," said the Ringer. "Gang meet the new pickup man."

They gave Harold appraising looks and went on with their work. Harold and the Ringer sat down.

"I wanted to bring you here to see how we work," he said. "You'll notice the revolvers on the boys' desks and the rifles and sawed-offs in the corner. That's in case we're interrupted. In fact, I'm afraid we'll be cooped up here most of the night. We've found the gang that's running the numbers now a little unpleasant. We've tipped off the police to them. They may get nasty."

They sat around and talked a couple of hours when there was a knock on the door. Frenchy opened it. A man burst in, dragging another man by the coat collar. He pulled him through the room where everyone was working and kicked open a door at the rear. They both disappeared. Frenchy got up and went after them. In a minute there were screams.

"Sorry you had to hear this," said the Ringer apologetically. "That guy's a holdout. He's been holding back slips and money for a week now. We had to teach him a little lesson."

Harold could hear kicks and then the steady rhythm of a strap interlaced with groans. Then there was silence. Frenchy came back wiping his hands.

"Won't he inform?" said Harold.

"If he does," said the Ringer curtly, "he'll get worse than that."

About two in the morning there was the sound of a truck.

"O.K., boys," said the Ringer. They took bundle after bundle of bills out of a drawer in the desk and great packages of policy slips neatly stacked and loaded them into a carton.

"Perhaps you'd like to see this," said the Ringer to Harold.

Harold watched them load the carton into an armored truck. On the front sat two uniformed men with revolvers in their holsters.

"They have to be in Boston at five sharp," said the Ringer. "At five there's a general accounting."

Just at daylight a man knocked and was admitted. He took a revolver out of his pocket and laid it on the desk.

"Here," he said to Frenchy, "clean this."

"Little trouble?" asked the Ringer.

"Little trouble."

"Well," said the Ringer to Harold. "We'll take a little run up to Falmouth. I've got a man to see up there. Then we'll come down Route 6. I make it a practice not to drive back and forth from the shore in daylight."

They drove to Falmouth and back and he dropped Harold at the house.

"What do you say?" he asked Harold as he got out. "Want to join us?"

"I've got a week's work on the wall to finish first," Harold told him.

"Give my regards to Mrs. Pierson," said the Ringer. "It's a shame for a fine woman like her to be driving that junky Olds. I think I'd join us if I were you. *I would if I wanted to keep healthy.*"

"What did he mean?" I asked weakly.

"What do you think?" said Harold.

I began to take down the curtains.

"Did he give you the twenty-five dollars?" I called.

"Yes," said Harold.

"Get out the book boxes as quick as you can," I said. "The boys are hitchhiking home for their Christmas vacation. They're due tonight. We'll take stock."

After supper everybody threw his money on the table. Rodney was broke, as usual. John was flush from running the laundry at Yale. It all added up to eighty-five dollars. Then I got a hat, some paper, and pencils.

"Everybody write down where he wants to go from here on a piece of paper and throw it into the hat."

The slips all read "New York."

I rushed down to Cap'n Dan Gould's store and did some fast telephoning. I arranged for a "return load" moving man to come and move us for fifty dollars. Then I got hold of Mrs. Armstrong, an old friend, in Scarborough, and told her our troubles. She said she could get us a house for thirty dollars in near-by Sparta.

"We're leaving here tomorrow at the latest," I telephoned Barbara. She dashed over.

"Let's go swimming," said the kids. So they all jumped into bathing suits and went down to the outside beach. Even Louise.

"My God, the temperature is only ten above," said Harold. "Now everybody will be sure we're crazy."

"Leave them alone," I said. "It's a farewell gesture."

The air was cold, they said when they returned, but the water was fine.

The moving men came late the next afternoon. John rode on one load. Rodney rode on the other. An hour later, I turned to Harold. "Thank heaven they're off the Cape," I said. "They're out of danger."

Barbara helped us throw our things into bags. It was just midnight when Harold, Louise, Frankie, our dog Honey, and I piled into the Anna Mae.

"Good-by," said Barbara, the tears raining down her face. "Good-by."

"Good-by," we said.

I turned to Harold.

"Give it all you've got."

The Anna Mae lurched forward. We tore along the deserted Cape Road. As we passed the crossroad to Hyannis, we saw a big convertible waiting at the light.

"I don't think it was yellow," said Frankie. But he wasn't sure. Harold pushed the gas pedal down to the floor. We could see the headlights in our rear window all the way to Barnstable. Then it turned off.

When we crossed the canal, I breathed a sigh of relief. We were safe. I shivered involuntarily. Harold put his hand on my shoulder.

"There isn't any easier way to earn a living than to be kicked around, is there?" I asked.

"Hell, no," said Harold.

MR. X, A FORMER CLERGYMAN

"MR. X, a former clergyman, made $176.89 last week,'" I read aloud to Harold. "What's a clergyman got that you haven't got?"

"He's got God on his side," said Harold.

"'L.G., a former bus driver, made $53.17,'" I went on. "'E.M., a former realtor made $98.80.'"

"I give up. I'll bite. How'd they make it?" asked Harold. "Hurry up and get to the plot. It'll be dark in a minute and you can't see to read by those damn candles."

We'd hit rock bottom—but before that we'd tried everything. When we arrived in Sparta a month before we had thirty-five dollars. Sparta was a slum sister of Scarborough, the English village Mr. Frank A. Vanderlip had planned to replace the shambles surrounding the lime quarry, a stone's throw from Sing Sing Prison. A few sturdy villagers still hung on, but the jungle was slowly closing in. We occupied a renovated 1905 asbestos-shingle job wedged in between an Italian family with seven children and Nick's saloon.

"It's not a very ritzy address," I said to Harold. "But Nick's got Venetian blinds now he's changed his speakeasy into a saloon. We'll never notice it."

We didn't till I instituted the new system of taking cold baths and drying yourself before an open window I'd read about in *Physical Culture*. The article said it would open up vistas. It opened up vistas all right. When Louise and I drew riotous applause the first morning we tried it, we realized Nick was with us late and soon.

"It'll do till we get on our feet," said Harold. "Young Frank Vanderlip's been swell about the rent. We'd have been licked if we'd had to pay in advance."

It looked kind of gloomy the night we arrived because the furniture hadn't come yet and we had to sleep on the floor. But we picked up some wood and made a fire in the fireplace. It was January 1 and pretty cold.

"Happy New Year," said Harold, throwing off the coat covers next morning. "A thousand colors to the rainbow of your happiness in this year of our Lord 1935. Ouch!" he added as he tried to rise.

"I wish we could get some coal," I said. "But I don't think we ought to dip into the thirty-five dollars."

"I'll jump into the Anna Mae and buzz down to the gas company and get the gas and light turned on," said Harold. "That'll make it more cheerful."

Five minutes later he came in with his tail dragging.

"The Anna Mae's stopped short never to go again," he said. "Damn thing froze up solid. The block's cracked."

"Well, get a paper anyway," I said. "I think the best thing is for each one of us to look in the paper and apply for every job there is. Out of the mess somebody'll land something."

In spite of our difficulties, I felt confident. It was fine to get back to civilization. My heart had bounded when we'd arrived in Sparta to find a wreath on the door and a note from the Armstrongs: "Come to our Tom-and-Jerry party." We hadn't, because we had nothing but dirty dungarees to go in. But it was a cheery thought. We were among friends. I always got a thrill out of looking at the help-wanted ads, anyway. There was the possibility that you might run across something novel, romantic, exciting. I had no idea of the depths of the depression; that no help was wanted but a truss fitter or a neat-appearing colored man on a bicycle.

Still I thought I'd better take steps. It might be a while before we got going. I hated to let my sister know how hard up we were. I'd seen her only once since she had visited us at the Cape. She'd taken a beating in the stock market, as everybody else, and for three years she'd been working night and day to give her two daughters bang-up educations plus bang-up coming-out parties. I saw no reason why she should be taxed because I was nit-witted. But I did have a little miniature of Marie Antoinette, surrounded by diamonds, that I thought she might be able to sell for me. It had been a present from my mother. Although I still had the receipted bill from Tiffany's for $485, I'd been unable to raise a cent on it. I put it into a box together with a golden arrow pin, and sent it to my sister, special delivery. Maybe, I wrote, she could find a market.

"On my way back from town I think I'll take a walk through the greenhouses," said Harold.

We were just a step from his uncle's greenhouse range. His uncle had failed two years before, in spite of a million and a half assets. He'd had cash in two banks that closed. The place had been bought in by Goldfarb "My Florist." His uncle at seventy-three was working in what used to be his own store in Tarrytown for a weekly wage of thirty dollars.

Harold came home pretty dejected.

"Goldfarb kept all the old men on. It seemed good to see them," he said. "But I wish I hadn't gone over to Briarcliff and looked at Father's place. It's gone to rack and ruin. Gates just swinging on the hinges."

His father had gone down in 1932 to the tune of $250,000. At seventy-five he was trying desperately to get a little cannery started.

"Our old house in Ossining has been torn down to save taxes," Harold went on. "It made me blue as hell. I kept remembering the Christmas Mother stood upstairs looking out the sewing-room window and Father drove up in a new Garford for a surprise. We all got in and rode to Tarrytown and back without 'anything happening.' That was a miracle in those days."

While he was talking I noticed how gray his hair was getting on the sides. Something in his expression made me realize it.

"I don't think you know how bad things really are around New York," he continued. "Suppose I *couldn't* get a job no matter how hard I tried? Suppose there just aren't any?"

"Oh, bosh," I said. "We've been busted before and we've snapped out of it."

"Don't forget you're forty-five and I'm forty-seven," said Harold. "I was talking to Buck Young, and he says they won't even interview men over forty. They don't want white-haired stenographers. And Louise can't do anything. They won't take anyone with crutches."

"Looks like we're all handicapped," said Louise. "Well, it's nice to have company."

"Take this cocktail shaker over to Nick's and bring back three stiff shots of rye," I said to Louise. "This is getting depressing."

I took a walk myself and came back with some good news.

"The Scarborough School will take Frankie on scholarship," I said. "And I ran across Warden Lawes' daughter Cherry. A trusty drives her to school every day and they'll pick up Frankie and bring him home."

"That'll be nice," said Harold. "Every night Frankie can tell us how the other half is living."

"For heaven's sake," I said. "Just because things don't look so good for the moment, there's no law we have to lie down in the gutter and pull the curbstone over us."

We were interrupted by the arrival of the boys with the furniture.

"Is there anything we can do?" they asked when it was unloaded. They knew there wasn't. They knew the only real tragedy to me would be to have them quit school or college. They could manage, with their scholarships. John said the laundry at Yale was doing so fine he could squeeze out some spending money for Rodney. The dollar or two Rodney made occasionally by washing cars about paid for tooth paste. "I think he'll get a scholarship at Yale, too," said John. "When I was in the office I saw his application. Somebody had written across it, 'Looks like a footballer; recommended for aid.'"

We put up sandwiches, and they started hitchhiking back to school.

"While there's education there's hope," I said to Harold.

"I was kidding about not being able to get anything," said Harold after they went. "I'll go down to Ossining and bring back a pound of hamburg and a ten-thousand-dollar job selling Christmas cards. I'll make you proud of me, darling."

"I'm going to try for this job in a laundry that's advertised," said Louise. "I'm a good ironer. I read where Henry Ford just eats up the physically handicapped. They work longer than anyone else because they don't care about getting home; it's no fun, anyway. I'll put on a long face and act as if I didn't have a friend in the world. They'll probably jump at the chance to exploit me."

I hated to have her go, but if I'd stopped her she would have been heartbroken. She came back an hour later, mad as a hatter.

"They're allergic to crutches," she said disgustedly. "The old fools said if I worked there it would raise their insurance."

Harold had better luck. He'd run across Jake Myers, the junk dealer. Jake was wrecking a building in Peekskill. He remembered a bum refrigerating plant from the Sleepy Hollow Club he'd once sold Harold at a war price.

"It was no good and I knew it," said Jake. "I'll pay you eighteen dollars a week. You always gave me a break when you had it. I'll give you one. I bet that's more than you can say for your swell friends."

"My swell friends are all pitching hamburgs. That is, the ones who didn't jump out windows," said Harold.

"That's where I got it on you," said Jake. "I know there ain't no Santy Claus. When I make money, I hang onto it."

Harold was all pepped up.

"We can eat, anyway," he said, "while I'm looking for something better."

When I came down to get his breakfast at six I found a note from Louise. She'd hocked her cornet and was hitchhiking to New York to look for a typing job. She was a pretty fair typist, owing to the winter evenings on the Cape she'd spent practicing on my old typewriter.

Tears came to my eyes in spite of myself. "Now, don't be upset," said Harold. "You've taught her to be self-reliant, and she is. You wouldn't want her any different."

"If you get something and Louise gets something, we'll have a toehold, anyway," I said. "I think maybe yesterday was the low spot."

While they were gone I got a wire from my sister saying she'd sold the pins for fifty dollars and was mailing a check. I knew she hadn't sold them. But she'd gathered we were strapped.

Louise got home first with no job, but in fine spirits. The police had picked her up in Tarrytown, where she was thumbing, bought her a pack of cigarettes, and picked out a good truck New York bound and placed her in it. The *Inquirer* had taken her picture; Perry Charles, Program Director at WHN, had let her broadcast and given her a ticket to the movies; Jack O'Brien, the old prize fighter, had let her join the fat women exercising on the roof under the sponsorship of the New York *Mirror*.

"I never had such a fine day in my life," said Louise happily. "And I've still got fifty cents of my cornet money left. Only I hate to tell you. I've broken my brace."

A new brace cost fifty dollars.

"Don't worry," I said. "We'll have it."

Just then Harold came limping in and lay down on the sofa. He'd fallen. He was on the roof of the building in Peekskill, paying out rope from a winch, when the rope tangled. When he tried to untangle it, it wound around his leg. He shouted to Jake to hold the winch, but Jake didn't hear him. He was halfway off the roof six stories up when he pulled himself loose and edged back. His leg was black and blue from ankle to thigh and had two deep gashes. The doctor said it would be two weeks before he could walk on it.

I went down town and got a *Times*.

"Wanted, a woman who can write the most brilliant, scintillating fashion copy in New York," ran the big display ad. "Salary $5000 up. Submit samples."

"All I know about fashions is what I see in the cleaners' windows," I said. "But here goes."

I hitched up my dungarees and pulled out my battered type-writer.

"Hi, Sailor!" I began. "Bretons rule the waves."

Two days later I got a telegram.

"Your copy selected from thousands. Be at our office for interview 2:30 tomorrow."

"What'll I wear?" I said. "I can't go to New York in dungarees. And my hair looks like Davy Crockett. I look like those women who scrub office buildings at four o'clock in the morning. I'm afraid some-body'll shove a mop and pail into my hand."

"I'll cut your hair with nail scissors," said Louise, "and you curl it.

Maybe you can rent a coat and hat at the Used Clothing Exchange."

The only coat that fitted me had stripes going around it. There was a cap to match.

"I wish my hair hadn't frizzed," I said to Louise, looking in the glass doubtfully. "I look like a cross between a tiger and a fox terrier."

"Never mind," said Louise comfortingly. "Even if you are fat and you hair's white, your face is young."

When I emerged from the house some big boys were coasting.

"Hi, Grandma!" they called gaily. "How about a date?"

I went right back in again.

"I can't go," I said to Louise, sitting down heavily.

"Now, Ma," said Louise, "buck up. They don't want a model. They want a writer."

"I feel so depressed," I said. "I think it's really because we haven't got a double boiler. I've met practically every disaster known to man head on with eyes front and a smile on my lips, but never without a double boiler."

"Hurry up or you'll lose the train," said Louise. "While you're gone I'll knit you a double boiler."

I started out again but I was shaken.

Going in on the train, I kept thinking, I can't go through with this. I just can't. But everybody's counting on me. I've got to.

The Fifth Avenue office where I was to have the interview turned out to be on the twenty-eighth floor. We shot up like a rocket, and I got out without my stomach.

I was ushered into an orchid-colored room with a chrome desk and two chairs against a background of nothing at all. I sat down, glanced out the window, and hastily glanced back again. I never could stand high places. My knees began shaking.

A high-powered executive upholstered in matching colors glided in and slipped behind the desk. She clasped her hands simply in front of her and looked me up and down.

"Tell me about yourself!" she said suddenly.

Tell me about yourself, I thought, yes by all means tell me about yourself. Well, I've had two husbands and five children. Louise cut my hair with nail scissors. I had a little pink silk dress from Liberty's I used to look fine in when I was ten.

"What fashion experience have you had?" asked the woman finally, gathering she'd hit a dead end.

"Fashion, fashion. 'I have been faithful to thee, Cynara, in my fashion,'" I thought vacuously. Oh, Mary, Mother of God, let me pull myself together and get this job.

The woman took my sample fashion copy out of the drawer and laid it on the desk.

"Did you really write this?"

"I did," I said earnestly. "It seems incredible, doesn't it?"

The woman put the copy back into the drawer and closed it.

"We had in mind somebody younger," she said, speaking loud and slowly and distinctly, as if she were speaking to a foreigner. "I'm afraid I have no more time to give you now. If we decide to interview you further . . ."

I didn't wait for her to finish. I stumbled out of the office and started for home.

When I got off the train, I walked slowly. I thought, I can't go home and tell them. I can't. They'll open the door, all smiles and eagerness. "Did you get the job?" "No." It was too awful. I saw why men took their last cent and went out and got drunk when they got fired or didn't get a job they needed. I wished I could.

Harold heard my step and opened the door.

"Sh," he said, when he saw my face. "If you didn't get the job, don't say so. The boys are home. I told them everything was hunky-dory; our trials were temporary."

I heard roars of laughter from the kitchen.

"The Westchester Gas and Electric turned off the gas and light," shouted Louise gaily. "Just after the boys blew in. It's mid-years already, so they're home for a couple of days. They're going to a party tonight. It's lucky they didn't turn off the electricity before I had time to press their tuxes."

The boys had gone up to a half-burned house on the hill and

brought down a lot of wood. There was an open fire roaring. Louise had made spaghetti and hamburg. When the boys went upstairs to shave with cold water and candlelight, Harold took me aside.

"You're doing fine," he said. "I know how you feel. I feel just the same, only more so. But what the hell! The kids are happy, anyway."

When a colored chauffeur came for the boys at eight and they drove off in their De Pinna tuxes we couldn't help being chirked up. "Pretty regal," said Louise proudly. We ignored the fact that John had paid for his tux by collecting laundry bills and Rodney had won his by matching pennies with Al Bloomingdale, a rich classmate.

"Rodney and John are wonderful!" sighed Frankie. "I wish they were always home."

He worshiped his older brothers and they idolized him. In fact, I had trouble in keeping the children from spoiling Frankie. They seemed to feel that he belonged to *them* rather than to me and Harold.

"It was silly my thinking I could get a five-thousand-dollar job, anyhow," I told Harold and Louise after the boys went back. "The state we're in. I'm going in to the ERA office tomorrow. They always need stenographers."

I'd returned the striped outfit, so I had to wear The Raincoat. I hated it. It smelled like ether. It had originally belonged to Harold, so it hung down around my ankles and you couldn't see my hands at all.

"At any rate, nobody'll know I've got on this old middy blouse and my gray skirt with the hole in the back. Maybe they won't even know I'm inside."

The ERA woman was very cordial.

"We need a competent typist this very minute," she said. "You're a godsend. Take your coat off. I'll give you a test."

"I'll keep it on," I said, "if you don't mind."

"Oh, no, you better take it off," she insisted. "It's warm in here."

"Oh, no," I said, my voice rising shrilly. "Oh, *no!*"

"Well," she said, a little surprised at my vehemence, "I suppose you can keep it on."

She dictated fast but I got it. A couple of times I had to wait. She stopped, and I ripped the paper out. I glanced at it. I couldn't believe my eyes. It looked like this:

In neferthctold peamubettstorefnhaet4ysek

The Raincoat sleeves had caught in some way, and I had been writing one line on top of another. The woman took the paper out of my hand.

She looked from the paper to me and back to the paper.

"Perhaps you better brush up on your typing and come in again," she said kindly. "So many older women find they have not kept up their skills."

"But I can explain it," I said. "Just give me another chance. I'm a wonderful typist. My psychoanalyst said maybe I would have been better off if I hadn't been such a good typist . . ."

"You didn't tell me that you had been under the care of a physician for a nervous disorder," she broke in.

"I didn't. I wasn't. It was years ago," I cried. "Damn this raincoat anyway. I never liked it."

"There, there," said the ERA woman. "You see, you're emotionally upset. Possibly we could arrange for medical advice of some kind. I blame myself for not having looked into your case history."

I cried going down in the elevator. But not while the ERA woman could see me. I was afraid she'd have me in the nut house.

"I'm hexed," I said to Harold when I got home.

"We're all hexed," said Harold. "The cop came about the Anna Mae. He wouldn't allow it to stand on the street any longer. I had to break out our last five dollars to have her hauled away."

For two days we had rice.

Then we began on split-pea soup.

Then we had onion sandwiches for five days.

The sixth day Harold put on his coat and limped out into the hall.

"I'm going down to Ossining," he said.

"Got your glasses?"

I always asked him that.

"They're broken," he said. "I didn't want to tell you. That's why I haven't been up and at 'em in spite of my leg."

He came back an hour later.

"They won't let me on WPA here," he said. "I was born and raised here and lived here for forty years, but we've been away five, so we're transients. I got a food order for eight dollars and thirty-five cents."

Frankie went down with his little red wagon and filled it.

"I got everything you had on the list," said Frankie, "but cigarettes. The man said he isn't allowed to give cigarettes to reliefers. The tax-payers raise hell."

"They do, do they?" I said angrily. "Well, you just watch a re-liefer raise hell! I've sold my soul for eight thirty-five and I'm going to get my money's worth."

I went downtown and came back with the cigarettes and a paper somebody had left in the grocery store.

That's when I saw that Mr. X, a former clergyman, made $176.89. " 'How much money have you laid away in the last five years?' " I read on. " 'What are your prospects for the next five? We want to talk with a man who wants to step out of a rut!' "

"Would they be interested in talking with a man who wants to step out of a canyon?" said Harold.

"It doesn't say," I said, "but they'll show you their books if you're serious-minded and adaptable. What kind of racket do you suppose they've got?"

"Lord knows," said Harold. "But we'll find out."

He left for New York early next morning on the greenhouse truck. Goldfarb had kept his uncle's driver on.

He got back about six that night. I opened the door when I heard his step. Harold removed his hat and bowed low.

"Has Mr. Smathers made an appointment for me?" he asked formally.

"No," I said, wondering.

"He told me he was going to. If you don't mind I'll come in and speak to you about it. I can't understand it."

"What's the matter with you? Have you gone crazy?"

"No," he said, producing an object that he had concealed behind him and pushing in past me. "I'm just practicing." He pointed to the object. "Look, darling, our future!"

"Good grief!" I said. It was a vacuum cleaner. "Selling vacuum cleaners is worse than begging," I said. "I'd rather go out and stand on the corner with a tin cup. You *can't* sell vacuum cleaners. You just *can't*."

"Now don't go up in the air," said Harold. "I saw all those bozos, Mr. ABC and what not. They actually did make $176.89 last week. Those damn things sell like hotcakes. They have a class to teach you. If you follow the directions in the booklet they give you, you can't help selling a vacuum a day even if you don't have leads. Just ring doorbells. Absolutely cold."

After supper, he said, he'd show us. Louise and I were to play hard to get.

"You haven't any money. You never buy anything at the door," said Harold enthusiastically. "You're busy cooking and you don't want to be bothered. You don't like my looks."

We went out into the kitchen. Harold put on his hat and coat and went out with the cleaner and a bag they'd given him. He rang the bell and I answered it.

"Has Mr. Smathers made an appointment for me?" said Harold.

We both laughed so hard we had to take it over. The next time he asked if Mr. Smathers had made an appointment for him I told him no.

"He told me he was going to. If you don't mind, I'll come in and speak to you about it. I can't understand it."

Before I could protest he whisked the vacuum cleaner from around the corner where he'd hidden it. Using it to block with, he followed his interference into the house.

"Have a chair," he said courteously, pulling one forward.

I sat down automatically. He sat down opposite me and put down the bag. He took out a pencil and pad:

"While I'm waiting for Mr. Smathers I might as well get your name and address. We're making a survey of automatic equipment."

"Mrs. Louise Pierson, River Road, Sparta."

"And your husband's name and business address?" he went on,

writing busily. "I wonder if you'd mind telling me your income. It's confidential of course."

"Harold C. Pierson. No business address. Income none."

"That's fine, Mrs. Pierson," he said cordially. "What kind of vacuum have you now? I'd like to see it, please."

"I'm sorry but I'm busy," I said. "I haven't time to get it. It's a National."

"I'll get it for you," he said, jumping up and starting toward the closet door.

I half got up in protest.

He said the directions said to start toward any door and the victim will instinctively rush and get the cleaner herself rather than have you disclose some horror of horrors or break in on the baby's nap.

Harold ran the National around disgustedly. Suddenly he opened his bag. He took out great handfuls of white lint and feathers and began throwing them around. He ran around like an adagio dancer trailing them behind him. In a second the room was a shambles. He took up the National and ran it around, halfheartedly.

"Aha!" he said. "You see your National won't remove this."

I didn't think anything would. I thought we'd have to move out of the house.

He sat down and began taking his vacuum apart as if nothing had happened. He showed me the moth sprayer, the furniture cleaner, and the shampooer. Then he put it together and ran it over one small section of the belinted rug.

"See," he said. "It takes it up perfectly. Now let us open the bag and see what we have."

Lint, feathers, and about half a pound of dirt and sand fell out.

"Why, Mrs. Pierson," he said reprovingly. "You are not giving that beautiful rug of yours the treatment it deserves. Now this is no fault of yours. I could see the moment I entered this home you were a perfect housekeeper. You just didn't know this condition existed."

He handed me the pad and pencil. "If you'll just sign this receipt I'll let you have this vacuum for your National and a deposit of five dollars."

"Is five dollars all I have to pay?" I asked.

"Five dollars, and a few cents a day. Here I have a little bank for you. Just put ten pennies a day in this bank and each month I will come and collect it for you."

"I don't want the vacuum," I said, trying to hand him back the pad and pencil. He ignored them.

"Kindly clean up this room," I said haughtily. "Then *leave* the premises. Or I shall call the police."

Harold fixed me with a stern eye.

"When we get tough babies like you we tell them the infantile-paralysis story," he said. "But I don't know it yet. I'm just a rookie. We aren't allowed to hear the infantile-paralysis story till the second pep talk."

The infantile-paraylsis story! That was the final irony. The whole setup was terrible, just as I'd feared. Anyone could sell one or two vacuums to his friends—if he got a foot in the door before it was slammed in his face. Then he was out and a new sucker was in. It was hopeless. But what could I say to Harold? I knew he knew it. And even the commission on one or two vacuums would help. We were desperate.

He wanted to go out again and try the whole thing over, but I was too exhausted. He vacuumed up the lint and feathers he'd thrown around and looked at the vacuum admiringly.

"It does the trick," he said, "damned if it doesn't."

He said he had to sit up and memorize the nine points when the housewife says no and he ignores it. At the tenth, he tells the infantile-paralysis story. Then he just sits there and talks till the housewife would buy the Washington Monument to get rid of him.

Next morning he set out hopefully. He waved good-by to us and patted the vacuum.

"Our lifesaver!" he cried gaily, skidding down the icy steps and landing flat on his back with the vacuum on top of him. He got up and brushed himself off. "I feel like a complete idiot lugging this bunch of junk," he muttered and trudged sullenly toward Ossining.

He came home that night too tired to eat. He took his shoes off and put his feet in a pan of water.

"By God," he said, "after all the times Doc Wrenn and I've done the sword dance together up at Nikko Inn it makes me pretty G.D. mad to have his wife send out word she won't see me."

It made him so mad he said, he went in the lunch wagon and had a hamburger. And it was a good thing he did. Alf who runs it had a hot tip on Sludgefoot and he plunked down fifty cents he'd won matching pennies. Sludgefoot paid off four to one. He handed me the two dollars. "Don't say I'm not a good provider."

In the afternoon he'd walked three miles out to our friends, the Brewers', but when he got there he didn't even knock on the door. He got to thinking if they'd seen the vacuum from the window and brushed him off he'd belt them in the head with it.

On the way home, he stopped at two houses. One woman shouted out the window to go away. The other one slammed the door in his face when he asked if Mr. Smathers had made an appointment.

"Maybe Mr. X, a former clergyman, wore his clerical garb," I said, "sort of sailing under false collars."

"I'm going over to Nick's," said Harold, "and call up somebody on the telephone. Every time I go in to call up he remembers the good old days when I threw money around like a drunken sailor and he was a bootlegger and this damn country was fit for white men to live in. Then he breaks out a shot of rye. I'll call some phony number so I'll get back the nickel."

The next day he came home furious. Three people he'd known for years refused to let him cross their thresholds. The fourth offered him her husband's old overcoat.

Two days later he almost sold a vacuum but he felt so badly for the woman after he'd high-pressured her into it he let her off. They were poor as church mice and it was too pitiful.

Then came a terrible week when he didn't even speak when he got home.

Every morning when he started out, his shoulders drooped lower and lower.

Suddenly his luck changed. He brought home ten dollars, eighteen, eleven. He was allowed to keep whatever sum the customer paid down when he sold a vacuum. Now he started out with eyes bright and head erect. He could hardly wait to finish breakfast.

The day he came home with twenty-five dollars I told Louise we'd go downtown. She could get some bed shoes and I'd buy a double boiler.

We were on our way home when Louise cried, "Look!"

There, leaning lonesome and neglected against the side of Tubby's poolroom, was the vacuum cleaner! I went over to the poolroom window. It was partly open. Harold was putting up his cue and some men were counting out money. "Nineteen dollars," said one, handing it to Harold. "That makes ninety-three dollars you've taken away from us this week."

"Don't give it a thought. It's all in a good cause," said Harold.

We hurried home and about fifteen minutes later Harold blew in.

"Has Mr. Smathers made an appointment for me?" he called cheerily as he burst into the kitchen.

"Louise and I were downtown," I said, fixing him with a cold eye. "Mr. Smathers has come and gone."

"Well, what the hell. I've made enough to carry us till I land something decent," said Harold. "We don't have to take any more charity."

"Do you honestly suppose Mr. X, the former clergyman, made $176.89?" I asked.

"Not unless he had something on the ball besides a prayer," said Harold.

DANCE OF THE
TRANSCONTINENTAL TRUCKS

*I*T WAS Louise and I who insisted on moving to New York City when Harold got his job as WPA Supervisor in the Park Department.

"If we're in New York, and I still can't get a job," said Louise, "I can take courses at night school."

"If we got an apartment in Greenwich Village, Frank could go to the Little Red School House," I said. Frankie had a terrific I.Q. The Little Red School House was experimental. I thought he'd find it stimulating.

Harold said it was no good living in New York unless you had a roll that would choke a horse. But when he saw the third-floor apartment on Hudson Street I picked out, he weakened.

"It's got plenty of room," I said. "The boys will be at Yale winters, and working summers. The little time they're home they can sleep on the couch. Of course it will need a little touching up here and there," I added. "That mustard-colored cupboard would give me the willies."

"Here we go round the mulberry bush," said Harold.

A week later we were settled. I was just painting the cupboard when Mrs. Froelich, our landlady, walked in.

"It looks good," said Mrs. Froelich admiringly.

"It looks better than it *did*," I said modestly.

"The last tenant, he paints it that fierce color," said Mrs. Froelich. "But he don't care what he does. He says he's an artist. All the time crates of pictures in the hall making fire hazards. He is *some* artist, that Thomas Benton!"

"Yes, indeed, some artist," I agreed absently. "Who? *Who?* My God!"

The brush dropped from my lifeless hand.

"I wondered where my predecessor got the idea of using souped-up chrome yellow for the background," I said to Louise. "It was ye olde wheatiefields of Minnesota, of course. I think my idea of crossing Canton blue with Red Tower spode is more stimulating. As we say in Greenwich Village, I feel Benton only gives us a surface record while I have made an organic statement."

"It's getting late," said Louise. "We better get going if we don't want to miss John."

John had asked us to drive down and meet the boat coming from West Island, a sandspit on Long Island Sound. He'd been over there tutoring some boys in sailing.

"He'll probably have a good sneer at the Stutz," I told Louise. "He'll accuse us of exhibitionism."

We got the Stutz because Harold was on WPA.

"Everybody on WPA but me has got a car," said Harold plaintively. "The men think I must have a screw loose. They won't take my orders."

The Stutz was "Today's Special" on the Greenwich Street used-car lot. It stood on a little platform with spotlights shining on it. The sign said "Take Me Home for $250." It had an aluminum hood and looked as if it had belonged to the Great Gatsby. As far as we were concerned, it was love at first sight. We tried to beat the used-car man down but we couldn't. He said it was a giveaway at $250. It cost $5000 when it was new; it was made to order for Vincent Astor. Vincent must have driven hell out of it, because the timing was shot and the top was gone when we got it. But it had front and rear windshields with wind protectors, though they were shattered. "The Rockefeller or Vanderbilt gang," said Louise, "must have shot at him." The upholstery was real Russian leather. It smelled so luxurious that every time the family got in the car they paused briefly to stoop and sniff at it.

"John will probably have kittens when he sees it," said Louise. "He'll really wish he owned it but he'll tell us we should have bought a Ford. He's gotten tight as a tick since he's taken up associating with the four hundred."

"He staked you to that Senior Lifesaving Swimming Course you wanted with the money he got for his last blood transfusion," I said. "Why should you care if he enjoys playing around with the filthy rich?"

"Because the filthy rich are usually so deadly dull," said Louise.

"I'm afraid they'll drag him down mentally. But John seems to get a kick out of them. He ought to write an article on 'How I Worked My Way Through the Ritz on Blood Donations.'"

I dropped her off at the movies at Bayshore. She said she didn't feel up to hearing John belly-ache.

I found John with a huge woman in an ulster and a yachting cap. She had straight white hair flying out from under the cap in all directions. She was carrying a basket with two cats in it. With her was an Indian who was holding a monkey who was holding what was left of a banana.

"Who are your friends?" I asked John gaily.

"Sh," he said. "They're wonderful people. I told them you'd drive them to New York."

"How am I going to accommodate that underslung group of undesirable aliens?" I said. "This is no Greyhound Bus."

But John said there was plenty of room. They piled in.

We picked up Louise at Bayshore. She came out of the theater whimpering like a dog because in the movie somebody shot Victor McLaglen.

"You might warn your friends," I said to John, "that when they hear a sound like machine guns firing, the Stutz has run out of oil. I carry four or five gallon cans in the trunk compartment. We have to stop and feed them into its maw at stated intervals."

"Oh, they think the Stutz is wonderful," said John. "It's just their type."

At the first red light the monkey threw the banana skin in the face of the driver of the car next to us. The driver threatened to get out and kill the monkey. The Indian sprang from the Stutz without even opening the door. We thought there was going to be a tomahawking. Quite a crowd collected.

"I'm the swarthy type," said Louise. "It's too bad we haven't got any baskets to sell. But if John will whistle something catchy I'll get out and pass the hat."

John told the driver to lay off the Indian because he wasn't a citizen. His tribe had never signed a treaty with Uncle Sam. This news proved so diverting that we were able to hustle everybody back into the Stutz and escape.

"We were afraid you might not approve of the Stutz," I said to John, as we drove along, mopping our brows. "It's a little conspicuous."

"I think it's a wonderful car, Ma," said John. "I do, really."

I told him I was glad he liked it, because when I went over to the Henningers' party and offered to drive Peg Shea home, she said, 'What in? That old silver number?' She told everybody afterwards that when she tried to get in the front, it was knee-deep in cigarette butts. She didn't dare light a match for fear of starting a forest fire. She said I drove like Jehu, on the left-hand side of the road all the way, screaming imprecations at fleeing pedestrians.

"I drove on the left because I need glasses," I said to John. "I came home from the oculist and told the family I had only thirty-three per cent eyesight and nobody even looked up from his reading. Now you ask me what the oculist said, and I'll say it isn't important and I don't really mind being blind because what difference does it make what happens to poor old Mother. At least I'll feel somebody's interested."

"I'm interested," said John. "I really am, Ma."

I should have known there was a catch to it.

"I was wondering," he said a moment later, "if, now you're settled in the new apartment, you'd have Ellen to dinner."

"I hope you won't think I'm being unfeeling if I don't remember which one Ellen is," I said. "You and Rodney have had so many girls I get a little hazy. Is she the one whose father commutes in a bomber, or the one who bet she'd come out of Vassar still pure?"

"She won the bet," said John. "I don't want you to get Ellen wrong. She's very conventional."

"That'll be a nice change from the last one you brought home," I said, "who practically threw a pack of cigarettes I offered her in my face because they weren't made by union labor."

"Ellen's the serious type," said John. "She's interested in remedial reading."

"She sounds terrible to me," I said, "unless she's awfully good-looking. I have a feeling she won't take to Greenwich Village. Why don't you tell her we all went down on the *Morro Castle* and you're an orphan? Take her to dinner at Schrafft's, and spend the evening at the Aquarium."

We stopped to let out the old woman, the Indian, the cats, and the monkey. They disappeared into the Fifty-ninth Street subway.

"How can you be on Mrs. Cutting's list and pick up a crew like that?" I said to John. "You ought to do something for that schizophrenia."

"I know Ellen will love the apartment," said John. "And I've told her all about Greenwich Village. It's just that she comes from Newton, her mother belongs to the Browning Club, and her brother's a Boy Scout leader. I've bragged so much about you all to her, see if you can't sort of pull the family together."

At first Louise said she couldn't take it; that the courses in trigonometry and Spanish she was taking at the Textile High School had lowered her resistance.

"Why do you always have to take an attitude toward things?" said Harold. "Why not take things as they come? Enjoy yourself. You're lucky Rodney isn't here to knock her teeth out. That's something." Rodney was spending his summer vacation behind the fountain at a Howard Johnson stand.

I told Louise that Ellen couldn't be any worse than the one Rodney brought home, the one who was taking the bride's course that taught you what to put with orchids so your dinner guests wouldn't go home and positively *hoot*.

"Don't forget you had to go to bed after we had the one who didn't want to merge her identity, and wouldn't help with the dishes," said Louise. "The one who was simply mad about those huge dizzy places that simply drip crystal chandeliers!"

"There's no use grousing, we've got to have her," I said. "We'll have roast lamb, mashed potatoes, peas, currant jelly, and rice pudding. God knows, that's banal enough. Harold regards it as a dinner fit for pigs, but it's certainly the acme of conventionality."

The day, which turned out to be the hottest day that ever dawned, started off badly. Louise in a burst of energy tried to wash the antique mirror.

"What'll we do now?" asked Louise anxiously, as I swept up the pieces. We'd run short of the imported Dickens paper with which we'd unwittingly camouflaged some of Thomas Benton, so we hadn't papered back of pictures, mirrors, or the secretary. It was the deuce of a paper to put on, anyway; while Harold was papering, one of his foremen had showed up to ask a question. "Get out of my way, you fat old fool," Harold had said, and the foreman had been all ready to turn in his time till he realized Harold was speaking to Mr. Pickwick.

All we had now to cover the bare spot back of the antique mirror was an old map of Cape Cod. It wasn't the same shape as the mirror, so it looked pretty funny.

"Just because the apartment looks funny," I said to Louise, "I don't have to. I'm going over and get a permanent."

It took longer than I had expected. I nearly went crazy under the drier, wondering if Louise had remembered to put the lamb in. I didn't wait for the hairdresser to comb my hair out. I said I'd comb it out at home. But when I combed it out it frizzed.

"I don't know whether I look more like Harpo Marx," I told Louise, "or a Circassian. I'm going down to the five-and-ten and get a bandana."

"Get gold earrings too," said Louise, "and a pack of cards. We'll tell her fortune."

Just before it was time for Ellen and John to arrive, I gave Frank and Louise a good bat and said for heaven's sake, this means a lot to John, everybody try to be decent and not ask Harold to do the one-armed flute player.

"She's never seen Greenwich Village before," I said to Frank, "and John's told her it's romantic. Don't tell her how you went up to see the little dead boy in the apartment house next door, or how you can't go out because the Hudson Street gang beats you with flour sacks. And if the patrol wagon comes for the drunk across the street, don't rush to the window."

I never thought to caution him not to talk about his Communist friend Dicky, because I knew he'd been mad at Dicky since Dicky had sneered at Louise because her picture had appeared in that capitalist paper, the New York *Mirror*. "But they ran her picture because she broadcast to help the Infantile Paralysis Campaign," Frank had protested. "That's a worthy cause." Dicky said that didn't make any difference. Besides, his mother was disgusted because I let Frank pour lead soldiers. "War," said Dicky, "is wrong." I told Frank to tell Dicky's mother she was old hat. I'd abandoned my silly prejudice against parades.

Frank and Louise said they'd talk about the weather, would that be all right?

"Sh," I said. "Here she comes."

Ellen, a surprisingly pretty girl, was panting when she got up the three flights.

"You ought to do something about your wind," said Frankie anxiously. "You're pooped."

"There's one thing about those stairs," said Louise, "you can hear people puffing a mile off. It gives you a head start on bill collectors."

John glared at us.

"Do sit down," I said to Ellen, pinching Louise and Frankie as I went by. But Ellen was walking around looking at the furniture. I hadn't seen anybody like Ellen since I had left Boston. Her hair had obviously been given a hundred strokes. Possibly one hundred and one for good measure. Even her severe dress of all wool a yard wide could not conceal the fact that nature had graciously provided her with curves. There was a distinctly stony look in her long-lashed gray eyes. "God pity the poor sailors on a night like this," I thought vacuously.

"This old secretary is definitely good," said Ellen suddenly.

"My great-great-grandmother thought so," I said, "or she'd probably have chopped it up for kindling." (After all, I too came from New England.)

"Is this *real* Lowestoft?" she asked, stopping to look at the plates on the mantel.

"We could break one and see," I suggested cordially. "You can always tell real Lowestoft by the texture."

I'd cleaned all the silver and I was pretty tired. I was glad to hear Harold's step on the stairs.

"Dinner's all ready," I said, rising.

Harold said hold everything, he had to shave.

"We'd have had cocktails," said Frank brightly when we finally sat down, "but Ma said to Pa, 'You know how the Piersons are. One drink and they want to climb telegraph poles. Now you're on WPA, the least you can do is——' "

"Tell me about your work with remedial reading," I broke in hastily. "It sounds fascinating."

But Ellen was taken with Frank. She kept asking him questions. I kept kicking him under the table to keep quiet.

"What little boys do you play with?" asked Ellen.

"I play with Dicky that lives across the street," said Frank. "That isn't Dicky's father that lives with them. His father got a divorce and his mother's on a music project. She expects her pink slip any day now. She promised Dicky not to get married again without asking him. The man that's living with them now used to train polo ponies in the Argentine. Dicky says he's a swell guy. He makes wonderful lamp shades and helps with the dishes. Dicky says he's told his mother to go ahead and marry him but she won't. He doesn't know what's the matter with her."

"Won't you have some more lamb?" I asked eagerly. But she wouldn't. Harold said he hated roast lamb, as I knew he would. It was fit only for pigs. He didn't blame her.

Then she saw the cupboard I'd left unfinished.

"What an amazing color scheme!" she said. "But amazing. One half seems to have been done by one person and the other half by another."

"It's the bourgeois-capitalist school of thought," I said, "versus the dunghills-of-Nebraska conception." I could see everything was off, anyway.

"Have you been working on any radio scripts lately, Ma?" said John, rallying bravely.

I told him I'd been working on the Deerfield massacre. I'd been reading Parkman and I realized what wonderful sound effects it would make as the Indians inched over the snow crust in the dark creeping up on the unsuspecting villagers. Just like leaves rustling.

Frank got up from the table and lay down on his stomach to show us. He crawled forward, hissing between clenched teeth and brandishing the bread knife. Ellen said it gave her the shivers.

"Do you suppose the women the Indians kidnaped and took to Canada really wanted to be rescued?" I asked John.

"Of course they did," said John.

"What do you mean *of course*," I said. "It's pretty funny the husbands had to foot it to New York to see the authorities and then up to Canada *twice* before they could get their wives to come home with them. Maybe the wives liked it better with the Indians. Maybe they found Deerfield depressing."

John and I got into a hot argument about it.

I looked at Harold appealingly. I hoped he'd stop me. I couldn't stop myself. It was a subject upon which I had felt strongly for years. But Harold always enjoyed seeing me frustrated. He just smiled.

I got so exhausted arguing with John that when we served the after-dinner coffee I kept drinking cup after cup. We passed the cup up the line to Harold, who was manning the coffeepot, and back to me as if we were fire fighters.

"Look out the window," said John to Ellen as we rose from the table. "That cobble-lined street with the dim light at the corner. Those funny old brick houses crisscrossed with the black fire escapes. Doesn't it look just like a stage set?"

"What are those children doing with that hydrant?" said Ellen. "Isn't it late for them to be up?"

Frank looked out. "They're trying to turn it on. We've got the only wrench in the block. Come on, John."

John ran into the bedroom to get his bathing shorts.

"We won't be but a minute," he said to Ellen. "Keep looking. We'll show you an old Village custom."

He turned to Frank. "Put on your shorts. Skin over to Washington market and get a barrel."

John ran across the street and turned on the hydrant. A stream of water gushed out. Frank came tearing back with the barrel. They threw it over the hydrant. It made a magic waterfall. Instantly, little figures sprang up from the gutters and areaways and circled it dancing. Big twelve-wheel transcontinental trucks rumbling along the cobbled street slowed up and stopped. Tiny lights flared up where the truck drivers lighted cigarettes in their cupped hands. Louise turned on the radio. Paul Whiteman's band blared out the *Rhapsody in Blue*. We set the radio on the window sill and turned it up loud. John and Frank started dancing around the waterfall hand in hand. The others joined them and made a big circle. A cop came up swinging his club, watched them for a moment, and took off his coat. Then he broke into the circle and danced with them. The shadows of the dancers bobbed and weaved on the old brick block. "Da da, da da?" The last plaintive notes of the clarinet were drowned out by the wailing sound of a siren.

"Cheese it. Minions of the law summoned by the irate taxpayers!" shouted Frank. They grabbed the barrel and turned off the hydrant. The figures melted back into alleys and areaways. The trucks rumbled on again.

John and Frank sprang up the stairs three at a time.

"Wasn't it marvelous, Ellen?" said John, his eyes shining, little pools of water forming on the rug beside him. "Wasn't it epic? It was Manhattan. It was Greenwich Village at its Greenwichest."

Frank triumphantly waved a wet arm in Ellen's face. "It was the Dance of the Transcontinental Trucks!"

Ellen flicked a drop of water off her cheek, and glanced down at her wrist watch.

"It's early, but I think I'll really have to be going," she said. "I *ought* to get back to Boston tonight."

John dressed and drove her to the station.

"What did she say?" we asked when he got back.

"She said we were nice," said John, picking up a dish towel and starting to wipe the dishes, "but definitely crazy. She said she didn't know Greenwich Village was the slums."

"Don't you dare to ever bring her here again," called Frankie from his bed. "She's mean. I hate her."

"Don't worry," said John. "I won't. In fact, phooey on her. I'm off women."

"Till when?" I asked.

"Till next Tuesday, to be exact," said John, flipping the dish towel over his shoulder, and starting to put away the dishes. "Next Tuesday, I've got a date with a babe from Park Avenue who has eyes like stars, teeth like pearls, and her initials in gold on a whole vintage of champagne."

CREAM OF LETTUCE, A USELESS
SORT OF SOUP

KNOCK, knock," said Harold, throwing his dinner bucket on the couch and scaling his hat onto the lamp.

"Who's there?"

"Wolf."

"Wolf who?"

"Wolferheavensake if I didn't get my pink slip from the Park Department today," said Harold gaily. "WPA rolls slashed and all that sort of bally rot. Upswing has begun."

"This is where we came in," I said gloomily.

"Now keep your shirt on, I'll get something. Just one of our periodical bumps," said Harold. Besides, he had a dandy lead. Somebody in the Park Department had told him that the Wallaces who owned the *Reader's Digest* had just built a big estate in Mount Kisco. "They want a superintendent," said Harold. "I've got a date with the man who sort of manages their affairs."

"Are you sure you'd like being a superintendent?" I asked doubtfully. "Isn't it a sort of superservant?"

Harold said he didn't care what it was. He needed a job. Here was one he could handle. He was going to get it.

"And I'm going to quit crawling on my belly," said Harold. "That doesn't get you anywhere. I'm going down to Barney's Seventh Avenue and Seventeenth Street and get a suit. I'm going all dressed up to the nines. I'm not going to hem and haw and say 'Please, mister, give me a nickel for a cup of coffee.' I'm going to tell them who I am."

He looked great when he started off. We'd cooked a big steak and fed him up like a lion.

"It's 'Pike's Peak or bust!'" he said as he departed.

It was bust. He had burst in upon the affairs manager in all his glory, and delivered the commercial in stomach tones. Before he could finish, the affairs manager interrupted him.

"I'm sorry we got you way out here for nothing," he said apologetically. "This job would just be chicken feed to a man like you. It pays only six thousand dollars and a house. If you took it, we wouldn't have you five minutes before somebody snatched you away from us with an offer commensurate with your abilities and experience—a really important position."

Harold argued and protested. But it was no use. The man liked him so much, however, he rode from Mount Kisco into New York with him and let Harold buy him two Scotches at the Commodore bar. Harold took two nickels and three pennies out his pocket and threw them on the table.

"Our total resources," he announced.

The job he got tossing hamburgers nights in a lunch wagon lasted only one night. Too slow, the boss said. Truck-driver trade didn't have no time to wait for no Oscar the Waldorf touches like parsley and onion strips. In-again, out-again, away-again Finnegan. That was their motto.

They wouldn't let him be an aluminum salesman because he failed in his test to cook four vegetables at once in a pressure cooker while getting the cowering housewife's Jane Doe on the dotted line. He kept saying he could do better if they would only let him try again. It was the spinach that licked him.

When the Supreme Finance Corporation repossessed the Stutz I felt it was up to me to get a position.

I'd hesitated, because now that Louise was at Bellevue Hospital having both legs broken and reset, there was nobody to keep house. The boys were away at Yale, of course. But there were Frank and Harold.

Louise had made her arrangements without consulting me. She'd gone over to Bellevue to see about learning to be an X-ray technician. She'd come home with the news that she'd signed up to have both legs broken and reset to fix her knock-knees. "But you were always knock-kneed," I protested. She said then it was time she wasn't. She confided to me later that the real reason she'd done it was that she'd got stuck on the intern who interviewed her, Dr. Nickerson. I told her I wished she'd said so. I could have worked out some easier way for her to get to know him than to spend six months with both legs in casts. To me, Bellevue was very depressing. But it wasn't to Louise. She zipped around in her wheel chair as if she were Queen Victoria. Down to the morgue, pulling out drawers to see what gunmen had been brought in; out on the dock and onto the Astors' yacht; up the street and into the Catholic church in casts and pajamas; then down the block to see the man who did cheap tattooing.

"I just wheel myself into the elevator and say 'Down,'" said Louise. "The place is so big they don't know what the dickens they're doing. Besides, I have to pass the time somehow. Dr. Nickerson just regards me as female—unusually robust."

"Even if Louise isn't here I guess you better see what you can do," said Harold. "I don't seem to be having much luck, and the money we got for the Governor Winthrop desk and the secretary is getting low. Don't worry. Frank and I can eat downstairs at Schiller's bakery."

Barbara, who came up from the Cape for a few days' visit, urged me to go ahead. She thought they'd make out.

My first two attempts to land a job through the classified section of *The New York Times* were a little discouraging. I escaped from the Spanish playwright, who lived three flights up and wanted someone to collaborate with him, by means of the fire escape. But I almost had to call in the police to spring me from the toils of the ethical dentist.

"We never did find out what he wanted, did we?" remarked Harold pensively.

I let it go at that. There was nothing to be gained, I felt, by pursuing it further.

I was almost ready to give up when I saw the ad for a woman "40 to 45, manage bar grill large midtown hotel salary $25." The fact that it didn't say "bust 34, waist 26, hips 34, will. to travel enc. photo non returnable" revived my courage. True, my management of our own bar and grill, on Cape Cod, had resulted in our losing or working away our entire capital of $12,000. But $12,000 would probably be only a drop in the bucket to a large midtown hotel.

My letter of application, which hinted modestly that I combined all the better features of Ralph Hitz and the Ramos brothers (of fizz fame), brought an enthusiastic demand for an interview. I figured the job was practically in the bag, if I kept my courage up and my trap buttoned.

When I crossed the marble threshold of the large midtown hotel I thought I had stumbled mistakenly into the Grand Central Station. Way over in the east corner where the train was supposed to leave for Peekskill a little band of uniformed bellboys was marching smartly around for inspection. I crept up to a gorgeous creature clad in spotless white behind the desk and asked him where the grill was.

The grill was not so imposing. I thought for a moment it must be the help's dining room. However, when my eyes got used to the dim light I was able to make out a soda fountain across one side and a tiny bar in one corner. The chairs and tables looked as if they'd been built by the bellboys in spare moments. There was a steady roar which I finally identified as the "air conditioner." The grill was evidently a stepsister of the hotel proper. I was a little disappointed, but it gave me courage for my interview with Mr. Cameron, the manager. If I couldn't manage this gloomy little eatery, I couldn't manage anything.

I had no sooner stepped into Mr. Cameron's office than I was hired. Mr. Cameron, a red-faced, white-haired man with gold-rimmed spectacles, looked at me searchingly.

"You look honest," he said. "I'll take you."

Most of the other applicants, I gathered, were either bent double with arthritis or no spik English. Gad damn it, said Mr. Cameron, he liked New Englanders. Born in Maine himself. And proud of it.

"Just one other thing," said Mr. Cameron. "I can't see your hair under that hat you're wearing. What color is it?"

"It's white," I said, "nor grew it white all in one night as men's are grown."

"You don't say!" said Mr. Cameron, thrown completely off base by this gratuitous bit of information. "Well, damned if I don't think a woman looks better with her hair white than she does with all this dyed stuff. I wouldn't take you for a day over forty if I hadn't read your application."

However, the subversive little crew of twenty-four which manned the bar and grill, where I went to have lunch with Mrs. Dietz, the head housekeeper, at Mr. Cameron's suggestion, apparently did not share his enthusiasm.

"Where did they dig up that old battle-ax?" a waitress asked the bartender, nodding in my direction.

"Probably some old dame who wanted to get in under the wire with old-age assistance," the bartender answered.

"The chicken livers are very nice today," suggested Mrs. Dietz hastily. "I'm sure you'll enjoy them."

The chicken livers, which weren't very nice, were followed by a little meeting in the steward's office. The steward, a short, fat man almost as broad as he was long, and also a New Englander, had summoned the grill help to give the new manager the once-over and pledge their allegiance.

"Now, Mrs. Pierson is no pushover like that Miss Burks from Cornell you ganged up on," said the steward warningly. "You better watch your step or you'll land in the gutter right on your fannies."

After a few ferocious scowls to give weight to his words, the steward asked me if I would like to say anything, but I said no. All I could think of to say was, "Hello, Mom, it was a great fight and the best man won."

"You'll have to look out for Artie," said the steward after they'd gone. "He's working his way through Columbia. He's a fool Red like all those college fellers."

Next morning I reported in fear and trembling. Mildred, the blonde waitress, took me in hand.

"You're supposed to go downstairs and look in the grill icebox and see what's left," she said. "Then you and Ella, the head cook, make up the menu. You have to get it to Alf, the hotel printer, by ten or he raises hell. Any stuff you need that you haven't got, you requisition from the hotel kitchen. They'll give you all the rotten lettuce and meat that's gone by, and charge you a war price for it."

She stopped to wait on a customer.

"I wouldn't order the bacon this morning, Mrs. Blitzstein," she said cordially. "It's terrible."

She explained that all the people who had big expensive apartments in the hotel ate in the grill to save money. As the steward's job depended on cutting down the $30,000 a year the hotel dining room was losing, this made him furious. The grill was really a thorn in his side. "He'll do anything he can to knife you," said Mildred firmly.

"I feel we ought to be loyal to the hotel management," I said with dignity.

"You'll get a whole lot further," said Mildred, "if you side with the customers."

I found the kitchen was equipped with an old warped coal stove heated by an oil burner. The icebox was one discarded from the hotel kitchen.

"It leaks," said Ella, the cook. "Look out for that puddle of water. There's no way to drain it. When the Health Department Inspector comes around you'll have to slip him five dollars."

The grill kitchen was connected with the hotel by a long dark underground passage. Supplies moved through this on a little wagon with wheels. This wagon was drawn by a boy named Griswold. Griswold's day ended, unfortunately, about two hours before we served dinner.

I was gliding around seating people about seven o'clock that night when I got an SOS from Ella. We'd run out of broilers. Ella and Annie, her assistant, were up to their ears in orders. I shot through the passage like a greyhound to the hotel kitchen. There I came up against a bottleneck named Marie. Marie, a striking peroxide blonde with a twenty-four-inch waist, forty-two inch bust, and seven charm bracelets, sat on a high stool guarding the narrow entrance to the kitchen. Everybody and everything which passed in or out of the kitchen had to be checked by Marie. She was a stickler for strict order of precedence. I had to wait while five waiters had their trays checked.

"You sneaking froggy, trying to steal an order of Melba," said Marie to the last waiter. As he handed her his check she bit him on the wrist.

"Why, I oughta kill you!" she said, adding the Melba to his check.

The telephone rang. "Lord Duveen?" said Marie in dulcet tones. "Good evening, Lord Duveen. Yes, I'm well, thank you. And you? Dinner in your room. Yes. May I suggest a *filet mignon* with sauce béarnaise; potatoes au gratin, and asparagus hollandaise?" Marie put her hand over the mouthpiece. "Be with you in a sec when this old bastard gets through drooling." In a moment she hung up. "What can I do for you, Countess?" she said brightly.

She O.K.'d my requisition.

"I don't give broilers," said the butcher, waving a huge razor-sharp cleaver. "We got no customers in the hotel dining room where we serve food, and not garbage, like you do. If we got none, you bet you got none. Why you want with these broilers? You sell stuff on the side?"

The hotel kitchen employees were all grill haters and ardent dining-room fans. I had to threaten to push him into the icebox and lock him in before he could be persuaded to part with the five broilers. I raced back, through the long dark passage, dumped them into Ella's outstretched arms, assumed a false and wooden smile, and went back to my hostessing.

I found running out of things was an old grill custom. We were not allowed to requisition a snip more than the steward figured we needed. Invariably during dinner we ran short of half a dozen items.

All this was very tiring and sometimes led to my being a little gruff with the customers. When some woman said she thought eighty-five cents was highway robbery for a little mess of Hungarian goulash made out of horse meat and wallpaper paste, and she could get fresh lobster at Schrafft's for $1.25, I was apt to give her the impression that the best thing she could do was beat it down to Schrafft's and get her old lobster. And it would be too soon for me if I ever saw her again.

The employees, although proud of my independent and dauntless spirit, felt I was playing the wrong horse.

"Why don't you tell the customer you know it's horse meat," said

Artie, the Red, who ran the fountain, "but you have to work here to support your old mother? She'll give you a dollar tip and think you're wonderful."

"I don't think that's right," I said. "And I've told you children to stop it. I think we all ought to be loyal."

"Loyal, hell," said Artie. "Who wants to be loyal to a place that employs spotters?"

A spotter was a spy paid by the insurance company that owned the hotel—in 1935 all hotels seemed to be owned by insurance companies —to be more insulting to the help than the customers were. He then reported back to the owners the help's reactions. I felt I could spot a spotter instantly. Nobody could be half as insulting as a regular customer. After one of these brushes I would just retire to my office behind the bar and discuss the depravity of human nature with Ed, the bartender.

Ed knew all there was to know about depravity. He had made a fortune trading on it—running dog tracks and showing illegal fight pictures in Texas after submitting public officials to a good stiff bribing. Depravity had also been his undoing. In his work he had run across a religious fanatic who would, he figured, if properly promoted, rival Aimee McPherson. But she had abandoned gospel spreading in favor of running off with a man with a wife and two children just after Ed had sunk a fortune in her. Old, broke, and thoroughly disgusted with human nature in general, he had been forced into the mean, low-down position of bartending. Clouds of smoke issuing from my little closet-office would indicate that Ed and I were having a bull session on the low estate of the world in general.

This often gave nervous customers the impression that the place was on fire and annoyed Mr. Cameron, the manager. Smoking was not "good hotel practice."

Nor was allowing the bus boy to carry Mr. Drake's dinner into his office behind the hotel desk "good hotel practice." Mr. Drake was assistant manager. I explained to Mr. Cameron that I sent Mr. Drake's dinner in to him so he could lay his teeth, which were new and hurt him, on the table and eat comfortably. (If Mr. Drake had followed my directions and put the dirty dishes in the safe and closed the door, Mr. Cameron would never have found out about it.)

"You've done a pretty good job so far," said Mr. Cameron. "But we can't let comfort interfere with business. Drake's on duty, and his teeth aren't your problem. And instead of spending your time smoking, I'd like to see you and Ed sell more liquor."

Ed and I didn't want to sell more liquor. Ed considered the prices charged exorbitant, and felt he had suffered enough disgrace already without gypping the public. I didn't want to because one man whom I had urged on to the consumption of seven Daiquiris—thirty-five cents, Tuesday's special—bit me on the ear while pretending to whisper to me. And the coaches of a football team who were staying at the hotel failed to show up at Baker Field at all under the delusion, after eight Martinis, that their team was playing Fordham. Besides, if customers stayed at the bar too long, their wives would telephone me.

"Have you seen anything of Mr. Lapham? This is Mrs. Lapham speaking."

The bar flies, not knowing who was wanted, but fearing the worst, would immediately begin signaling—an outward, downward-pushing motion of the arm and hand, meaning, "You haven't seen me."

"I haven't seen Mr. Lapham but if I see him I'll tell him you want him," I would reply weakly.

It troubled me. I could see Mrs. Lapham snapping the burners on and off under the double boiler, when she could tear her nose loose from the window.

"Where's Pa?" I could hear the children asking.

"Down at the office," Mrs. Lapham would reply, adding that, since this man Roosevelt had got in with his ideas about feeding the poor, the bottom had been shot out of Pa's kippered-herring business. Which didn't for a minute fool the children. Sometimes this gruesome picture would seem so real to me that instead of propping Mr. Lapham up against the bar and shoving another Horse's Neck down him, as duty demanded, I would call a taxi and Mr. Lapham would find himself zipping home at my expense before he could say Jack Robinson.

Naturally this was very distressing to Mr. Cameron. "Bad business," was the way he put it.

Mr. Cameron also expressed himself as annoyed that I could not get the countermen to clear the dirty dishes off the counter faster and onto the dumbwaiter. The little dumbwaiter, which worked on a rope, was supposed to whisk the dirty dishes down to Tony, the dishwasher. The truth, which Mr. Cameron didn't care to face, was that the dumbwaiter was of a medieval type and was usually busted and in no condition to do any whisking. Nor would the hotel engineer fix it. "Who do you think you are, the Queen of Sheba?" he replied brusquely when I asked him. I didn't like to tell Mr. Cameron this because he liked to think of the staff as just one big family.

We had meetings every Thursday morning in Mr. Cameron's office to stress the family angle. These had originally been planned to allow the department managers of the hotel to talk over their problems with Mr. Cameron. But as years had passed they had developed into a half-hour bawling out by Mr. Cameron during which the staff sat stunned and dormant.

"Look here, Lyons," Mr. Cameron would say to the first assistant manager. "The housekeeper tells me she sends up five clean towels a day to your apartment. What the devil's the matter with your wife, anyway? I use one clean towel every three days, and if you think I'm dirty you're crazy. Then, I noticed Mrs. Pierson down in the housekeeper's department watching the teletype. What business of yours is it who goes in and out of this hotel?"

"I only wanted to find out if any large parties were expected so we could be ready," I said meekly.

"It's your business *always* to be ready," said Mr. Cameron. "And I don't like to be interrupted when I'm talking. Another thing, where did you get those Parker House rolls you served last night?"

"I made them," I answered.

"What do you want to do, wreck the hotel dining room? Well, get to work everybody. Remember we're in the hotel business to make money. There's no sense giving anything away. This is not an eleemosynary institution."

The family went its various ways, cursing softly.

I was so provoked about the Parker House rolls that I joined Marie, the bottleneck, in taking rhumba lessons from Tony, the dishwasher. During slack time in the afternoon Tony would hitch up his dirty white ducks, brush the crumbs off his hairy chest, rough up his black curly hair, and stick a carrot over his ear. Ella and Annie, the cooks, would beat time on the pots and pans with mixing spoons. Marie and I and Tony would sneak around the dishwashing machine after each other, taking care not to slip on the water from the leaky ice chest. When Mr. Cameron caught us at it he almost had a stroke. This was one of the situations against which he thought white hair was insurance.

But I had to do something to keep up my courage. Things weren't going smoothly at home. Louise was still at Bellevue, Harold was trying to sell insurance, and Frankie had come down with chicken pox. I couldn't get a practical nurse anywhere. Frankie said he was all right but I worried. I'd gone home two nights before to find Miss Kearney from the Little Red School House talking with him.

"I'm in despair," I began.

"Why should you be?" she said in calm, experimental tones. "He's perfectly all right."

"But it itches," I protested.

"Would it itch any less if you were here?" she asked.

I knew it wouldn't but I still worried. I subsidized the neighbors to come up every hour. The next night when I got home I found a sign on the door: PLEASE DO NOT DISTURB. Frankie said he'd been terribly annoyed by people coming. He'd just get set reading *Analytical Chemistry* when he'd have to leap up and open the door. After that I calmed down.

I was glad when the boys came home from Yale for Christmas vacation. They played chess with Frankie and took my place in going to see Louise. I couldn't stand it after the ward got so crowded Louise had to sleep on a mattress on the floor under the Christmas tree. She said it was fun, just like a CCC camp, but after seeing her I always went downhill for a week. I wished she could have been home to see the boys taking off in sartorial splendor for Ethel du Pont's party at Pierre's and Hope Procter's (Procter & Gamble) coming-out at the

Ritz. She always got a kick out of seeing them beat the economic rap, as she put it. She had Surgical Ward LI eating out of her hand with her account of how the Ritz fountain broke down at Hope Procter's party and her brother was the hero of the evening when he fixed it with a hairpin. I liked to see the boys togged out in their royal regalia as much as she did, but I did wish they could learn to pick up their things. I left at eight in the morning and it was after nine at night when I got home. I didn't have much time for housework. Harold said he came home one night to be met by the janitor who'd been up to fix the pipes. When the janitor saw the shambles Rodney and John had made of the apartment he said he "feared foul play." But Harold said what the hell. They were paying their way through college. John had brought Louise a hand-knit Angora sweater, Frankie a microscope, Harold a check for eighty-five dollars for a new suit, and me a suede handbag with my initials in silver. And—surprise—a subscription to *Fortune!* And it hadn't been done with mirrors, either. They'd washed dishes, minded kids, tutored, waited on table, and John had made a whopping success of running the laundry. "Aw, let 'em have a little fun," said Harold. "Let 'em relax for a few minutes and take it easy."

They sometimes ran across my sister's daughter at the hoe-downs of the rich, they said. It seemed funny. Her children and mine arrived at the same place, but by such different routes.

My courage renewed by their visit, I went at my job at the grill hammer and tongs. I got the steward to let me put *filet mignon* on the dollar dinner. I made *minuten Fleisch* for Mrs. Blitzstein. I finagled a roll warmer away from the hotel kitchen. Things prospered. All was quiet on the managerial front. The month the grill cleared a thousand dollars I even made good old New England red-flannel hash for Mr. Cameron.

I think Mr. Cameron sensed the fact that I was becoming almost too lighthearted. He enjoyed seeing people dutifully depressed. He paid me back for my airy attitude by not warning me about the bridge tournament. The lady experts snowed us under. At one o'clock the dumbwaiter quit entirely and couldn't be fixed. This was fatal because the dumbwaiter not only whisked dirty dishes down but whisked hot orders up—any orders too fancy to be kept hot in the tepid water of our homemade *bain-marie,* or steam table. And the orders of the ladies from the bridge tournament were plenty fancy.

By one-fifteen my ankles began to swell. The waitresses and I staggered down the crooked little stairway to the kitchen with great trays of dirty dishes. A second later we staggered up again with heaping trays of broiled chicken and stuffed tomatoes. By one-thirty the place was a pandemonium. I was so dizzy I carried down three trays of dirty dishes, forgot to set them down, and carried them right up again. One lady claimed she burned her hand on a dish of ice cream. She probably did. We ran so short of china that a dish would go into the dishwashing machine and be thrust red-hot right into circulation.

At three o'clock the holocaust was over. I called the help in to my office to bind up their wounds and thank them for not dropping dead on me. Our little mutual-admiration meeting was interrupted by a bellboy bearing a salver with a message on it for me from Mr. Cameron.

"As I walked through the grill at 1:35," I read aloud, "I noticed a number of dirty dishes on the counter. Another instance of your utter disregard of my instructions."

By the time dinner was to be served I was in no mood for trifling. Otherwise I might not have replied to the man in the tweed suit who asked me what I was doing after eight o'clock that night that unless he had something more dynamic to propose I planned to drink up all the wrong drinks Ed, the bartender, was saving for me, and go upstairs and kill Mr. Cameron. Nor, if I had not been tired as a dog, would I have allowed the help to play their favorite and forbidden game of state capitals. This game consisted in a waitress saying to a counterman, "One chicken patty, rolls on the side, coffee, Colorado," to which the counterman would reply, "One chicken patty, rolls on the side, coffee coming up, Denver." I had forbidden them to play it because the customers often joined in. I didn't think the insurance company would like it.

I might have stopped them, tired as I was, if I hadn't had something else to distract me. A man at the bar began pulling out another man's necktie and a good fight was in the making.

"See if you can get this drunk out of here," hissed Ed, the bartender.

I knew it was no use to appeal to an assistant manager.

"You sold it to him, it's your problem," would be the answer.

I approached the drunk warily.

"Don't you think," I began.

"Saints above," said the drunk falling on one knee and stretching out his arms supplicatingly, "those green eyes. That white hair. If it isn't my old mother!"

A dead hush descended on our swank little beanery. Old ladies paused with their forks halfway to their mouths. Waitresses stood with trays transfixed. Fountain men held fire with chocolate malteds as our little drama unfolded.

"Please," I said firmly.

The drunk looked at me.

"I'll go if you'll shake hands," he said suddenly.

I extended one hand cautiously. Seizing it in a viselike grip he whirled me round and round past tables of gaping diners. Past the cashier we whirled right through the revolving door across the sidewalk into the gutter. As I started to get up, he yanked me to my feet, threw both arms around me, and kissed me.

"Night, Toots," he said as he signaled to a passing taxi. "I wasn't as drunk as you thought I was, was I?"

I brushed off my dress, took a long breath, squared my shoulders, and marched resolutely into my office past the accusing eyes of the horrified customers.

"Say," Ed, the bartender, called to me, "that guy in the tweed suit you told off at dinner watched the whole business. Then he beat it. The housekeeper's department just phoned up he beefed like hell about a towel with a hole in it in his room. When Mildred waited on him he asked her if she didn't feel her love-life had been neglected. We think he's a spotter."

"Isn't that just dandy?" I said wearily.

"Psst!" said Ed. "Here comes Mr. Cameron!"

Mr. Cameron came in and sat down at a table by the window. He glanced out, then stared fascinated.

"Maybe your friend the drunk's back," whispered Ed.

I walked as nonchalantly as I could to the window. It wasn't the drunk. It was Harold and Louise and Frankie, waiting for me in the re-repossessed Stutz. Louise had evidently come home unexpectedly and they'd decided to surprise me. They succeeded. Louise was wearing a peasant costume of bright red and yellow with puff sleeves and billowing skirt, evidently constructed in secret during her long sojourn at Bellevue. She had topped this Yugoslavian dream of heaven with a matching bandana. She looked more like a peasant than any peasant I had ever seen. Deprived of cigarettes at the hospital, she was now smoking one in a long holder Dr. Nickerson had given her. As she exhaled luxuriously, long curls of smoke issued dragon-like from her nose. Frankie, his eyes shining expectantly, had on a torn sweater and an old aviator's helmet with the ear muffs hanging down. Harold was slumped down in the driver's seat, reading the evening paper and racing the motor absent-mindedly. Great clouds of black smoke issued from the exhaust.

Mr. Cameron tore his eyes reluctantly from the window and met my startled gaze. "Who on earth are those crazy people?" he demanded. "Gypsies? And why should they park here?"

"I'm just getting ready to go home," I said hastily. "I'll find out."

I told Harold to drive around the corner. Then I jumped in.

"I bet you were never so surprised in your life!" said Frankie.

I laughed. "I bet I never was!"

Next morning I got word from Mr. Cameron to report to his office immediately.

"I have here," he began as I entered. I didn't even bother to listen. I knew what he had here. It was the report of the spotter.

Count by count he read off the indictment. Each time he looked up for confirmation, I nodded.

"And did you," went on Mr. Cameron, "when the occupant of room 106 complained that you had sent up champagne without champagne glasses, say, 'You can drink it out of your hat for all I care and I hope it chokes you'?"

"I might have," I said evasively. But I felt better. Room 106 was occupied, as I suspected, by the spotter.

"Well, don't hesitate to call on me for a reference. It was too bad things had to end this way," said Mr. Cameron in conclusion.

As I stood shaking hands with Mr. Cameron, my eye caught the final paragraph of the report which Mr. Cameron hadn't included.

"She served cream of lettuce, a useless sort of soup," it said. "And," had been added in pencil, "I hope it chokes her."

ARE YOU a stenographer? And a good one?" wrote Miss Molly Dewson, Chairman of the Women's Division of the Democratic National Committee from Campaign Headquarters at New York City's Hotel Biltmore.

"Tops," I wrote back instantly. "When do I start?"

I'd written Miss Dewson six months before the 1936 election when my job at the hotel bar and grill folded, asking where I could fit in. I was tired of working just to get money. It was so uninspiring. I wanted to do something that really counted.

"I'd rather help re-elect Roosevelt than anything I can think of," I told Harold. "I think he's aces."

There was no reason now why I shouldn't have a job. Louise was a tower of strength with the housework. Frankie was visiting Barbara down on the Cape. The boys were away; Rodney had his usual summer job at the Howard Johnson stand; John, now graduated from Yale, had already started on a year's tutoring job to get the money to start a four-year course at the College of Physicians and Surgeons. He'd decided to be a doctor. Harold was the only one left to cook for. And he was away all day, supervising a small field project for a landscape firm.

He'd suggested that as long as he was earning I might rest awhile. But there was no telling what would happen when his present work was over. I couldn't believe he'd really get the job he'd set his heart on—the super-dooper position of Superintendent of Planting at the coming New York World's Fair.

"What makes you think you stand a Chinaman's chance for that?" I asked him.

"Because everyone but the Duke of Windsor has written in recommending me," said Harold, "enclosing box tops. And I'm the best damn man in the country for the job."

It was nice dreaming. But I thought I had better keep my feet on the ground.

"This job at the committee is the most exciting thing that's happened to me in ages," I told him, waving Molly's letter in his face. "Think of me helping elect a President of the United States."

"I thought that was old stuff to you," said Harold. "To hear you tell it, you practically elected Hoover singlehanded."

He meant the telegram I sent to Mr. Charles B. Hilles, New York Member of the Republican National Committee, who was balking at nominating Hoover in 1927.

"I was born on Adams Street, Quincy, and went to the First Unitarian Church, where I sat over the bodies of John Adams and John Quincy Adams," I wired him, "but so help me, I will vote for Al Smith if you don't nominate Herbert Hoover. Al Smith cocks his hat over one eye, is generous with money his own and the state's, and isn't afraid of the devil himself. What's more, he has 'it.'"

Next morning, Sunday, my little message appeared in a box at the top of the front page of *The New York Times*. It seems that when Hilles read the telegram he was so mad he threw it on the floor and stamped on it. A roving reporter picked it up. The item was reprinted in newspapers all over the United States. I had started a controversy. Up to 1927, "it" had never been regarded as a masculine characteristic. There was even an editorial on the subject in *The Boston Transcript*. My mother was horrified when she read it.

"I cannot imagine any circumstances," she wrote me, "which would justify your voting for this man Smith." We had always been stanch Republicans. As a matter of fact, I wasn't a Democrat now. I was a Rooseveltite. There was a world of difference.

"That Hoover stuff was just a flash in the pan," I told Harold. "This time I'll really be in there punching. I'm wild to see how the women handle their end of the job."

"If you see Perkins," said Harold. "Ask her why she doesn't can that hat."

"I don't care," I said. "You're just prejudiced against women."

He said he wasn't prejudiced against *all* women. But as long as I'd introduced this controversial subject he'd admit, confidentially, that he thought woman's place was in the home; and it would be all right with him if she were further restricted to the two rooms especially designed for her by an all-wise Providence—bedroom and kitchen. "You selfish beast," I said. "You make me sick."

He said he was only kidding. Go ahead and muddle around the committee if I got any kick out of it. It couldn't do anybody any harm.

I set off for the Hotel Biltmore in high spirits. The Democratic National Committee was housed in regular hotel rooms, each with bath. I was ushered into the presence of the office manager of the Women's Division. The manager said I must take a test.

She dictated a short letter and then asked me to transcribe it. The only typewriter available was a broken-down Remington perched precariously on a window sill. I had to write standing up. I handed her the letter and she threw it into the wastebasket without looking at it.

"This is just a form we go through," she said. "If Dewson wants you it doesn't make any difference to us if you can't read and write. You're in. Salary twenty-five dollars."

I'd heard politics was like that but I'd never believed it. I was a little disillusioned.

I was assigned to Miss Louisa Wilson, Publicity Head of the Women's Division.

Miss Wilson could not see me immediately because the Women's Division was in a stew about Ruth Bryan Owen Rohde. She'd resigned as Minister to Denmark because of the new rule disqualifying diplomats who marry subjects of the country to which they're accredited. She had offered her services in the campaign. Somebody had thought up the bright idea of having her campaign in a trailer. The trailer had arrived outside the Biltmore all painted up to beat the nines. Her husband had hopped in but she hadn't. The trailer she evidently regarded as a crown of thorns. A crowd of photographers was waiting impatiently. Mrs. Rohde was photogenic as well as famous.

Finally, somebody had an inspiration. "Get in, Mrs. Rohde, and tell us what you don't like about it," she urged.

Mrs. Rohde got in. The photographers' bulbs popped. She hauled away from the Biltmore cross as a tiger, with her husband driving.

It was quite a relief when Mrs. J. Borden Harriman drove up in a modest Ford. Mrs. Harriman, a handsome, commanding-looking woman with an iron-gray permanent, had been assigned the yeoman task of swinging rock-ribbed Maine into the Democratic orbit. The Ford was to show Maine that, Harriman or no Harriman, we were all just "old potatoes" (remember?) under the skin.

"Oh, dear," said the head of the Radio Department as we went upstairs, "we forgot to ask Mrs. Rohde for her itinerary. But we'll probably hear from her."

I thought we probably would.

Miss Louisa Wilson returned to her office, looking pretty frazzled, and sent for me.

"Telephone this order, Pierson," she said crisply. I waited eagerly, pencil poised. "Leg of lamb not over five pounds," she dictated. "Two pounds of fresh peas and three pounds of sweet potatoes. Tell them to get it over to my apartment by ten or I'll change butchers. Here's the number." While I telephoned she tried to get her gum off a blotter where she'd parked it. She'd taken up chewing gum, she said, in an effort to cut down on cigarettes.

After I'd telephoned the order she asked me if I thought I could write a speech if she gave me some notes.

I said I thought I could.

"We've got to write a speech for one of the Gish girls. We'll give her the Organization Speech," she said.

I didn't know what the Organization Speech was then but before election night I bet I typed it a thousand times. It began with the banks, the wild bands of boys and girls on freight cars, and the apple sellers. Cut-back to the treatment of the bonus army on Anacostia flats. Mention prosperity just around the corner and two chickens in every pot, sarcastic-like. Millions of people being dispossessed from homes and starving. Hint at revolution. The rich are fleeing to their cyclone cellars. *Such* were the conditions when Our Gallant Leader took over. *Now* what have we? (At this point hurry a little. There might be hecklers.) Begin again with Saving Deposit Insurance, CCC and CWA. PWA. AAA. (Ignore any cracks about the little pigs.) Go on to SEC, RFC. Democracy is *on the march. No longer will one third of a nation be ill-housed, ill-fed, and ill-clothed.* The *forgotten* man has been *remembered.* If it's an industrial community, throw in collective bargaining. If it's an agricultural community, throw in soil erosion.

I was pretty proud of it when I got it done. But the Gish girl didn't like it at all. She sent over notes for her version. "Begin with little white hands foraging pitifully in garbage cans. Long queues of white-faced men and women, with collars turned up and shoes tied with string, outside bread lines. Suggestion: God must have been happy when he made Roosevelt."

"And what's good enough for God is good enough for me. Period," I added.

"We can do without any further suggestions from you, Pierson," said Miss Wilson.

That was why I didn't say anything about the coal miners. Miss Wilson wrote a speech about how badly schoolteachers were paid in Kansas, Landon's state. She added that a deplorable situation existed among the Kansas coal miners. I figured she'd find out sooner or later there were no coal mines in Kansas.

By the time we got the speech to suit Miss Gish, Mrs. Rohde was heard from. She and her husband had got into a slight argument about parking the trailer. Mrs. Rohde had fallen off the running board and broken her leg. She was going to broadcast from a hospital. She wanted a speech written quick.

I got out all her father's gems and larded the organization speech with them generously. Miss Wilson said it wouldn't do at all. Mrs. Rohde didn't like colorful speeches. We had to begin: "When we recall the deplorable conditions which existed prior to the election of Franklin Delano Roosevelt, we are aware that no little progress has been achieved . . ."

Of course, we didn't spend all our time writing speeches. There were the daily releases to the "Usual Release List." This meant the thirty-four newspaper and press services in Manhattan, Brooklyn, and the Bronx.

The releases were always about some forthright character who had switched to Roosevelt.

"Mrs. Eugenia C. Picklepuss, who graduated from Vassar in 1893 and has been for forty years President of the Mechanicsville Garden

Club and a stanch Republican, says she will vote for Roosevelt."
This dynamic declaration was accompanied by a glossy print of Mrs.
Picklepuss in a high stock with a moonstone brooch. Caption: Will
vote for Roosevelt.

These items were supposed to be a shot in the arm for doubtful
voters. They were known in the city rooms of New York newspapers
as "hogwash."

Two minions were employed to cut these items out of the papers
—if by any chance they were printed—and paste them in a large
scrapbook. This book was tangible proof of the sterling work being
done by the Women's Division of the Democratic National Committee on behalf of Our Gallant Leader. On the day after election it was
to be sent to Washington to the President. He could have it to thumb
through during the long winter evenings when his wife was out.

Every night when I got home, the family begged me for tales of
the women's great accomplishments. I hated to admit that we weren't
accomplishing anything. In the first place, it was obvious that the
Women's Division was just a stepchild of the organization, tolerated
but unloved. We were supposed to putter harmlessly around our own
little garden and keep strictly on our side of the fence. What little
we did do, the men could have done better. Worse still, we were dull.
If I tried to put any life into the proceedings, I was frowned on.

When I wasn't busy writing newspaper releases, I made up
bundles of Rainbow Fliers and sent them out to newspapers all over
the country. Each flier told of accomplishments along one particular
line during the Roosevelt regime. Brown: what had been done for
the farmers. Red: what had been done for labor. Then Miss Bolton,
Miss Wilson's secretary, had a bright idea. Why not have "mats" of
the Rainbow Fliers made up so a newspaper could simply slap them
on the press? It would save typesetting. She phoned the company who
said they'd make up the mats for $400. When the mats came, it
seemed she'd made a mistake. The man had said $1400. But it didn't
make any great difference because nobody wanted the mats anyway.

There was a great deal of general correspondence to be answered.
People wanted buttons, or donkey banks. Somebody's husband was

out of a job and they'd lined up forty votes for Roosevelt. What were
we going to do about it? These had to be answered carefully.

DEAR FELLOW DEMOCRAT:

We are glad to have you write us of the fine work you are doing. More power to you!

It is indeed sad to hear of your husband's difficulty in obtain-
ing work, but conditions are improving steadily. This is, as you
know, due to the efforts of Our Gallant Leader, Franklin Delano
Roosevelt. He *must* be re-elected in November if the good work
is to go on. We know you will do your part to bring this about.

At present we have no more buttons but we expect some more
in shortly. When they arrive you may be sure you will be first
on our list.

We are enclosing a donkey bank. Anything you may care to
put in it will be appreciated.

We hope you will write us again. We are counting on you to
help "put us over the top."

Sincerely yours,

It was pretty monotonous. Politics wasn't a dirty business, I decided, as some people hinted. Just a boresome business. I was low in
my mind, anyway, because Rodney had come home from his summer job, with the news he wasn't going back to Yale.

"But you've got a five-hundred-dollar scholarship," I protested.
"And you'll be stroke on the crew."

He said he'd been sick of crew ever since he'd caught the crab.
He'd been so proud of rowing on the Yale freshman crew, I'd suggested Louise and Harold drive to Princeton to see him row in the
Yale-Princeton freshman race. I couldn't go because I was typing
some case histories to help pay Frank's tuition at the Little Red
School House. Louise and Harold were cheering wildly at Yale's six-
length lead when the Yale boat stopped dead in its tracks. "Something's happened," bawled the announcer. "Number Seven's caught
a crab." Louise groaned and shut her eyes. "Is it?" she asked Harold
fearfully. It was. "Now Number Seven's lost his oar," the announcer
went on. "He's almost upset the boat." "Let's get out of here," said
Louise, "before he drowns everybody." He had showed up at the
apartment that night blue as indigo and with a big gash where the

oar had caught him in the chest. "I dreamed all last night I'd catch a crab," he said gloomily. "And then I did it." It was all we could do to get him to go back to New Haven.

Now he was through with Yale, he said. Finished. He'd been think-ing about it all summer. He was going to learn the steel business from the bottom up. The only thing he'd ever done that he'd really liked was work in the rolling mills. He'd keep on with his education. He'd take courses nights and pay for them himself. It was the hard way. But it was real. He was sick to death of stained-glass windows and ivory towers. He got up next morning, went over to Crucible Steel in Harrison, and landed a job. I knew it was the right way for him but I couldn't help feeling badly. I wanted my plans for the boys' education to go through on schedule, as advertised. I couldn't get it out of my mind.

I was glad when, by luck, I was handed a real job at the committee. There were some ructions out in Chicago, and Farley suggested it might help if Cardinal Mundelein said a word.

"Who'll ask him to?" inquired Michelson, Publicity Head of the Democratic Committee.

"The President," Farley replied.

But the letter to the President wasn't so easy to write. Farley wrestled with it, passed it on to his secretary, Mrs. Duffy, who gave it to Molly Dewson, who passed it on to Louisa Wilson, who dumped it into my lap.

"Here, Pierson," she said blandly. "See what you can do with this."

A letter to the President! I hauled up my chair and began to bat out "Dear Frank." Me with two husbands and five children and bills you could chin yourself on, telling the President of the United States what to tell Cardinal Mundelein to tell the world! Where but in America, land of the free and home of the brave!

I'd just finished the letter when Louise called up in great excite-ment to say that while she was over at the butcher's all the silver had been stolen. "Call the police!" I directed her. "Thank you," she said politely and hung up. I took it she was pretty rattled. When I got home I found that not only the flat silver, but candlesticks, cake dishes, fruit bowls, everything was gone. "My wedding presents!"

I moaned. "Which wedding?" asked Harold roguishly. Being married twice, I reflected, was hard.

I was just about to dilate upon this dismal fact when my sister called up, saying she was in New York on business. "Could she spend the night with us?" She sure could! I hadn't seen her for four years.

We sat up half the night catching up on the news. I told her how thrilled we'd been to see her crackerjack article on society in the *Satevepost*. She thought Louise and Frankie were wonderful, she said, to go to Textile High School nights. I told her Louise was preparing for college. And the Little Red School House people didn't think night school on top of day school would hurt Frankie, even if he was only eleven. There was no other way, at his age, he could work in a chemistry laboratory. His "drive" for chemistry should be encouraged at all costs, they said. Textile High was glad to let down the bars to a boy who knew more chemistry, they claimed, than the average college senior. He could help teach the class.

"I haven't asked you," she said. "How are the women on the committee making out?"

"They aren't," I said.

All we were doing, as a matter of fact, was trying to return the barrage the Republicans were keeping up on the Democrats about the hidden taxes. We wrote article after article throwing the hidden taxes back into their camp. I got pretty sick of it. One afternoon I got out a Bughouse Release to entertain the office force, entitled "Who Hid the Taxes in Mrs. Murphy's Overalls?" It suggested all sorts of quaint places where the taxes might be hidden. They were finally located in Republican Headquarters, where they were being used for campaign material. Some enemy placed the Bughouse Release on the desk of Mr. Michelson, Democratic Publicity Director. He changed a few words and released it over the radio. It was the only consciously humorous note struck in the campaign.

When the Republicans stuck the sour news in workers' pay envelopes that a percentage of their pay would be deducted when the Social Security Law went into effect, the committee went wild. Nobody had ever heard of Social Security. "Maybe it's something women's clubs know about, like *Social Justice*," they said. I dug up a copy of the law and pointed out in passing that it allowed the government to use the cash and let the credit go. Everyone was furious at me. They wondered if I was a "good" Democrat. I came within an ace of getting fired.

I might have, if everybody's attention hadn't been distracted by an attack of hair-pulling in the Radio Division. The woman in charge had worked out a terrific card system to keep track of speakers all over the country and their speaking dates. It was all done with colors. She lost Mrs. J. Borden Harriman—mauve. Words were had. The woman in charge of the cards went into hysterics. She grabbed up the cards, screamed, and threw them up to the ceiling. It was weeks before some of the speakers were located.

At this point I was given the proud privilege of managing the Park Avenue-for-Roosevelt luncheon at Sherry's. Forty ladies whose husbands had incomes in the upper brackets showed up. The press didn't. The potatoes were simply *frightful*. Instead of being those marvelous crispy little things, they were positively *limp*. Who did this? I mean, *who* was responsible? I took the rap. Toward the end, a reporter from *The Brooklyn Eagle* drifted in and lapped up four Martinis. He said we were worse than the Republican Committee Chairman, John D. Hamilton. Every morning John D. Hamilton called up the city editors and said he had some hot news. Everybody would rush over, and it would turn out the news was that Landon was running for President. What the hell, he said, the luncheon didn't mean anything. He bet those dames' husbands didn't know they were there.

As the campaign gathered momentum, the committee began to get a little impatient with the President. They couldn't understand why he kept on saying he meant to go on with social reforms. "Why does the Boss keep pulling those gags?" they asked plaintively. "Doesn't he know he's in?"

"I have a hunch he means it," I said. "That's why I'm for him."

They shook their heads sadly. It wasn't good politics.

They got so worried for fear he wouldn't get elected that the Women's Division decided to give a tea at the Biltmore for the Tammany lady leaders. Miss Dewson, an ardent New Dealer, was in charge. She was a large, efficient, kindly woman who wore ground-gripper shoes and had been born two houses from me on Adams Street, Quincy, although she now made her home in Maine.

If there was a rift between the New Dealers and the organization, there was a crevasse between the organization and Tammany. They all hated each other's guts.

"I hope you will all make every effort to get out the vote," said Miss Dewson to the Tammany ladies in her best Boston accent.

"Trust us, lady," said one old party. "We'll conk 'em on the head if they don't vote right."

"Dear me," said Miss Dewson. "I don't—I mean—really . . ."

"Do ye want the vote got out or don't ye?" demanded another forthright Tammanyite.

"Why—yes," said Miss Dewson.

"We bin gettin' it out for twenty years," said the speaker. "There's nothin' for gettin' out votes like a length o' pipe."

There was one fly in the ointment of the Women's Division. They couldn't get out a human-interest story. They'd dragged an old ninety-four-year-old Republican out of a deathbed to register Democratic, but the papers turned up their noses at it. The scrapbook testifying to the women's sterling efforts was pretty thin. It didn't contain much but Picklepuss releases. The men were twitting the women about it.

I spoke to Louise. "You've been wild to do something to help Roosevelt," I said. "Here's your chance."

She said: "I'll tell you what I'll do. I'll put a 'personal' addressed to the President in *The New York Times,* explaining that I'm offering the letter he wrote me on White House stationery for sale to the highest bidder. Proceeds to go to the campaign. I'll start it F. D. R. Everybody will read it out of curiosity. It might get results."

She wrote out the ad:

F.D.R.: Am offering for sale to the highest bidder my most cherished possession—letter you wrote me from the White House. Will contribute proceeds to your campaign to make democracy safe under capitalism. Am 19, ambitious, but walk with crutches. You told me

"Keep your chin up!" Same to you. Remember, sunflowers die in November!

Louise Y 2369 Times Annex

She went down to the *Times* with it. They went into a huddle. They finally said they had to see Roosevelt's letter. She came back and got it. They hemmed and hawed. For a while they thought they'd have to get Adolph Ochs out of the grave to pass on it. They finally said they'd print it and it would be seventeen dollars. They sent a spy back to the apartment with Louise to look things over and collect the money. It meant letting the rent go, but we'd made up our minds to go through with it.

Next morning, the ad appeared. By the time I got up I had to eat breakfast in the kitchen. The apartment was full of reporters and photographers. Harold was disgusted. Louise said, "What shall I tell them?" and I said thoughtlessly, "Tell them anything as long as it's true." When I got down to the Biltmore I kept mum about it. I got the *World-Telegram* and the *Post* on the way home and found she'd told them how she'd gone to Washington and the President had said, "You look as if you'd gotten on in the world, Louise," and she had said, "Well, you look as if you hadn't done so badly yourself," and he had allowed as how he hadn't. She also added that Harold was an "unemployed florist walking the streets looking for work."

People sent money galore, an offer of marriage, and several dirty postcards. A doctor offered her electrical treatments, which she accepted but abandoned after she discovered he'd never found anyone who would consent to take them before. They were, she said after trying one, a not very mild form of electrocution.

Michelson, Democratic Publicity Director, picked up the item in the *Democratic News Digest*: "A girl crippled from infantile paralysis offers to sell her letter from the President."

"That's a real story," he said. "The kind of story we ought to get after."

He sent for Louise. When she got to Democratic Headquarters, everybody groaned.

"We only have to take one look at you to know whose child you are," they told her. "You're the spitting image of your ma."

Louise said what of it? They said if they played up the story and the newspapers found out her mother was working for the committee, they'd say it was a put-up job. It might leak out to the Republicans. They'd make a mountain out of it.

Louise said what did they mean, a put-up job? The Roosevelt letter *was* her most cherished possession; she *did* walk with crutches; we'd paid the seventeen dollars for the ad out of our own pocket; she'd collected sixty-three dollars for the Cause. They said they were sorry; it was no soap. She'd better keep the sixty-three dollars and go home. Louise was furious. She wired Mr. Morgan, the kindly Democratic Treasurer, and made an appointment to turn over the money. Then she called up the photographers and newspapers and tipped them off. She and Mr. Morgan made a double spread in the *News* and all the morning papers. She got in some wonderful plugs for Roosevelt.

"He'll need 'em, Ma," she said. "You and I are the only people for Roosevelt. Everybody else is just Democrats."

Her pictures and publicity filled pages and pages in the Women's Division scrapbook. It made the scrapbook look fatter, really impressive. But everyone acted as if I'd done something dishonorable or unethical. They seemed to forget they'd paid for the "spontaneous" Park Avenue-for-Roosevelt luncheon out of the till! Then suddenly something so upsetting happened that everybody forgot me. Tammany was putting on a rally for Roosevelt at Madison Square Garden, but, as they hated the organization, almost nobody on the Women's Committee could get tickets. A steady line of ticket beggars got the receptionist pretty frazzled. Toward night an aristocratic-looking old lady with a cane came up to the desk.

"Can I get a couple of tickets to the rally?" she asked courteously.

"No," snapped the receptionist. "Tammany hates our guts. The best thing you can do is to buy an apple and a bottle of milk, go down to the garden, and stand in line."

"Could I speak to Miss Nancy Cook in the New York State Division?" asked the old lady.

"I don't think so. But I'll ring her. Who'll I say wants her?"

"Mrs. James Roosevelt, Senior," said the old lady.

Election night, Harold and I and the children all went to the nineteenth floor of the Biltmore to hear the returns. It was pretty dull. We could hear sounds of revelry from all the other floors where the Democrats who had worked for Our Gallant Leader for big salaries were having a party.

"Let's go over to the Republican Headquarters and see what's doing," said Louise to Rodney. Frank said he'd go along with them.

"It's a landslide," I said to Harold. "We might as well mush along home."

It was midnight when the children blew in.

"Wait till you hear!" said Louise. "You'll die."

When they got over to Republican Headquarters, it seems, they found the place shrouded in gloom. But there were free beer and sandwiches. Old ladies hung with diamonds and orchids, and old men with white walrus mustaches and dripping with Rolls Royces, were moaning around.

"Look, Pennsylvania for Roosevelt," said one of them to Louise. "The only place left is Spain!"

"Not Pennsylvania! How awful," said Louise. "I can't believe it."

"Kansas, not Kansas! My God, how horrible!" cried Rodney.

The man reading the returns broke down. He turned to Rodney. "Will you read for me?"

Rodney said he would.

"New York. New York for Roosevelt," bellowed Rodney. "There is only one recourse left. There is only one thing for this man who has destroyed our way of life. Impeachment!"

The crowd cheered.

After the returns were all in, a short, stocky man in a Brooks Brothers trench coat, who said he used to be manager of Altman's, took Louise and Rodney down to the Hotel Commodore bar and bought them Daiquiris. Frankie went along, too. After the man had had two drinks he asked Louise confidentially if she knew that infantile paralysis affected your brain—made you crazy. She said sure she knew it. She'd been crazy as a bedbug for years. Booooo-ooo-ooo! Clear the tracks. She was coming at him!

He jumped for his life, hustled Louise, Rodney, and Frankie out onto the street, and called a taxi.

"That's the rich for you!" said Louise as she finished the story.

"You shouldn't talk about the rich like that," said Frankie. "It's not democratic. The rich have just as much right to live as we have. Can they help it if they stink?"

"Are you sure we're doing the wise thing in sending Frankie to the Little Red School House?" asked Harold. "Maybe it's *too* stimulating."

"If I was Louise I'd be mad at the Democrats, though," went on Frank. "They never even invited her to their party after her getting up the human-interest story and giving them the sixty-three dollars. I think they're mean!"

"I don't care," said Louise. "I did it for Roosevelt. I think he's swell. I know what he's been through."

"He'll know you do," I said comfortingly, "when he gets the scrapbook from headquarters. If he ever looks at it."

Next morning I went down to headquarters to wrap up the scrapbook and dispatch it to Washington and clean out the files. I was the only one there in the Women's Division besides the office boy, who was drunk. I was a little disappointed. I wanted to point out to my coworkers that the only states the Democrats lost were Miss Wilson's native state, Vermont; and Miss Dewson's home state, Maine. As the scrapbook didn't seem to be anywhere around, I thought maybe somebody'd sent it the day before without telling me. But that didn't seem likely. While I was working on the files, one of the cleaners came in for a mop she'd forgotten.

"I wonder if while you were cleaning you happened to see a huge scrapbook that was on this desk," I asked her. "I can't seem to locate it."

"Oh, that!" said the cleaning woman. "Sure I seen it. I thought it wasn't no good to nobody. I throwed it out for junk!"

WHEN the Japanese Commissioner's chauffeur came around the day the New York World's Fair opened and asked if the Commission could park three cars in our yard "regular," I told him absolutely not.

"It's against the law," I said. "No parking within one thousand feet of the Fair grounds. Besides, I hate the Japanese."

"For four dollars a week in advance do you hate the Japanese?" he asked. "Just daytime?"

I told him for any damn sum he could name I hated the Japanese, daytime *and* nighttime.

After he went, Louise said maybe I'd been hasty. Why should I let politics interfere with business?

"But Harold would lose his job if we parked," I said.

We would have cut off our right arms rather than jeopardize Harold's supercolossal job as Superintendent of Planting at the New York World's Fair of 1939, Inc., which he'd landed in spite of my skepticism. That's why for the past two years we'd been living in a rugged Queen Anne number right in the shadow of the Soviet pavilion. He could hardly drag one foot after another after planting ten thousand trees, two hundred and fifty thousand shrubs, acres of lawns, miles of hedges, half a million perennials, and a million tulips. "The fact that nineteen thousand feet of hose are in use daily," he said in his speeches to Kiwanis Clubs, "may give you some slight idea of the magnitude of the undertaking."

"What does the Fair care whether we park or not?" said Louise. "They've got their money from Sam Rosoff."

Sam Rosoff had the parking concession at the south parking field. Everybody on Queensborough Hill blamed Sam Rosoff for the fact that we were "zoned."

"If the Fair doesn't care, Sam Rosoff does," I said. "Even if we don't get arrested I don't want to stick my neck out. Sam Rosoff is allergic to competition."

Louise said bushwah, nobody else was scared. Look at Walter Rau just above us. He had eighteen cars. Look at Cantelora's yard. Look at Kowalski's. They were parked solid.

I said I'd speak to Mrs. Kowalski about it when I went over for a pack of cigarettes. Mrs. Kowalski was a Polish peasant with a shrewd tongue and a heart of oak, who owned the candy store.

"We ain't afraid of Sam Rosoff," said Mrs. Kowalski. "What if he is a sewer magnet? The city ain't going to crack down on us. They'll figger if we make a dollar they'll get back taxes paid they'd give up for lost. 'Course the police'll have to make a big noise like they're protecting Rosoff. But they won't make no arrests."

Johnny Cantelora, who was over getting a bottle of pop, said they figgered to make five or six hundred dollars. He said Rosoff's field wasn't so hot. People didn't want to walk two miles to get into the Fair.

"We're handy," he said. "We're going to park anyhow. Let's see anyone make us stop it!"

When I got back, I told Louise we'd watch for a week and see how they made out. It would give Louise something to do, I thought. She'd been lost since she'd given up Queens College.

"Is Queens College that little bunch of Spanish outhouses off Horace Harding Boulevard?" Rodney inquired when he heard she planned to go there.

It was. One year finished off Louise.

"It was nothing but a battle between the American Student Union and the Cardinal Newman Club to see who could get control," she said. "I was an oppressed minority." To her, the courses seemed vague and impractical. "I can't get excited over the social significance of the great advances made by the proletariat in Russia," she said. "It's all I can do to brush my teeth and get on the trolley."

She'd become so tired of lofty generalities that she'd wangled a job washing dishes afternoons in the college cafeteria. She scrubbed the floor too for good measure. She said it was filthy. It made her mad, though, to get only twenty-five cents an hour for working, when the NYA students got forty cents an hour for watching her. The pay-off came in the English class, over the discussion of an essay. In it the author stressed the sad fact that the cream of the crop in England had been killed in the last war. How many in the class disliked the essay, asked the instructor. A forest of hands went up. How many liked it? Louise! The whole class turned and glared at her.

"Do you mean to *imply*," the instructor asked Louise reprovingly, "that the products of Eton and Harrow are *superior* to, say, a truck driver?"

Louise was always a little hazy about definitions.

"I don't mean to *imply*," she said. "They *are!*" She was hissed from the room. She came home bringing her books. "I'm through with higher education," she said.

Parking, I thought, would be something she could get her teeth into.

By the time a week had passed, Queensborough Hill was one great parking lot. Cars were parked fender to fender on lawns, in flower beds, on front walks, in driveways—everywhere.

"Park here; park your car; park; *park!*" rang out day and night like a great battle cry. Fifty cents for strangers; twenty-five cents for steadies. "That was my customer!" "Oh, yeah, let's see you prove it!" Neighbors turned against neighbors. Blows were struck. Competition was fast and furious.

"Why should we be holdouts?" asked Louise. "Everybody's cleaning up. You could chop down the apple tree, and we could grade the rock in the middle with ashes. Nobody'd notice unless they had one of those underslung Auburns. I figure we could park thirty-three cars."

"Don't forget we'll have nobody to help us," I reminded Louise. "We'll have to go it alone."

John was already firmly entrenched at the College of Physicians and Surgeons (where he was already running the laundry!) and was booked up for years ahead with summer jobs. Rodney had left Crucible Steel. He found at the Harrison plant they were still using the same cranes and derricks and trucks they had used in 1916. They didn't use the same toilets because they were stopped up. The CIO staged a rally one Saturday night, and nine hundred of the one thousand employees (including Rodney) signed up. The next day his foreman said, "You weigh two hundred and twenty-five and you're six feet two. We want you to go to Van Cleve, the vice-president, and stand over him like this and say, 'You're going to put in new toilets and you're going to install new machinery, you blankety-blank so-and-so.' Van Cleve was the man who had hired Rodney! He saw he was going to be fired whichever way it went, so he quit and applied for a job as laborer on the open hearth with U. S. Steel. When the letter came, "Job open in western Pennsylvania," he telephoned the Personnel Director of Carnegie-Illinois, U. S. Steel Subsidiary, at Pittsburgh, "Hold everything. Coming by next bus." Naturally, everyone was curious to see who would telephone Pittsburgh long distance to cinch the worst, most dangerous, and poorest-paid job in the steel industry. He was met by a deputation at the station and in three days promoted to pit foreman in charge of six hundred and fifty hunkies with orders to rush production. He'd already signed up for courses in management engineering at Carnegie Tech.

Frankie was also riding high. He'd written a letter to Du Pont telling what kind of junior chemistry exhibit they ought to have at the Fair. They'd turned his letter over to the American Institute of Science, which engaged Frank to demonstrate chemistry experiments at the Westinghouse Building, at the same time ad-libbing over a loudspeaker. This kept him busy from ten to six. Evenings he spent lolling in the lounge of the Du Pont building, discussing advances in chemistry with visiting notables.

Louise said were we mice or were we women. We could manage it.

"O.K.," I said. "I'll chop down the apple tree and we can see how the place looks."

I chopped down the pear tree, too, while I was at it. When Louise had dumped a few buckets of ashes on the rock you couldn't see it at all.

Louise said we'd have to work like beavers because we were the last house on a one-way street. If a car got past our driveway it would have to keep right on going; the police wouldn't let it turn around. She said we'd have to sit on the big stone at the entrance and take turns hollering "Park" through John's Andover megaphone.

We didn't do so bad for beginners. By the time Harold got home to supper we had twelve cars parked. Walter Rau, who had the lot above us, made us pretty mad though. Walter was a big husky guy who wore a turtle-necked sweater and a checked cap down over one eye. He looked like Liliom, if no stars had been involved. Just as a car would be ready to turn in our yard, he'd come running down and jump on the running board and tell them to back up.

"Don't tell Harold about the parking till after he has his dinner," I told Louise. "He doesn't like to be surprised when he's hungry." The driveway was at the back and there was a high hedge either side of the front walk. Harold couldn't see the cars on his way in.

He'd just started to carve the roast beef when a man tapped with a fifty-cent piece on the window.

"What kind of place does he think this is?" said Harold, jumping up angrily.

"Don't, don't," screamed Louise. "That's the Vermont Chrysler. I told him he could pay when he came out because I didn't have change for ten dollars."

While she went out to collect the money, I explained to Harold. He said we were crazy. He said he washed his hands of the whole business. When we landed in jail he wouldn't even bring cigarettes to us.

The next night, when we showed him fourteen dollars we'd taken in, he said maybe it wasn't such a bad notion. But about midnight, when the Massachusetts Lincoln hit the rock and ricocheted off onto the side of the garage, he said we'd end up in the state prison.

"Maybe we'd better put up a sign, 'Park at Your Own Risk,'" I said to Louise. But Harold said not to put up any sign that had the word "Park" on it. If we did, we were liable.

By the end of the week we had the place going full blast. We filled it up with workmen at seven in the morning. As they parked by the week, we charged them a quarter. When they went out along about two or three in the afternoon, we replaced them with fifty-centers. We could get in only twenty-six workmen because they had such big cars. Electrical Local 3 had Buicks and Chryslers, and Plumber's Local 95 had Packards.

We did so well, Walter Rau came down and accused us of cutting prices.

"You're rich," he said. "You're just parking for the hell of it. You don't care what you charge."

"If we were rich, what would we be living in a dump on Queensborough Hill for?" I asked, but he said rich people were funny.

"He thinks he's the cat's whiskers," said Louise bitterly, "because he's got Edna May Oliver and we've only got Bruce Cabot."

"But we've got Mrs. Smith Ely Jeliffe," I said. "Dr. Smith Ely Jeliffe was the alienist in the Thaw case."

Louise said she told Walter, but he said tell it to the marines. She said nobody remembered the Thaw case but me and a couple of other Confederate soldiers. She said Walter made her tired.

Every day she went up and counted the cars in Walter's lot and he came down and counted the cars in ours.

It was because she couldn't bear to have Walter beat us that she told the Frenchman to drive in when we were parked solid. I'd told him I was sorry, we were full up.

"But this is a so very convenient place to park," insisted the Frenchman. "In me you will have a steady customer. I will be here every day till the Fair closes."

"Drive in," said Louise. "Leave your car in the middle with the keys in it. We'll run it into the first space we have vacant. I've got an old party who drives cars around."

The Frenchman drove his Ford coupé into the driveway between the two rows of parked cars, got out, bowed deeply from the waist, handed Louise a quarter, and departed.

"You shouldn't have told him that," I said to Louise. "You know I can't drive cars around without ripping bumpers off and smashing fenders. Especially the way you've got them jammed in. I don't think we ought to take any more cars than we can park decently."

"Oh, don't worry about that old Ford," said Louise. "Did you see the guy's brief case? I think he's got his apron in it. I think he's a waiter in the French pavilion. When Electrical Local 3 goes out at 2:30 you can stick him in Augie's place. Or you might squeeze him in beside the garage. I don't care if we have to park cars in the living room. I'm not going to have Walter Rau lick us."

After that we put two or three cars in the middle every day and I had to drive them around. I couldn't seem to get control of the new models at all. It seemed as if every day I hit something. Even my new glasses didn't help—I was a bum driver. Louise and I would have to polish up the scratches and dents with furniture polish and then wipe dust on them. Once I got into a car and pressed a button and the whole blame thing sprang into action—the lights went on, the radio played, the windshield wipers wiped furiously, and the car leaped forward. I was so scared I jumped right out again. Luckily, a chauffeur parked in the yard took over.

Walter Rau came back by cutting down his hedge so he could park three more cars than we did. But next day he got a summons. Sam Rosoff's lawyer had got busy and the police had to make motions.

"Ya! Ya! Ya!" yelled Louise through the megaphone.

"You better not crow over him, we might get arrested ourselves," I said.

"Don't worry," said Louise, "the police can't give you a summons unless they actually park in the yard and you accept the money. Walter was just dumb. I know Doubrava and Hoffmann, those Keystone detectives from the hundred and ninth. I'll never park them."

Doubrava and Hoffmann were typical Metro-Goldwyn-Mayer dicks; fedoras at an angle, dark suits, suspicious glances, and guns on their hips which they fingered nervously. Nobody but a blind man could mistake them.

Next morning Louise was lining up the workmen when a new customer drove in. He had on old working clothes, a cap, and was carrying his lunch done up in a newspaper. He was wearing dark glasses.

"I'm a workman at the Fair," he said getting out of his old Dodge. "Some of the fellers in Electrical Local 3 tells me this is a good place to park. I'll be here regular. Here's your quarter."

"Let's see your workman's button," said Louise.

"I'm new, this is my first day," said the man. "I got to hurry. My foreman's waiting for me."

"O.K.," said Louise, taking the quarter. "Here's luck to you."

"Here's luck to you, sister," said the workman, taking off his black glasses. "Bad luck!"

It was Doubrava. Louise was so mad she threw the quarter on the ground. She and Doubrava had to go down on their hands and knees to look for it. Then he went in the shed and wrote her out a ticket.

She stayed in the house all the rest of the morning because Walter kept yelling, "Who's loony now?" at her.

When I went over to Kowalski's I found Stanley Kowalski had got a summons. Mrs. Kowalski was furious.

"This man comes driving along and stops," said Mrs. Kowalski. "He says to Stanley, 'Where can I park, sonny?' and Stanley jumps on his running board all full of power and gladness. And what does he get for it? A summons."

By night everybody on Queensborough Hill had got summonses. There was a mass meeting. Rosoff was picking on the 109th Precinct, that's what he was. Over in Corona they even had neon parking signs. But Corona was in the 110th. The cops in the patrol car said it wasn't Rosoff, it was the Skipper. The Skipper was Captain Sayre of the 109th. They said the Skipper was a swell egg but tough as nails. He enforced the law, that was what he did. That was how come he got hustled the hell-and-gone out of Manhattan and stuck in a dump like the 109th.

Queensborough Hill was deserted the morning the cases were called. About noon everybody got off the trolley with a broad grin on his face. The cases had been indefinitely postponed. Rosoff's lawyer had left court, raging. He'd said he'd fix those wildcat parking lots.

I had good news for Louise. While she was at court I'd got Johnny Green, the orchestra leader. But that afternoon Walter got Kate Smith's chauffeur, so it was a tie. Then for a solid week we got more cars than Walter. He accused us of getting the traffic cop on the corner to send them up to us.

"It's because we take an interest in our customers," said Louise. "We discuss their problems with them."

Harold said he didn't approve of our discussing the customers' problems with them. But Louise and I said if people paid fifty cents to have their differential smashed and their fenders scratched, they had a right to have their problems solved. He said we'd get into trouble if we didn't mind our own business.

That was why he wouldn't listen when we told him that Cusick's affairs were approaching a crisis. Cusick was one of his own men, too.

Louise and I grew more and more worried about him. He had a wife and three children in the Bronx. But a waitress in the Polish pavilion had fallen in love with him. She wanted him to elope with her, and when he refused she'd put poison in his coffee. He'd found out just in the nick of time. He'd bought a widow spider to kill her with. He had it in a box. He showed it to us.

"It really was a widow spider," I said to Harold. "I think you ought to do something."

Harold said we ought to have our heads examined.

We were pretty relieved when Cusick showed up next day minus the spider. He'd got drunk in a saloon in the Bronx and showed the spider around. Dr. Ditmars dropped in and took it away from him. The spider was now over at the Fair on exhibition.

"If you don't believe us, go and look at it," we urged Harold. Harold said the hell with it. He had troubles enough. One of the fifty-foot elms they'd planted in old bedsprings and concrete slabs didn't look so hot. He said they expected him to make Versailles gardens on a dump.

He had so much on his mind we didn't tell him when Cusick's affairs took a turn for the worse. It seems his wedding anniversary was approaching. He'd promised his wife he'd take her out to dinner in celebration and he'd promised the Polish waitress he'd elope with her down Long Island.

"I think something is going to blow up," said Louise. "We better get him to pay a week in advance."

It was good we did, because the morning of the anniversary, while we were eating breakfast, somebody came over from the Fair for Harold. Cusick had stepped in front of a trolley car.

"Good God, now look what you've done," said Harold.

At ten Cusick's wife showed up. She'd told him particularly not to fracture his skull that day because he went and fractured it on their fifth anniversary. She said he was in awful shape. He looked worse than Max Baer when Joe Louis finished with him. She couldn't understand it. He'd come in that morning at three o'clock happy as a lark and left for work at six cheerful as a cricket. After she'd gone, the Polish waitress came over. She said she was to have met Cusick at six that evening and they were to leave for Montauk. She'd left him at ten minutes of three that morning, happy as a lark.

"Now you're murderers," said Harold. "With your larks and crickets. He was probably stewed to the gills. After this, for heaven's sake don't listen to people. This is no Court of Human Relations."

We didn't have time to listen to people, anyway, because we had company. My sister came to see the Fair and insisted on my going over with her. I nearly dropped dead waiting for her to inspect every heraldic device in the British pavilion. Then we had tea and crumpets.

"That reposing you did when we were young certainly paid dividends," I said. "You're stronger than I am and you don't look a day over thirty-five."

She said that was because she went to a gymnasium.

"You'd look better and feel better," she said, "if you took off some weight."

I said as soon as she went I'd start doing exercises.

I didn't have any time to exercise except late in the evenings. I was lying on my back on the floor, doing the bicycle ride one hundred times, when Frank blew in.

"You look as if you were going to have a stroke," he said critically. "Besides, you aren't doing it right. Why don't you just give up and *be* old and fat?"

"Because I don't want to," I said angrily.

"When your mother gives up on anything," said Harold to Frank, "let me know so I can make the funeral arrangements."

"Thanks for the ad," I said.

Harold was stingy with compliments. They were usually back-handed.

My sister had barely gone when Barbara and her husband came. They brought their baby and left it with us while they did the Fair. He was a fat, good-natured, handsome baby but full of the dickens. While I was out helping Louise park a car, he crawled under the ice chest and drank water out of the pan. He had to be watched every minute.

They'd no sooner gone than Skipper, our police dog, named after the incorruptible police captain, had eleven puppies. We sent out engraved announcements to all our friends. Every time we opened the door to the shed to go out and park a car, Skipper and the eleven puppies rushed out. It took us half an hour crawling under cars to capture them and get them in again.

Walter Rau told everybody not to park with us because we kept vicious dogs.

Louise was so mad she stopped his customers as they walked past our driveway and said, "Next time why don't you park in a good place?" She got two away from him. Next morning we found one hundred and twenty-five nails in the lot. We showed them to the sergeant from the 109th, but he said he couldn't do anything because we couldn't prove who did it.

"We don't have to *prove* who did it, we *know* who did it," said Louise. But he said he couldn't do anything for us.

"There's one thing, Walter'll never get the Frenchman away from us," said Louise. "He'd park if there were a hundred and twenty-five thousand nails."

Every day he stopped and talked with us. He told us he was twins. Louise said she didn't believe it.

"He says anything he feels like," said Louise. "Sometimes he says he's Spanish."

He wanted Frank to wash his car, but Frank said he wouldn't under a dollar.

"I see Frankie is the intellectual type," said the Frenchman. "He is above car washing."

Louise told Frankie he was pretty darn mean to ask a waiter a dollar.

"You may be the little round button on top with Du Pont," said Louise, "but pipe down when you get home."

If we hadn't been busy picking up nails we might have been able to keep the Virginia car from backing over the bank. There was a steep bank to the right of the parking space. We'd put logs in front of it. When cars backed up to it Louise would yell, "Whoa—slow now—hold it, *hold it!*" But we were down on our hands and knees looking for nails when the Virginia car came zooping in, swung around, and backed right over the logs. The crankshaft hooked onto the logs and the rear end hung out over the crevasse; the car rocked back and forth like a seesaw. The driver climbed over the front seat and sat down beside a man and woman in the back. They began laughing and rocking the car.

"Good heavens," said Louise. "They're drunk as lords."

We told them to get out, but they wouldn't. Everybody came rushing over from the other parking lots. Walter Rau opened their car door.

"You better get out; your car's ruined, mister," he said. "If I was you, I'd sue."

They staggered out, shaking their fists at me and Louise. I got them to sit down on the back steps and drink some ice water while I sent for the tow car. The tow car had hardly got them safely off the logs when they jumped in and tore out of the yard, yelling imprecations. In five minutes they were back. And it had cost us five dollars to get them out.

"Very, very lovely people," they said shaking hands with us. "This besh ol' place in whole worl' to park."

"Go away," said Louise. "It's a terrible place. There's a rock in the middle that'll smash your car to smithereens if my mother doesn't."

They left the car locked up tight right in the middle of the lot, so we couldn't get a car in or out, and dashed over to the Fair. All our customers had to wait till they came back and got their car out at two in the morning. Walter waited outside the driveway and told them to park in his lot next time. *His* lot had supervision. He didn't allow drunks in it.

We were pretty discouraged. On top of that, the next night we lost the Rumanian waiters. It was cold and rainy. They'd just parked and left for the Fair when we heard a tapping on the window.

"Good-by," they called, "you'll never see us again. We're sailing at midnight. We just got word from the consulate. We've been called up."

Louise cried, it was so sad. We knew it meant the war was on.

"Tomorrow," she said, "I suppose it'll be Old Faithful."

Old Faithful was the Frenchman. But Old Faithful still hung on. We were glad because he was the only person willing to park between the driveway and the garage. Every incoming and outgoing car grazed his fenders, but he didn't seem to mind it.

We felt better when we got Mrs. Loew's car of Loew's theaters. But Harold said we'd better make the most of it. He said there was a rumor over at the Fair that the police had been ordered to "clean up." When the King and Queen of England were at the Fair, they were accompanied by a lot of high-ranking police officials. Queensborough Hill was one solid mass of parked cars. Rosoff's field had only a dribble.

Next day was Sunday, and when we looked out the window, squads of policemen were getting out of cars and off trolleys. The whole Bronx division had been commandeered to clean up Queensborough Hill. Two cops took up positions at each parking lot.

I went out and talked to the two guarding our entrance but I didn't get any answer. They were tough. Word went up and down the hill by grapevine: "These boys mean business."

It was when I dashed over to Kowalski's for a cigarette that I saw Johnny Weissmuller's car parked in the sand lot. He spoke to the policeman standing near by and went on into the Fair. The sand lot didn't belong to anybody, but it was against the law to park there.

"Officer," I said, "I wish to protest against this car parked in the sand lot."

"But that's Johnny Weissmuller!" said the cop.

"Why should Johnny Weissmuller be allowed to park in an illegal place?" I said. "And for nothing, at that? What's Johnny Weissmuller got that I haven't got? While that car stands in that sand lot, Louise and I park cars. If you make one move to stop anybody from driving into our yard, I'll call up Valentine and report that car."

"Who said anything about you not parking cars?" said the cop.

He called off the two men stationed in front of our place. All the rest of Queensborough Hill was shut up tight as a drum, but we were parked solid.

"By golly," said Louise. "For once we've got the drop on Walter."

About three o'clock that afternoon, Johnny Weissmuller drove out. Our guard returned. They wouldn't even let anybody come down our street. They just let cars out.

Bob Kingsley, an old friend from the Cape who'd moved to Jersey, called up. "What is this, Russia?" he asked. "I drove way over from Montclair to call on you people and the police won't let me by. I told them I was a friend of yours and they said, 'Gwan, we've heard that one. Maybe you're their old aunt.'"

Harold said, thank God, nobody could park. For once he'd have a good night's sleep. We didn't feel too badly. We'd set Walter back on his heels and made fourteen dollars that day.

Monday there wasn't a cop in sight, but Walter came down. He said he'd fix us. He said the police had to *act* when a taxpayer called up and complained about illegal parking. He felt pretty good because he'd just got a Dusenberg with a coronet on it.

"I wish you hadn't refused the Japanese Commissioner's Cadillacs," said Louise. "They had Rising Suns on them."

About five minutes later she called that she was coming in pretty soon. The place was nearly full, anyway, and she'd seen Doubrava and Hoffmann pass on the lower road in a new Buick.

"Not that I'm really afraid of them," said Louise. They'd been friendly. When they weren't in an arresting mood they'd drop in and sit on the rock beside me and Louise. While Louise was eating the Good Humor they'd brought her, they'd help park cars and collect the money.

"But I haven't seen them in days," said Louise. "We can't be too careful. Walter might have called up."

A minute later I heard screaming. I went out. Louise had got a ticket for "soliciting."

Doubrava and Hoffmann had driven up the hill in the Buick and, when they were out of sight, changed into an old Willys. Hoffmann lay down in the back. Doubrava put on glasses. He drove the Willys down toward Louise uncertainly, as if looking for a place to park. Louise couldn't see him because the sun was on his windshield. She needed one more car to fill the lot, so she motioned him in.

"It's Walter all right," said Louise bitterly. "He must have complained."

I parked while she went to court. When the Frenchman got out of his car, I thought I was seeing things. There were two of him, exactly alike. I could hardly wait for Louise to get home to tell her he *was* twins. She got home in high spirits. The judge had dismissed the case.

"As long as you didn't wave a red flag and jump on running boards," he said to Louise, "I don't see any harm."

The next day Walter got a summons for jumping on running boards, and the judge gave him a call-down. Walter blamed it on Louise. He came down and shook his fist at her.

"While I was at court, your mother got that blue Rhode Island Packard away from me," he said. "You better look out. If he parks in your yard tonight I'll flatten his tires."

Louise said scram or she'd hit him over the head with a crutch.

We sat up guarding the Rhode Island Packard till we were so tired we couldn't keep awake. The owner was night electrician at the Fair, so we knew he'd be there all night. Next morning before we got up we heard swearing and cursing. His tires were flat.

When I went over to Kowalski's for a pack of cigarettes, Walter Rau was standing outside.

"I wish I walked with crutches like Louise," he said, "so I could give everybody a sob story and park every car in Queens."

"Maybe you will," I said, leading with my right. He weighed over two hundred but he went down like a plummet. I got the cigarettes and went back.

"I shut Walter Rau up," I told Louise.

We were eating supper when the bell rang. Harold answered it.

"The police are looking for you," he said to me. He went back to the door with me. Walter Rau and a cop were waiting.

"Are you the lady who called this man a so-and-so and knocked him flat?" asked the cop.

"That's no lady, that's my wife," said Harold.

The cop handed me a paper:

SUMMONS   Officer on Post Please Assist
IN THE NAME OF THE PEOPLE OF THE STATE OF
NEW YORK
To Mary Pierson the name Mary being fictitious, full name un-
    known, but who can be identified
COMPLAINT HAVING BEEN MADE THIS DAY BY   Walter
    Rau
THAT YOU DID COMMIT THE OFFENSE OF   Assault 3rd
    degree by unlawfully striking deponent in the face with
    your hand.
YOU ARE HEREBY SUMMONED, etc.

I wanted Harold to go to court with me, but he wouldn't. The judge gave Walter an awful call-down after he heard the story. He said he'd like to call him just what I called him but the dignity of the court prevented.

"Thank God the Fair's got only two more days to go and this thing will be over," said Harold.

But it was the last day that broke our hearts. Walter got Myrna Loy!

"We've made fifteen hundred dollars," said Louise sadly next morning. "But it doesn't seem like anything. Walter's still crowing."

She was brokenhearted. She wouldn't even go over to Kowalski's for cigarettes.

It was late in the afternoon, when I was reading the paper, that I ran across a picture that looked vaguely familiar.

"Look!" I cried to Louise. "Look who's dining at the Stork Club with the Duchesse de Talleyrand!"

"Holy mackerel, Jeepers creepers, wait till I show Walter this!" shouted Louise.

There, chatting chummily with the Duchesse, was the Frenchman we thought was a waiter, whose battered Ford had been given the lowly position between the driveway and the garage.

Underneath the picture was the caption:

"Prince de Bourbon."

O. M. BLODGETT, SOLE OWNER
AND PROP.

It was the night Maurice Hindus broadcast from Prague that I got the funny feeling in the pit of my stomach. He turned the mike toward the crowd so we could hear them yelling for arms and singing the national anthem. General Sirový came out on the balcony to quiet them. "Such trouble as the world has never seen—" Maurice Hindus' voice trailed off thinly. The Prague radio was silenced.

For a moment nobody said anything.

"We're alone. America's alone," I said suddenly. "France and England must be nuts to hand over the Skoda works and the Czech army and the Sudeten forts—Hitler's last barrier. The Russians can't hold him off with their gun butts." Nobody commented. "Well, don't just sit there," I said. "We ought to wire our Congressman, whoever the dickens he is. We ought to do something."

"The hell with those guys for going back on Czechoslovakia," said Harold. "I feel like taking my British uniform and burning it on the steps of the British pavilion."

A year later, when England declared war on Germany, Harold got out his old British war posters, "Forward to Victory" and "Your King and Country Need You," and put them up.

"Good old England," he said. "I knew she'd come through."

The day his job with the World's Fair ended, Warsaw fell. That night when the broken bugle call sounded from the Polish pavilion, the lights went out. There was no more Poland.

"I can't stand it any longer," said Harold. "I can't keep my mind on my work with those Huns on the loose again. It isn't Hitler, it's the German people. They're born barbarians. Let's get our passports. Let's go to London."

Louise said she'd go too.

"What could you do?" I asked her. "Park tanks?"

"She could be a camp follower," suggested Frank.

"Do you know what a camp follower *is?*" asked Harold sternly.

Frank said he didn't exactly, but he'd always read where they had them. He thought they probably dished out coffee and hot doughnuts. Harold said was I sure Frank's I.Q. hadn't been exaggerated.

Frank said if we all wanted to go to London not to worry about him. He'd be all right. Through his work at the Fair he'd been granted a full scholarship at the Hill school. He was to have a *private laboratory* for his chemistry.

The boys and Barbara were furious. They said we had no right to go and get ourselves killed.

"Good Lord, we can't live forever," I said. "I'd rather be popped off by a bomb giving the RAF a great hand than die of senile decay puttering around the kitchen."

We jumped into the car and drove to Washington. It was two A. M. when we got there.

"Let's drive around and see the lights burning late in the embassies," I said. "It always tells about it in the papers."

The embassies were black as pitch. Harold said maybe they were expecting an air raid.

The next morning Harold went to the British Embassy. He came out quick. He said they were almost afraid to talk to him. They said they couldn't accept enlistments from Americans. If they did, the American people might think they were drumming up an expeditionary force or something.

Sol Bloom, Chairman of the House Foreign Relations Committee, said there wasn't a chance of our getting passports. The government felt the high seas were too dangerous for Americans. If Americans were sunk, public opinion might be "inflamed."

"American public opinion is about as inflammable as a wet dishrag," I told Harold. "The only things Americans get excited over are boogie-woogie, electric iceboxes, and going down to Jones Beach. What's happened to the freedom of the seas? How come that's been handed over before Hitler even asked for it?"

Harold was so mad because he couldn't enlist with the British that he didn't even listen.

"My God," he said, "that paperhanger with the hives has got

everybody buffaloed. If you want to fight him you're out of bounds."

We drove dejectedly home, and Harold picked up the classified-ad section of *The New York Times.* "I might as well look and see what the cat's dragged in," he said gloomily.

"Listen," he said. "This sounds possible. 'Wanted, man who loves the country as overseer of large hotel property. Blodgett's Point, Lake George, New York. O. M. Blodgett, Sole Owner and Prop.'"

"Count me out," I said. "I'm not the peasant type."

Harold threw down the paper. "Now I'll tell you one thing. I'm not going to walk up and down Sixth Avenue again with all the other bums out of work reading those 'Help Wanted, bus boy' signs. I'm going to take the first job I can get. And pronto. Take a letter."

I took one. I also wired my sister telling her I was threatened. Rush reinforcements.

She arrived just as we received an answer from O. M. Blodgett. I read her the list of the overseer's duties:

Overseer must know how to do work listed below and be able and willing to do it himself:

Repair all electrical equipment in hotel and 50 cottages
Take care of all motors, generators
Repair, adjust, and install oil burners
Take care of refrigeration plant and iceboxes, pumping back
    ammonia and starting in spring
Install power and light lines. I would like to rewire whole place
    this fall. This means cutting holes and installing additional
    power line for motors
Drain all water pipes in fall and put together in the spring
Install complete bathrooms and run sewage lines
Repair automobiles
Repair furniture
Build cabinets
Build cottages
Draw and shovel gravel for fixing grounds, roads, paths
Repair and overhaul boats
Cut ice and wood in the wintertime
Shovel snow

Overseer's wife must be willing to cook for 8 to 10 men as needed.

"What, no large-scale projects?" asked my sister. "I'm disappointed. But you could always run up and harness the St. Lawrence in your spare time."

Harold said, now be reasonable. It might not be bad at all. He'd spent a winter in the Adirondacks when he was young and he'd never forgotten it. Going out early to get wood, when it was so cold the snow squeaked under your boots and your breath froze. Rubbing your numb hands over the cheery little pot-bellied stove in the kitchen. Steaming coffee. Pancakes loaded with honest-to-God maple sirup. Homemade country sausage.

"How much are the tickets?" said Louise. "I'll take one."

"Harold feels about the Adirondacks just as I did about the Cape," I said. "He can't see that it was because we were *young* that everything looked so good to us. He doesn't realize that he's changed. And so, doubtless, have the Adirondacks."

"I tell you, Harold," said my sister, "if you take that job it will be the death of you. It sounds to me like the Georgia chain gang. That man doesn't want an overseer. He wants ten men and a bulldozer."

I asked Harold what there was for me and Louise to do when we got tired of listening to our boots squeak and rubbing our numb hands over the pot-bellied stove. He consulted Mr. Blodgett's letter. There was "little diversion," according to Mr. Blodgett, during the winter. The six families who lived at the Point, mostly Indians, went to the movies occasionally at Whitehall, twelve miles distant, or listened to the radio if the roads weren't open. But, added Harold, there were lots of interesting places to see around Blodgett's. Louise and I could drive over to Fort Anne and Fort Ticonderoga.

"There's nothing I like better when it's seventeen below," I said, "than to dash out and inspect a few old redoubts."

"You and Burgoyne," said Louise. "Me heap much better like movies occasionally if road open."

"You all make me tired," said Harold disgustedly. "You and Louise haven't done anything but mope anyway since you haven't got the boys to wait on."

This was a bull's-eye. I missed the boys and Barbara dreadfully. I was right, I thought. I should have had nine children. I tried not to think about it. I was afraid I'd get like the women I'd made so much fun of all these years who wrote in to Dorothy Dix asking what to do with their lives now that their children had grown up and left home.

I saw Harold was getting discouraged.

"Maybe the job wouldn't be so bad," I said hopefully. "Maybe we could make something of it."

"I had hopes of you," said my sister, "when Harold got this wonderful job landscaping the Fair. But they're fading fast. For thirty years you've lived in a world of fantasy. Every few months you'd call me up or write me about some great new astounding undertaking. Everything was going to be different. It was 'the most wonderful job in the world' or 'the finest house you've ever seen' or 'the brightest child that ever drew breath.' You hoped!"

"I did more than hope," I said. "I believed!"

"And you never once noticed during all those years," said my sister, "that after faith and hope usually came charity. Now look. If you go through with this hitching yourselves up to a plow again, I'm through with you."

Harold said, look at it sensibly. He had to have a job. Right? Right. Did we know of another? No. Were landscaping firms on their uppers or weren't they? They were. Then prospects were bum. Here was a job he could do and he was going to do it. He had a family to support. Besides, he was worried about his father. "I'll have to help him," he said, "though it'll about kill him to accept anything. He was always the giver." His father had just written that the doctor had forbidden him to work any more. He'd had to give up the little cannery. Bad heart. "But it's my own fault," he added. "Everybody told me not to try to lift things but I was bullheaded." Harold's father was eighty.

"Well," said my sister. "I don't know why I should set myself up as the Voice of Experience. It's up to Harold to decide what's best."

I told her she had every right. She'd been successful. We hadn't.

"Oh, now, you aren't being fair to yourself," said my sister. "You can't measure the results of your efforts, and mine, with the same yardstick. I'm a materialist. You're an idealist. I only rave on because I hate so to see you struggle."

"But you've never wanted worldly things for yourself since you were twenty," I protested. "You've only wanted them for your children."

"I hate to break up this fascinating discussion of the divergent philosophies of the beautiful Randall sisters," said my sister, "but I've got to catch a train."

Let her know what we wanted for Christmas, she called as she went out the door. Harold looked after her affectionately.

"Your sister," he said, "is my favorite Tory. I've been meaning to tell her so for a long time."

After she'd gone, Harold told us that Mr. Blodgett suggested that he go up for two weeks and get things organized. Then he was to come back for me and Louise. "Oh, I forgot to tell you," he added. "Mr. Blodgett says the house we're going to have is furnished. We'll have to stick our stuff in storage."

It would have solved everything, I thought sadly, if Harold could have connected with the British. It would have been wonderful to go to London. I could just see us standing on the deck of a liner, Harold in uniform, Louise and me with orchid corsages on our fur coats purchased with the parking money. Pulling out of New York Harbor at dusk. Waving au revoir to the Statue of Liberty. Heading for ringside seats at the biggest battle in the world's history.

"Well, what do you say?" said Harold. "Shall we try Blodgett's?"

We'd just be strings to somebody else's bow, I thought. There was no future in it. But what else could we do? Maybe it wouldn't be too hard. Mr. Blodgett had said Harold could have helpers; two or three in winter; eight in summer.

"O.K.," I said. "Wire Mr. Blodgett."

We'll make a go of it, I thought. Somehow.

Mr. Blodgett wired back, "Come at once," and Harold departed. Louise and I were blue. We were bluer still when we got a wire from Harold saying, "Everything under control. But Blodgett doesn't like dogs. What about Skipper?"

"But we can't get rid of Skipper," said Louise. "He's one of the family."

Skipper was really a she but we called him he. "Because," said Louise, "there's nothing catty about him. I think Skipper was as surprised as we were when he had those eleven puppies."

Getting rid of Skipper was such a dreadful prospect we didn't even discuss it. I kept putting it off and putting it off. I'd made up my mind not to send Skipper to the SPCA. He never could bear to have a stranger touch him. The day Harold and the moving men were due to arrive I got up early and dug a grave. I cried all the time I was digging. I couldn't help it. I didn't want Louise to see. Later, while she was busy packing china, I went up to the drugstore and asked for "enough chloroform to chloroform a big dog." The druggist gave me a Merck's chloroform bottle half full, twenty-five cents' worth. When Louise went out for the *Times*, I took some cotton and put it inside Skipper's muzzle; then slipped the muzzle on. Skipper sat looking at me patiently. I sat down on the floor beside him, tears streaming down my face. Slowly, I started to pour the contents of the bottle onto the cotton. Skipper leaped in the air with a piercing yell, tearing his muzzle off, and knocking over the bottle so the rest of the chloroform spilled on my hands. Before I could stop him he streaked it out the back door. I raced after him.

"What's the matter with Skipper?" called Louise as she came down the hill. "He tore past me without his muzzle. I'm afraid he'll bite someone." I stood there wondering what to do. "My God," said Louise, as she came up. "What's happened to your hands?"

I looked at them. They were swollen double their normal size. They felt as if they were burning. "And what's that hole in the ground you've dug? Oh, Mother!"

"I didn't know what to do," I said. "I couldn't bear to turn him over to strangers."

"What's that funny smell?" said Louise. "Like carbolic acid. And your hands are turning black."

"I think the drugstore man made a mistake," I said. "I better go up there."

He had. He'd handed me an old Merck's bottle into which his clerk had poured left-over carbolic and nitric acid.

"Quick, rub this on your hands," he said. "I'll bandage them."

When he'd finished, I rushed back to Louise.

"Skipper's mouth must be raw," I said. "I'm going to telephone the police to shoot him." I called up the police. They sent around the sergeant. "You broke the law buying chloroform without a prescription," he said. "I'm going to hand you a summons."

"I *didn't* buy chloroform!" I shouted. "I bought nitric acid! You can't arrest me for that. Why don't you do something about Skipper? He's suffering."

"Skipper's playing with another dog now," said Louise, comfortingly. "I think he feels better."

"I sent for the SPCA to come for him," said the sergeant. "I ain't allowed to shoot him."

"But you threatened to shoot him dozens of time," I said, "when I let him out without a muzzle."

The sergeant said that was different. Skipper wasn't bothering nobody now. He was playing. "But I gotta warn you," he said. "When I told the SPCA what you done they said by rights they otta arrest you for cruelty to animals."

"Go on, arrest me! Everybody arrest me!" I cried, waving my bandaged arms. "What do I care?"

"Now, lady," said the sergeant. "You got no call to get excited." If there was anything he could do for me, short of shooting Skipper, he added, he'd be glad to do it.

"You can go down to the state store and get me 'Today's Special. Green River. $1.29.' Here's the money. If the Captain kicks, tell him it was to save a woman from going crazy."

Louise and I retired to the shed and got glasses. When the SPCA man came for Skipper, we cried so we could hardly sign the release. We tried not to listen when the man said, "Now I've got you," and Skipper gave a pitiful whine. We didn't look when they drove out of the yard.

Fortunately, the sergeant came buzzing up just then with the

Green River. "Join us?" I asked. "It's against regulations," he said, reaching for a glass. I raised my glass in my bandaged hand. The sergeant and Louise raised theirs. "To Skipper," I said. There was a step at the door. It was Harold. He took one look; Louise sobbing; me with my arms bandaged to the elbows; the Green River; the sergeant. "For God's sake," he said, "what's happened? Are you all on a crying jag?"

"It's Skipper," said Louise. "The SPCA."

"You haven't done anything with Skipper!" said Harold. "Why all the way down I kept thinking we'd sneak him back with us and Mr. Blodgett would be crazy over him. I didn't think you'd do anything about him till I came."

"Well, I guess I'll be going," said the sergeant, sliding out the back door. Luckily, just then, the moving men came. An hour later, the house was empty.

"Now, snap into it," said Harold. "Throw all our things into the La Salle. I've got to get back tonight."

As we swung onto the Parkway and headed north, Harold put his hand on my bandaged arm. "Listen," he said. "It's going to be a new life. Let's do the best we can. It would have been wonderful if we could have gone to London, but we couldn't. The British Embassy hinted I was too old, anyway. So all right. The hell with the war!"

He wasn't going to think about it. He didn't want it mentioned.

The war wasn't mentioned all the way up to Blodgett's. Of course, we did have Kaltenborn, Elmer Davis, and Wythe Williams on the car radio. Harold was pretty sharp with Louise when she wanted Artie Shaw's orchestra. It interfered with the 4:15 news from Europe.

When we began to go up hills in low and down in low, Harold said we were in the Adirondacks. Blodgett's was over the mountain from Whitehall. We crawled up the side of the mountain like a fly. Then we went down, down, down. Suddenly we shot out of the woods onto a small plain dotted with bungalows set on stilts. At either end of the plain were two large hotels. Lapping the edge of the plain were the waters of Lake George.

With our brakes burning merrily, and our floor mop waving waggishly in the breeze, we drifted to a stop in front of a large square house, completely surrounded with a glassed-in porch, right on the shore of the lake.

"Home!" said Harold. "We live in one half. When the Blodgetts are up from Albany they live in the other."

Mrs. Blodgett came dashing out in *Vogue*'s dress of the month and diamond earrings. Louise and I looked gloomily at our plaid lumber shirts and dungarees. Mr. Blodgett was a large man with lots of gold emblems dangling from his watch chain. His slightly disapproving manner conveyed the impression that anyone who had not been as financially successful as he had was guilty of criminal negligence. Harold hopped out, sprang around to my side, and opened the door with his most courtly manner. Instantly, *The New York Times,* the vacuum cleaner, a bottle of hydrochloric acid that I was supposed to be holding upright, and Harold's Park Grammar School Diploma for the year 1901 fell out on Mrs. Blodgett's feet.

"Why, what is the matter with your hands?" asked Mrs. Blodgett.

"Oh, nothing at all really," I said. "I just burned them."

"Well," said Mrs. Blodgett doubtfully, "I hope you'll get on all right. Your boarder will be here in about half an hour. I suppose Mr. Pierson told you. We're going right back to Albany after my husband gives Mr. Pierson the orders."

Boarder! I shot Harold a dirty look. He ignored it and hurried in after the Blodgetts. I'd forgotten that Mr. Blodgett's letter said "wife willing to take boarders."

"Maybe we should have chloroformed ourselves," I said, "instead of Skipper."

"We might as well get out," said Louise gloomily. "We've got to sometime."

The glassed-in porch proved to be reeking with plants. Aspidistras and the more pernicious forms of coleus.

"I make it fifty-five," said Louise. "The Blodgetts' half is crawling with them, too. Pa can't look a plant in the face since the Fair. We'll have to water them."

Before we'd had time to get our hats and coats off, the boarder arrived.

"I'm an electrician," he said affably, sitting down beside us. He looked at his watch. "My gosh," he said. "We almost missed it. Time fer the furrin broadcast. I orries listen to this here now Ed Murrow."

Bob Trout was just winding up with "And that's the world today," when Harold came in.

"Oh, listening to the war," said Harold.

"Let 'em stew in their own juice," said the electrician. "This God-damn war's no business of ours. I fought in the last war. I know what war is. They'll never git me inter another one. I got me a good job and I'm gointer hang onto it. Security. They ben fightin' ever since they wuz born over there in Yurrup. It ain't got nothin' to do with us. Let's we keep outta it."

"What outfit were you with?" asked Harold.

"Machine-gun section of the eighty-second," said the electrician. "I was all over. The Argonne, the Moose, Shatto Teary."

"I was with the Royal Canadian Dragoons," said Harold. "Cavalry machine-gunner. Sergeant Major. Those Vickers guns we had were something."

"They didn't have nothing on the Brownings," said the electrician. "Take that Browning I had——"

"Those Brownings were a lot of crap," said Harold. "Listen! At Vimy Ridge, how long do you think it took us to get a Vickers into action? I'm riding lead horse, at a stretch gallop. I'm leading a pack horse with gun and tripod. Behind me comes another man riding at stretch gallop, leading a pack horse with ammunition. We get the order. How long do you think it takes us to stop, dismount, set up the gun, load and fire? Eleven seconds!"

The electrician picked up a pillow, dropped it on the floor, and threw himself down on his stomach behind it.

"Look," he said. "We're on this little rise in the Argonne. The Heinies is firing at us from that clump o' trees——"

Harold hurled two pillows into the opposite corner and threw himself down on *his* stomach.

"How many yards? Ratatatatatat!" he said, tentatively, swinging his imaginary Vickers into position.

Mr. Blodgett opened the door.

Harold and the electrician jumped to their feet.

"We were talking about the war—" began Harold.

"This is not our war," said Mr. Blodgett. "If we know what's good for us we'll keep out of it. We made the world safe for democracy last time and look what's happened. The best thing we can do about the war is forget it. Put it out of our minds. It's not the German people, it's just this damn Hitler. The British were fools to let him get the Skoda works. Now he's got his eye on the Rumanian oil fields. Look, if he takes his troops out of eastern Poland and sends them to the border——" Mr. Blodgett picked up the inkwell. "This is Rumania." He took the ash tray. "This is Poland."

The boarder turned out to be no trouble at all. He went upstairs after dinner every night and drank himself to death. In the morning he came down with his eyes red as a mongoose's and sipped delicately at a cup of coffee.

The work turned out to be harder than Harold had expected. Mr. Blodgett was a strictly self-made man. He'd worked like a dog all his life and expected everybody else to. He'd made a success of Blodgett's. It was the biggest, most popular resort on Lake George. Now that the doctor had forbidden him to do physical labor, he felt the least he could do was to see that everybody else worked twice as hard. He'd left a list of projects for Harold a mile long. Harold and the Indians worked like beavers, repairing, draining, building, and installing. Every night when the cheap rates went on, Mr. Blodgett called up from Albany to see how we were doing.

The Indians were a disappointment. They didn't wear blankets and they had crew haircuts. The only really convincing one was Bob Allen, a big, dark, beady-eyed man with muscles of steel who had married the daughter of Eliphalet Jakeaway, a basket maker from over the mountain. He could fell a tree with ten blows of his ax, which he kept sharp as a razor.

Every morning Louise and I gave the house a thorough going over. Mrs. Blodgett was very particular. Despite her chic, she was a worker like Mr. Blodgett and quick as a flash. She could clean her half of the house, cook up enough food for an army, and embroider a needle-point chair seat before Louise and I could get the rugs out. We felt she would not look with favor on our usual method of letting the work pile up and then digging in like happy sandhogs.

When we'd cleaned the house, all there was for us to do was listen to the radio. We'd tried taking walks, but it was already getting cold and the roads were icy. After Louise fell flat on her face twice, we stayed inside.

At first the radio ran amok among unfamiliar letters like WGY and KIAK. Before we got it under control we learned that Sally Sears of Boston had sent in:

> *It is so cold and dreary alone on Beacon Hill*
> *Because my debut next year will not be until.*

We switched hastily, only to discover that on Halloween in White River Junction they had a parade of Horribles in front of the Hotel Coolidge, led by the chief of police; and that a man known as the Murderer of Murderer's Gulch, who was awaiting execution, had authorized a sale of his belongings to defray the expense of his imminent funeral. The hay brought $7.50 a ton, but they only got $28.75 for the little bull calf which, in happier days, the Murderer had trained to follow him around.

"It hardly seems enough," said Harold when we told him.

The Canadian stations proved more cheerful. There was somebody just like Charles Boyer (whose very *bon soir* can cause me to swoon like any debutante). Just the way he said "Monnrayahl, Kebeck," and the passion which he could put into the simple declarative *"Maintenant le Chipso programme"* made you feel that not only did Chipso take the cuss off washday but it had all the mystery and efficacy of a love potion.

Even though Harold got so tired working, he managed to sit up and listen to the news from Europe. Wythe Williams and Kaltenborn. He wouldn't discuss the war news with us, though occasionally we heard him mutter, "Damn Chamberlain." One of the Indians informed me, however, that "Mr. Pierson sure had the war down fine." There was always a heated forum on foreign affairs at the post office every noon, when all Blodgett's gathered to wait for the mail. Everybody but us, I discovered, sat up till eleven every night in order to hear Paul Sullivan. At eight, Harold limped off to bed.

"I'm failing fast," he said. "I guess the British were right in not taking me. But I think old OMBSO & P is going to be tickled to death when he comes up. He won't expect to find the wood cut and the new dock built. We're ahead of schedule."

When Mr. Blodgett came up, however, he seemed disappointed. Harold hadn't cemented the floor in the hotel liquor room. Harold said he didn't know he wanted it cemented. Mr. Blodgett said he didn't want a man who had to be told everything. He wanted a man with vision.

Mr. Blodgett was "surprised" at me because I'd given the ferrets hamburg with salt on it. The ferrets lived in a box chastely shrouded in an old rug, out back of the kitchen. They were long, furry things. I knew they were ferrets the minute I saw them, because of my long and unsuccessful tussle with the *New York Post* Puzzle Contests. The reason they were ferrets, not stoats or ermine, was that you have to have the two *r*'s in ferrets to combine with the name of the Secretary of State under President Harrison or the final word won't come out. (And don't let it fool you, either—there were two President Harrisons and that grizzled old sourpuss is Horace Greeley.) Salt was bad for ferrets, Mr. Blodgett said. It killed them. He wanted to know why they were collecting bottle tops. Every time I let them out for a run, they came back with a bunch of old bottle tops.

"Maybe they've read the writing on the wall and think war is coming," I told Mr. Blodgett. "That's their war effort."

Mr. Blodgett didn't think this was funny. He'd been in a bad mood, anyway, ever since the tractor got lost. The tractor was made by Jim, Harold's predecessor on the job.

"Jim can make anything," said Mr. Blodgett.

After seeing Jim, I told Harold his next project should be a set of uppers and lowers. Then we'd find out.

The tractor was Jim's Big Moment before he retired to his muskrat farm. If you used the tractor you had to go over and get Jim to come back and drive it. Nobody else was sufficiently foolhardy. It had one gear, a very fast high. When it started, it took off like an airplane and didn't hit terra firma for about fifteen feet. Then it simply streaked it in whatever direction it was headed. With infinite optimism Harold had been using this instrument of death to plow up a bog back of some of the cottages, with the idea of turning it into a lawn. Jim bestrode the Speed Demon. Behind it they dragged a plow manned by Bob Allen, the authentic Indian. This caravan tore through the muck, making turns as if they were on Bonnevelle Flats.

But one day they goaded it too far. It just plain sank. It fought and kicked and reared and plunged for a while, then gave up the ghost. Harold and the Indians got cordwood and threw pieces into the mire in front of the tractor. As each piece was set, the tractor would leap aboard and pause shuddering. They almost had it out when Mr. Blodgett came up. He accused Harold of carelessness. Harold and the Indians were pretty mad. That was why they wouldn't do anything when Mr. Blodgett set the place afire.

He set the place afire with the flame thrower. He'd bought the flame thrower to kill poison ivy. Every time he came up he got all dressed up in his flame thrower's costume, an outfit suitable for deep-sea diving, and dashed out tugging the flame thrower. Five minutes later he would stagger into the house all pooped out, dragging it behind him. Something had gone wrong with it. But the day the tractor got lost nothing went wrong with it. I smelled smoke and looked out to see billows of black smoke rolling in from the meadows.

"Come on," said Louise. "Let's take to the boats."

After two hours of hard work Mr. Blodgett finally got the fire out.

"I think you were mean," I said to Harold, "not to help him."

"To tell you the truth," he said, "I don't think it makes a hell of a lot of difference what I do. We're not the kind of people the Blodgetts expected."

We weren't. Yet they'd really been very kind. Mrs. Blodgett was always dashing in with plates of hot biscuits. They urged us to help ourselves to anything they left in their icebox when they went back to Albany. Mr. Blodgett said there was no use in the stuff spoiling. Mrs. Blodgett always invited me and Louise in to talk while she embroidered.

The trouble was, I reflected, they were never there long enough to see just how hard Harold was working. And he was never one to blow his own horn. There was so much to do on fifty cottages, two hotels, a casino, a golf course, garage, trucks, boats, tennis courts, and docks that the finished jobs just seemed a drop in the bucket. Instead of the three helpers he'd been provided, Mr. Blodgett had cut Harold down to one helper, then none. Harold was literally breaking his back and getting nowhere. Besides, it was getting colder and colder. It's pretty hard to get much done outside at a temperature of five below zero. It wasn't Harold's fault that the storeroom roof caved in before he could get the snow off it.

"One man can't shovel three feet of snow off sixty roofs simultaneously," said Harold.

"That's what you think," said Louise. "Mr. Blodgett could."

"He probably could," Harold said wearily. "I never saw people in my life who could do as much work as the Blodgetts. If they've made money, they've earned it."

"Don't you think they're satisfied with us?" I asked him.

He said frankly, he didn't. He had a hunch we were on the skids. Mr. Blodgett had asked him if he had anything in mind, if things didn't work out. "But it's no use worrying," he said. "We can't do any better than our best."

We were glad when Christmas came and John and Frank got off the Laurentian all weighed down with skis and skates, looking like Abercrombie and Fitch, Incorporated. They were a little taken back to find how desolate and deserted Lake George was. They'd pictured it a gay paradise of winter sports. They helped Harold stack wood. Harold was glad to have them because he'd broken a bone in his hand. Besides, he had to spend a lot of time under the back porch with a blowtorch. The pipes kept freezing. Louise and I dished up Washington County sausage and pancakes with Adirondacks maple sirup every morning to keep his courage up. At night, we all listened to W. L. White in Helsinki.

"Damn it, John," said Harold. "I don't know how much longer I can stand it not to be *doing* anything about this war."

I didn't either. Just as W. L. White signed off we'd hear the droning whine of the Canadian mail plane. Frank looked out at the snowy mountain and watched the beacon flashing.

"Gee," said Frank. "This place sure is lonesome."

He felt better next morning when I showed him my mink trap. Every morning I'd seen a mink run across our back lot. It was the first mink I'd ever seen that wasn't in Jaeckel's window and therefore out of my reach. I could hardly decide between the Oneida Victor, sixteen cents, Sears Roebuck, page 977, and the Oneida Number 1 Jump Stop-Loss, thirty-two cents. Both had death-grip steel jaws. I'd sent for both. I'd also sent for the four-hundred-page free booklet, *Tips to Trappers*, and some mink scent. I didn't know you had to have scent till I read about it in the Sears Roebuck catalogue. I thought the animals had it. Frankie went out faithfully every morning and looked in the trap.

"I could do with a pair of mink mittens," he said.

John told us that he was in the top third of his class but he'd made so much money selling subscriptions to *The New York Times*, giving blood transfusions, tutoring, and running the laundry that the College of Physicians and Surgeons had withdrawn his scholarship.

"If the doctor business ever palls," said John, "I can always open a laundry as a hobby. I've been running one now at one school or another for going on twelve years."

Frank and John seemed to be having such a dull vacation that I was glad when Mrs. Cramer called up and invited the whole family to the Christmas party at the church. Mrs. Cramer was the social leader of Blodgett's, a determined-looking woman with masses of jet-black hair and snapping black eyes.

"It's our annual entertainment," she said. "Supper too. If you care to bring something in the line of food we'd appreciate it."

"How about an apple pie?" I asked her. She said that would be fine.

"While I'm doing it," I told Louise, "I might as well make two. One for us, and one for them."

Christmas Eve it was colder than Greenland's icy mountains.

"The thermometer says ten below," said Frankie. "But it feels colder than that. I think it's broken."

Frankie and John got their ears nipped riding the half mile to the church in the rumble seat. I rushed in first with the apple pie so it wouldn't freeze and rushed out again.

"Go right home and get the other pie," I said to Harold. I'd caught a glimpse of two tables sparsely set with edibles. Those "vittles" wouldn't go far with the thirty-five sturdy inhabitants of Blodgett's milling around the little room which comprised the church.

"There's one thing," said Mrs. Cramer as we entered and handed her our pies. "The summer folks remembered us good. There's plenty of presents."

Sure enough, the little Christmas tree in one corner was banked high with gaily wrapped packages.

"Sit down and make yourselves at home," said Mrs. Cramer. "We were afraid you might be busy packing. We hear you're leaving."

"We are?" I said aghast. Harold pinched me. "Oh no," I said. "You must be mistaken."

"Well, good enough," said Mrs. Cramer in a doubting tone. "I hope you're right."

Somewhat shaken, we sat down on a bench in front of a platform across the front of which two sheets strung on clothesline were drawn. Encouraged by our example, the rest of the customers reluctantly tore themselves away from a large lukewarm stove optimistically named the "Good Cheer" and joined us. A silence fell. We sat expectantly, if coldly, waiting. But Ellen McCallum, the teacher, was having difficulty in rounding up the performers who still stuck to the stove.

"Angels!" she called imperiously. Five nervous angels, their white cheesecloth costumes prudently topped with sweaters, filed onto the platform and disappeared behind the sheets.

"Wise Men!" demanded Miss McCallum. The Wise Men wore lumber jackets.

Mrs. Cramer advanced to a commanding position at the front of the room. Laying one hand firmly on the "Good Cheer," she raised the other imperatively for silence.

"As you can see from the piles of bundles underneath the tree," she said, "our friends from the city have remembered us, thank the good Lord. We also wish to give thanks, O Lord, for the *strangers in our midst.*" She fixed Harold, Louise, John, Frank, and me with a basi-liskian eye. Everybody turned to look at us. "And for the two apple pies they brought."

There was a sprinkling of applause. We blushed modestly. At this point, the door burst open, and Kissy Fuller, a local belle, entered, triumphantly escorted by three guards from the state prison at Com-stock. A ripple ran through the audience. It was a thrill to have visi-tors from over the mountain.

"The entertainment," went on Mrs. Cramer, frowning down this vulgar display of snobbishness, "is about to commence. I hope there will be no hooting and yelling as there was last year. Ellen McCal-lum, as you know, has been working under difficulties. There are six-teen now in our school. She was put to it to find good parts for every-one. The first number will be a recitation of 'Jingle Bells.'"

A few hardy souls removed their hats, thought better of it, and put them on again. The sheets parted. A little girl about five, in sweater and hunting boots, dashed out on the stage.

"Jigga bayoo, jigga bayoo, jigger awa dayoo," she began.

Ellen McCallum touched me on the arm.

"You may find it a little hard to understand them," she said. "They've intermarried for years, and way back, somebody had an impediment in his speech."

The little girl bowed and dashed off the platform to wild applause. Then a tousle-headed boy of ten rendered "Home on the Range" or, as he sang it, "Hoah oh ve Wayuv." After that came a play involving a rock, a good fairy, a bad fairy, three wishes, and a lot of miscel-laneous characters in sheepskin coats and skating boots. By the time the Angels and Wise Men came on, there were a few catcalls. The audience was becoming impatient. They wanted Santa Claus.

"Santa Claus will be with us in a moment," said Mrs. Cramer re-provingly.

"That's what you think," came from a seat in the rear.

Ellen McCallum explained *sotto voce* that was Bob Allen, Jr. He was mad because they wouldn't let him be Santa Claus again, because he'd been drunk last year.

"Where's Santa Claus? We want Sant Claus!" came from all parts of the room. Somebody opened the door and looked out. "He'll be here soon's he gits inter his suit." To create a diversion the reciter of "Jingle Bells" was brought up on the platform and induced to sit on Ellen McCallum's lap and call up Santa Claus on a toy telephone. She had just urged him to hurry when the door burst open with a crash and Santa Claus staggered in.

"Well, well, well," he shouted in terrible tones.

The little girl burst into tears. Santa Claus began shaking hands with Mrs. Cramer, pumping her arm up and down.

"That's enough, Santa Claus," said Mrs. Cramer sternly. "Let's get to the presents."

Santa started to mount the platform, misjudged it entirely, and fell flat on his face.

"Santa Claus forgot his glasses," said Mrs. Cramer apologetically.

"He didn't forget that pint o' rye he had in his hip pocket," came from the back of the room.

"Who will help Santa Claus hand out the presents?" said Mrs. Cramer hastily. "Santa Claus needs help."

This was putting it mildly. He couldn't even get up on his knees. Several recruits rushed forward. One picked up a package.

"Mr. Pierson," he called.

Evidently our names had been sent in to the city people, but before Harold could step forward it was seized by an outstretched hand and disappeared. It seemed to be an old Indian custom. The fourth time Harold's name was called he leaped like a gazelle—and made it. Everyone watched breathless as he opened the package. It was a lace runner for the table.

"The *very* thing I wanted," said Harold.

Although we sat down at the table where our pies had been placed, they seemed to have disappeared. But there were cold baked beans, corn pone without butter, cole slaw, and jello. The men talked about what a trimming the Finns were giving Russians and when we'd get in the war. "Better git in now," they said. "Have it over."

"We had a wonderful time," I said to Mrs. Cramer when we left.

"I've meant to ask you," she said. "How are your hands where you burned 'em?"

"Fine," I said. "Just fine."

"I don't care," said Mrs. Cramer forgetting it was Christmas. "You'll get revenge on that druggist who sold you that acid if you've got any Indian in you."

When we got home we opened our presents. There were big boxes of things from Barbara and Rodney and my sister. And five dollars for Harold from Mr. Blodgett. Barbara wrote she was naming their new baby John Randall for my father. Rodney wrote he was transferring to the University of Pittsburgh. He'd taken every metallurgical course they had at Carnegie Tech. My sister wrote she was looking for us any day now.

"It's the best Christmas we ever had," said Frankie.

I asked Harold after we went upstairs if he thought our number was really up. He said he did. But not till after the icing.

"What'll we do?" I asked.

"Nothing," he said. His policy was "watchful waiting."

The boys had no sooner gone than the icers came. There had been nine days of twelve-below-zero weather. Every night Mr. Blodgett called up from Albany to ask how thick the ice was. When we told him it was twenty-four inches he said if it didn't snow again the icers would be there Sunday.

Old Man Slight showed up first. He was seventy-two and bent double with rheumatism. He owned the only ice-cutting machine in the county, so everybody had to employ him.

"I'm a lineal descendant of King James I," he said as he came in the door. "My ancestors founded Washington County. The sooner we get in this war, the better for everybody. And that goes for my black-hearted Catholic neighbors." And did we have a copy of *The New York Sunday Times*? He was lost without it.

Mr. Hopkins was next. "He's got a boy in N.Y.U. but he can't read or write, got to make his mark," whispered Mr. Slight loudly.

The third was a red-faced man named Jake.

They all ate like horses. Louise and I cooked from morning till night. One night they ate seventy-seven raised biscuits.

There were eight other local men and two trucks working on the icing.

Every morning Mr. Slight got up at five and went out and started cutting. By six he'd have cut himself off on a little island of ice. Then he and the icing machine fell in. It would be ten before we'd get him and the machine dried off again. When the ice started rolling, the trucks carried it to the icehouse and dumped it onto the conveyor belt. Harold stood at the top and piked the one-hundred-and-twenty-five-pound pieces off the conveyor belt into position. At five everybody crawled back to the house, half dead and hungry as hunters. After supper, they took off their shoes and put them in a ring around the stove. Then they draped the stove with steaming socks and sweaters.

"First, Kattleborn," Mr. Hopkins would say, pointing at the radio. Next we had to have the European news. Then right on through every commentator. After that came open discussion.

"The trouble with this country," Mr. Slight would lead off, "is too many women. Boys raised by women nowdays. Taught by women. When they get married their wives lead 'em around by the nose. No guts to fight for freedom. Women don't want war. Afraid they'll lose the old meal ticket."

The other men said Mr. Slight had the biggest farm in the county, but women had been the ruination of him. Mr. Slight said what if he did moggige the farm and shoot the money on women. He had sense enough not to marry any of 'em.

Mr. Hopkins said it wasn't our war. He heard on the radio how bad England treated people. He heard England promised them Hindus they could rule theirselves. Then they wouldn't let 'em.

"Good Gaddamighty," said Mr. Slight. "Who cares? Nobody but that Gandy, goes round in a didee. Rest of 'em's infidels. When my ancestors come over nobody promised 'em anything. What they got they fit for. They was met on Plymouth Rock by Indians with bows and arrows loaded for bear."

By golly, said Mr. Slight, he only had a privy but he could set on it when he wanted to. And by God, he'd fight for that privilege.

"This country's made progress sence *your* annsisters come over," said Mr. Hopkins. "An' don't you fergit it."

Mr. Slight picked up his shoes and started for the door. Halfway, he turned and looked at Mr. Hopkins. "Some calls it progress," he said. "And *some* calls it discontent."

It was the last night the icers were there that Mr. Blodgett invited us into his half of the house to see the pictures. He was a candid-camera fan. When we got across the hall we found everything in utter darkness. There was a table with a gadget on it, with three chairs in front of it, as we found by feeling. In one of the chairs was Mr. Mullaney, Mr. Blodgett's father-in-law. He turned out to be a spry old duffer of seventy-four who said his biceps was as good as ever and he didn't know he had a heart. He ascribed this desirable state of affairs to the fact that he'd spent sixty years working under a steam hammer at the Arsenal. A forger, he was, and at one time had eight men working for him.

"Have they found out yet how to temper copper?" asked Harold eagerly, ignoring Mr. Blodgett, who was seated before the machine and had already thrown one picture on the screen upside down.

"It's a lost art," said Mr. Mullaney, sighing deeply, "but take an old German was in the shop—this was in 1888 mind you——"

"This is Miami, and that is Mrs. Kelly's sister," said Mr. Blodgett. "Hell, it's upside down again."

"He was a dirty old beggar," pursued Mr. Mullaney. "Fingers flat like thumbs. They put it up to him to make a rifler for one of the big guns."

"This is Blodgett's Point," said Mr. Blodgett doggedly.

"Didn't take us long to get here from Miami," said Mr. Mullaney. "Well, do you think they had any blueprints in Washington? You're dern right they didn't."

"This is the lake," said Mr. Blodgett, raising his voice and throwing a picture of the lake on the screen.

"You showed us that once, Oscar," said Mr. Mullaney. "Well, that rifler called for three sixteenths by a eighth, turn and a quarter—what's that, Oscar, fog, or you got it upside down?"

"It's taken through a glass-bottomed boat," said Mr. Blodgett angrily.

"So what I thought was a freighter is a sculpin after all," said Mr. Mullaney happily. "As the man said, it's all in the way you look at it

—well, this German he went out and he collected the gol-derndest bunch of junk you ever saw——"

"Now I've burned myself," said Mr. Blodgett loudly.

At that moment there was a knock at the door.

"James Chase, Republican Supervisor, town of Dresden," said Mr. Blodgett, doing the honors, "and *she*," he added, pointing at me, not daring to vent his wrath on Harold and Mr. Mullaney, who were about halfway down the bore of the gun, "*she* is the Democratic Leader of Brooklyn!"

Mr. Blodgett was a rock-ribbed Republican and that was the worst thing he could think of.

There was a moment of stunned silence. We rose with dignity, thanked Mr. Blodgett kindly for a pleasant evening, and retired to our side of the house.

"Now you've done it," I said to Harold. "That's the finishing touch."

"We're out, anyway," said Harold. "The icing's done. We never fitted here anyhow. I guess it's been as hard on the Blodgetts as it has on us. Mr. Blodgett didn't want a superintendent who would take charge of things. He's always been boss. Always will be. He wanted a handy man—a regular truck horse he could order around. He's only kept us on because he got us up here and he thought we didn't have anywhere else to go. He barks a lot but he's really a kindhearted son-of-a-gun."

"If we're footloose and fancy free again," I said, "why don't we do something about the war? You've wanted to. And I've wanted to. But we thought we ought to be sensible. I've felt like a heel ever since I read that piece in *Time* about 'Where are the Americans hiding?' Well, here's three, present and accounted for. Remember that broadcast of W. L. White's? The one where he said if people were knitting it would be nice if they knitted a few bombers? Well, let's! You're an A-1 mechanic and you took engineering at Cornell. Let's get going right now. Don't let's wait to be fired. Let's quit."

Harold hugged me. "Maybe you think I haven't been about crazy draining toilets and cleaning up after ferrets, with the whole world cracking up in my face," he said. "I'll go in and tell Blodgett."

He met Mr. Blodgett in the hall. Mr. Blodgett had started twice to come in and tell us the bad news but felt so badly about it he'd retreated. He said he was sorry it didn't work out but he honestly thought we'd be happier elsewhere. He saw from the start we weren't used to working.

Next day Mrs. Blodgett cooked us up a wonderful dinner with roast pork and lemon-meringue pie. Mr. Blodgett helped us tie the rugs onto the fenders of the La Salle. "Personally we liked you fine," they said. "Good luck."

When we got up to the top of the mountain, Harold stopped the car. We looked off at the world stretched out before us.

"Oregon or Santa Fe?" I asked.

"Philadelphia, Workshop of the Nation," said Harold. "That's headquarters for tanks, ships, and bombers. I figure I can get a job in one of the factories. If I make enough I'll brush up on my flying."

"I can learn to run a lathe," said Louise.

"I'll write letters to the papers about defense," I said, "if they won't let me count bullets. I'll tell how the best defense is a good offense. Remember how Greasy Neale used to tell the boys at Yale that the place for the line is in the other feller's backfield. We'll save this country whether it likes it or not."

"Believe me, any country where we've been free to fail in all the different ways we've failed deserves to be saved," said Harold.

He took off the brake and pressed down on the pedal. The La Salle shot forward like a jack rabbit. I put my hand on his arm. "You know," I said, "I have a feeling this time maybe we won't fail——"

"Fail, hell!" said Harold. "All down but nine, set 'em up in the other alley!"

THIS IS WHERE WE CAME IN

NOW IT was the year Franklin Delano Roosevelt took the oath of office as President of the United States for the third time, with Fala at his side. It was OPM, CIO, SPAB, Leon Henderson's cigar, Harry Hopkins' hat, John L. Lewis' eyebrows, a fifth wife for Tommy Manville, a third term for New York City's Little Passion Flower. It was no gasoline, some gasoline, business as usual, but better rush bombers. It was going around in circles, getting nowhere. 1941.

And then suddenly it was 7:55, the morning of Sunday, December 7, at Pearl Harbor.

Everything was different.

When the Philadelphia firm Harold was working for ordered him to Boston to inspect a war construction job, I said I'd go with him. There was talk of his being sent to Eritrea. In a time like this every minute counts.

I didn't realize we were going by way of Quincy till all of a sudden I looked up and there was the Fore River Shipyard sprawled out for miles and miles. Its fantastic network of steel girders stretched as far as the eye could see. It was hard to believe it was the same Fore River I'd thought so "big" when I worked there thirty years before.

"We ought to be in Quincy in a minute," I said to Harold.

"You're in Quincy now," he said.

I looked around bewildered. The Adams farm was gone; the Coddington School; the old Jeffrey Brackett House. Swallowed up by miles of new highways, rows of defense houses, forests of chain stores. The little old historic town of Quincy we Randalls thought we owned was gone. John Adams and John Quincy Adams, I thought, must be whirling in their graves. In the battle between the Past and the Present, the Present had won hands down.

"I thought we'd go by way of Adams Street," said Harold, "so you could see your old home."

Home. The trouble was, my mother said, your father endorsed notes. We shall of course have to sell this house. Sell *our house?* Our house, my father said, was our castle. And a damned good one at that, he always added. Our house was big. Make no little plans, my father said. You'm a hard nut, you'll make out, said Fred. Sure. I'll make out. I'll be like my father when I grow up. I'll be on the inside looking out. I'll never be on the outside looking in. Nobody can tell me what to do. I'll be a free spirit.

"What are you crying about?" said Harold. "I thought you'd be tickled silly."

"I don't know," I said. "It's just that life turned out so—so different from what I expected."

"What did you expect?" said Harold.

"Nobody told me life was a battle," I said. "I expected to have life, liberty, and the pursuit of happiness served up to me on a silver salver. *Plus* a bank balance of six figures and my name in electric lights."

"You and a hundred thirty million others," said Harold.

I hardly heard him. I was looking at the old Vassall House. It was closed and the shutters were boarded up. The little yellow moss rose-bush by the door was gone. The boxwood borders of the garden were shrouded in muslin. In the twilight, they looked like ghosts.

Harold slowed down.

I didn't want to look at our house. Maybe it's a roominghouse, I thought. Or maybe it's torn down. And then I looked.

It was just the same! I couldn't believe my eyes. Our castle, I thought, there she stands. The widow's walk on the roof where we used to go to watch fires; the massive bulk of the main house "four square to all the winds"; the opaque glass in the windows of the serv-ants' dining room so they couldn't look out; the summerhouse with the well in it because my father wouldn't touch "city water"; the drooping cut-leaf maple. It was all just as I remembered it. Nothing was changed.

In the dusk, I could see Fred waiting at the front door with the carryall, ready to go down to meet my father at the station. In the library, a light flashed on. It's Christine, I thought, lighting the tall green lamp on the carved San Domingo mahogany table, with a long waxed taper. Suddenly, the light was gone. Christine had drawn the shades. I knew my mother was standing at the top of the stairs in her kitten's-ear broadcloth with the long train, the diamond butterfly from Tiffany's sparkling at the black-velvet ribbon around her throat, her "face on top." But I couldn't see her for the mist in my eyes.

We started slowly on. I looked back. The house was just a dark shape now, receding into the past. At last, like the familiar spirits who had peopled it, it was gone.

As we reached the hilltop, I looked off over Boston Harbor. Boston light was dimmed. Past the tiny islands, a convoy of ships carefully picked its way. Over it, protecting planes circled and dipped.

I thought of what my mother had said: "The things which are seen are temporal; the things which are not seen are eternal."

Whether my father's castle stood or not, one truth was self-evident. The spirit that moved him to build it and defend it against all comers still lived on. There were still millions of Americans who believed, like him, that freedom was a fighting word; who'd rather die than live without it.

A warm feeling swept over me. I felt good. I thought, I didn't get rich and I didn't get famous. Who cares? I had a good time trying. I did as I liked. And so, God willing, would my children and their children after them. Liberty, I thought. That's all that counts.

I put my hand on Harold's arm.

"What'll you have?" he said.

"America," I said. "I'm glad we didn't give it back to the Indians. It's a mighty fine place."

ABOUT THE AUTHOR

Louise John Randall Pierson was born on Adams Street, Quincy, Massachusetts, with an eighteen-karat gold spoon in her mouth. (This quickly became tarnished.) Upon graduation from Simmons College she plied her trade of secretary until she ran across Arnold Bennett's reference to stenography as "the attribute of the slave."

Louise Pierson has been married twice; she has five children and three grandchildren. At present, when not busy reporting industrial news for *The Philadelphia Record*, she bakes oatmeal bread, runs the mop around the seventeen-room mansion she lives in because it has a Dutch fireplace, plays with Toughy, her dog, and Queen Wilhelmina, her cat, telephones her husband and daughter, who work different shifts, and envies people who have the time and money to have a nervous breakdown.